Cultural Encounters in Near Eastern History

CNI Publications 44

Cultural Encounters in Near Eastern History

Edited by
Thomas K. Hertel
Mogens T. Larsen
Kim Ryholt

DEPARTMENT OF CROSS-CULTURAL AND REGIONAL STUDIES 2018
UNIVERSITY OF COPENHAGEN MUSEUM TUSCULANUM PRESS

CNI Publications 44
Cultural Encounters in Near Eastern History

Cover design by Thora Fisker
Text set in Times Roman by the editors
Printed in Denmark by Specialtrykkeriet Arco

ISBN 978 87 635 4387 3
ISSN 0902-5499 (CNI Publications)

Published and distributed by
Museum Tusculanum Press
Dantes Plads 1
DK-1556 Copenhagen

www.mtp.dk

CONTENTS

PREFACE

THOMAS K. HERTEL, MOGENS T. LARSEN, AND KIM RYHOLT

Contact between different cultural, social, linguistic and political units or societies has occurred countless times throughout the history of the Near East. Whether as a result of war or peaceful contact, they all provide for numerous interpretations of just how individuals and societies have historically approached "the other", be it traders, nomads, religious movements, ethnic groups or conquering armies. The processes whereby groups of individuals invent or redefine their social identity seem to be given an added impetus in these encounters. Though historical examples are abundant, traditional theoretical and analytical approaches often seem inadequate in interpreting such encounters within a comparative and interdisciplinary framework. Needless to say, understanding cultural encounters is not only a concern for the ancient historian. Questions of conflict, prejudice, interaction and adaptation are of primary importance in our contemporary globalized society, where contact between different groups and societies on many social levels is as common as never before.

The present work represents a selection of contributions that were presented at the international conference *Cultural Encounters in Near Eastern History – An Interdisciplinary Conference*, organized by the *Center for Canon and Identity Formation*, University of Copenhagen Programme of Excellence, May 10–11, 2012. The conference had the aim to discuss and establish meaningful analytical categories for the description and understanding of cultural encounters by way of both theoretical discussions and the presentation of empirical material. The cases presented in this book come from a range of different fields of research within the overall history of the Near East, including Mesopotamian history, the impact of Hellenism in Central Asia and the Near East and the spread of Islam.

The motivation for arranging a conference on cultural encounters springs from the work on the Old Assyrian merchant colonies in Anatolia in the Middle Bronze Age (c. 1900 BCE) that has occupied the Assyriological group in Copenhagen. The material on which we have been working consists of large archives of texts found in private houses in the lower town of the ancient city Kanesh in central Anatolia, about 20 kms from the modern metropolis Kayseri. A rich repertoire of architecture and material culture is available to complement and interact with the textual evidence. Palaces and other official buildings have been found on the mound itself, and hundreds of houses flanking streets, alleys and squares in the lower town give a vivid impression of a once flourishing, cosmopolitan town, where people of different cultural, ethnic backgrounds lived and met. Some 60 of the houses excavated in the lower town at Kanesh contained archives which show that they were inhabited by Assyrians, and it seems that they lived shoulder to shoulder with local Anatolians. A few Anatolian archives have also been found here, but nearly all textual assemblages stem from the households of Assyrian merchant families, people whose home town Assur is located in what is now northern Iraq on the river Tigris, ca. 800 kilometres from Kanesh in a straight line.[1]

The precise relationship between Assyrians and Anatolians has been discussed from the moment when the texts began to be read. For a long time, some scholars maintained that the Assyrian presence was the result of a political and military conquest of central Anatolia, but that paradigm has been completely abandoned in favour of a purely commercial expansion. The presence of Assyrians in Anatolia is to be explained by their participation in a vast network of overland trade that reached all the way from Central Asia to the Black Sea. Donkey caravans carrying luxury textiles and hundreds of tons of tin went from Assur to Kanesh and other Assyrian settlements in Anatolia in a regular stream, and the Assyrian merchants also exploited an inner-Anatolian network for the trade in copper and wool. The merchants were in a position to provide essential goods, primarily to the palaces in the many small kingdoms in the area, where the local elite had an interest in or direct need for the textiles for largesse and display, and for the tin to establish a production of bronze. Despite the monopoly of power that the Anatolian kings maintained, their successful participation in the long-distance trade required a peaceful interaction with Assyrians and legal measures that guaranteed the safety of the merchants operating in Anatolia. This situation led to the creation of a kind of balance of power, where both sides accepted the need for an ordered interaction. The trade was protected by treaties with the local kings who in return for hefty taxes secured the roads, gave the traders the right to settle in the various towns and allowed them the freedom to make use of their own political and judicial institutions, councils and popular assemblies within the Anatolian cities.

The texts provide some evidence concerning the daily contacts between the groups, even though they are first of all concentrated on the

---

[1] For the Old Assyrian Period in general, see Veenhof, 'The Old Assyrian Period', 2008.

commercial activities. Remarkably, the evidence from material culture is much less clear-cut, for there is in fact very little in the archaeological record that indicates the presence of the Assyrians in Anatolia, let alone their commercial activities. Apart from the texts it seems that all other artefacts found in the houses, primarily pottery, as well as the houses themselves are of purely local style. It is understandable that the merchants would not have seen the transport of commercially uninteresting objects such as pots and pans from Assur to Anatolia as meaningful. It appears that they did not ask the local potters to produce wares in the style used in Assur either – although it must be remembered that so little is known of the Old Assyrian record from Assur itself that it is in fact very doubtful whether we can identify typically Old Assyrian pottery. But it is clear at least that the pots that are characteristic of the houses in the lower town quite clearly belong in an Anatolian tradition with links both to the Early Bronze tradition and to later, Hittite ceramics.

The adoption or appropriation of foreign cultural elements is also attested for the Anatolian population. Above all, they took over the Assyrian communication technology, writing texts in (sometimes pretty bad) Assyrian, and made use of the characteristically Mesopotamian cylinder seal rather than continuing the local tradition of stamp seals. The production of cylinder seals in Anatolian workshops resulted in the creation of a new artistic style that mixed elements from Mesopotamian and Anatolian traditions. We have a large number of sealings made with such cylinder seals in the Anatolian style, highly elegant and accomplished miniature works of art, and it has been shown that several prominent Assyrian traders in Kanesh preferred to buy them in preference to seals in the traditional Old Assyrian style.[2]

On the level of personal contacts we can see how the Assyrian merchants in time established closer links to the Anatolian population, culminating in a common practice of mixed marriages.[3] During the last phase of the existence of these merchant colonies the Assyrian community appears to have been divided into at least two fairly distinct groups: those who still maintained close commercial links with the home city Assur, and those who could be referred to as "settlers", apparently families originating in Assur who now based their existence on a primarily agricultural way of life in Anatolia. A couple of late treaties make it clear, however, that even these settlers were regarded as

---

[2] Lassen, *Glyptik Encounters*, 2012.
[3] Veenhof, 'Old Assyrian Merchants', 1982.

"Assyrians" and in that capacity enjoyed certain privileges, for instance freedom from *corvée*.[4]

The concrete, daily experience of cultural encounters is therefore a defining trait in the Old Assyrian evidence, and various attempts to create a satisfactory analytical framework for our understanding of this fundamental feature of Old Assyrian society have been made. Grand theories regarding socio-cultural interaction and development have offered little but tautological reproductions of models except for those we have been able test against a detailed and varied dataset in such a way that it allowed us to ascertain the appropriateness and limitations of the chosen theories when applied to the Old Assyrian case. A few preliminary analytical steps have played a crucial role in our own search for satisfactory analytical frameworks: integrated approaches that combine textual and archaeological datasets, micro-historical analyses and an acute awareness of micro-temporal developments (years, decades, generations), and concrete comparisons to other historical cases and explanatory models.[5]

Even if we are only in the early phase of understanding the developments that took place during the 250 years that mark this particular cultural encounter, our initial attempts to combine textual and material culture have shown that integrated approaches are of crucial importance to our critical assessment of exactly which models and theories are relevant to the analysis and ultimately to an appropriate description and understanding of a particular society. For instance, we know that the presence of "Anatolian style pottery" in a household at Kanesh does not *per se* signal an "Anatolian" household, and that a Mesopotamian style cylinder seal cannot necessarily be attributed to an "Assyrian" individual. The same ambiguity characterises what one might call "hybrid" artefacts that blend different cultural traditions into new forms, objects that appear to have been appreciated by individuals within the multi-cultural population at Kanesh irrespective of their own cultural and ethnic background. A comparable analytical issue exists for the analysis of the textual record, especially when it comes to the question of ethnicity. Personal names have traditionally been regarded as a key diagnostic criterion in this regard, and in the Old Assyrian material a

---

[4] Barjamovic, Hertel & Larsen, *Ups and Down at Kanesh*, 2012.

[5] Larsen, 'Individual and Family in Old Assyrian Society', 2007; Dercksen, 'Subsistence, surplus and the market for grain and meat', 2008; Lumsden, 'Material Culture and the Middle Ground', 2008; Hertel & Larsen, 'Situating Legal Strategies', 2010; Stratford, *Agents, Archives, and Risk*, 2010; Barjamovic, *A Historical Geography of Anatolia*, 2011, Hertel, *Old Assyrian Legal Practices*, 2013; Michel, 'Considerations on the Assyrian Settlement at Kaneš', 2014.

general division has been made between names rendered in the Assyrian dialect of the Akkadian language on the one hand, and non-Akkadian names drawn from a variety of non-Akkadian (mostly Indo-European) languages on the other. Not surprisingly, the former group of names has typically been attributed to ethnic "Assyrians" and the latter group largely to those population groups we indiscriminately call "Anatolians" – understood as the indigenous population of Central Anatolia. Whereas this is relevant for the first generation of traders attested in our texts, a development over time may be observed. For instance, mixed marriages came to be an ordinary phenomenon of the multicultural society in Kanesh, in which mixed Assyrian-Anatolian couples could name their children in whichever language they preferred.

During a period of about 250 years the Assyrians and Anatolians managed to maintain a system which was built on mutual interests and a willingness to negotiate and innovate. The study of both the textual and material records shows how a diachronic perspective can throw light on the way in which the two communities influenced each other; but that is less easy to describe for the political and social structures.

The inherent ambiguities of the empirical record obviously leave room for the application of a variety of conflicting models and different writings of history depending on how data are selected and accentuated. Although Old Assyrian studies do not have a long history and many fundamental problems have never been properly addressed, the last fifty years have seen a dramatic development in our understanding. Micro-historical and chronological analyses of a dense and detailed textual corpus correlated with the archaeological record have allowed us to if not resolve then at least make the problem of ambiguity manageable. As a first step, this involves the identification of archival assemblages, the writing of detailed prosopographies and biographies of individuals, and the reconstruction of families and social networks, all of which is fixed on a micro-chronological timeline with yearly increments. In the second step the results of the micro-historical analysis are combined with whatever material culture can be associated with certain individuals and families so as to form a total socio-cultural context and backdrop for a more general analysis.

General theories concerning the fundamental socio-cultural developments and the relationship between the political and cultural groups present in the material have hardly ever been applied to the Old Assyrian material. Specialist scholars have been more concerned with the elucidation of technical terms and procedures, to some extent inspired by a desire to get rid of some of the unhelpful theories and ideas inherited from previous studies – where the analyses offered by scholars like Julius Lewy and Karl Polanyi stand as prominent examples.[6]

The only example of a general theoretical approach has been offered by Gil Stein who recently attempted to apply the model of Merchant Diasporas to the Old Assyrian case. In our view his analysis is only partly successful, since it places a heavy emphasis on the colonists' need to retain their own cultural distinctiveness. Stein sees his interpretation in contrast to hybridity or hybridization, stressing that trade diasporas place a strong emphasis on their own distinctive cultural identity – "being different is the essence of a trade diaspora."[7] His model is relevant for an understanding of the specific Old Assyrian experience in Anatolia because it stresses the commercial basis for the very existence of the colonies. It is also obvious that the two groups retained their different traditions, but our focus on the contacts and the process of interaction between the two groups makes Stein's model less useful for our purposes. His view that the traders "actively maintain a social identity very different from that of their local host community" risks downplaying the complexities in the social and cultural relations that can be directly observed and described. Highlighting the differences rather than the on-going process of negotiation and manipulation in our view presents a one-sided picture of the interactions.

We have instead been inspired by the theory defined by the American historian Richard White as The Middle Ground.[8] He defined this model to explain the ingenious way in which the meeting between the French and the Indians in the "Pays d'en haut" took place. He suggested that the two groups structured their contacts in a metaphorical space where they could interact on the basis of a set of rules that referred to what each side in the interaction understood (or more often misunderstood) as the traditions and practices of the other side. This set up a virtual space where problems and controversies could be resolved, while the participants in the exchanges could retain the essential part of their own group identity.

In such a situation, certain elements were necessary, as defined by White: "a rough balance of power, mutual need or a desire for what the other possesses, and an inability by either side to commandeer enough force to compel the other to change." He furthermore noted that "force and violence are hardly foreign to the process of creating and maintaining a middle ground, but the critical element is mediation."[9]

---

[6] Lewy, 'On some institutions of the Old Assyrian Empire', 1956; Polanyi et al., *Trade and Market in the Early Empires*, 1957.
[7] Stein, 'A Theoretical Model for Political Economy', 2008, p. 31.
[8] White, *The Middle Ground*, 1991.
[9] White, 'Creative Misunderstandings', 2006, p. 10.

This model is clearly of particular value for the analysis of socio-political contacts, and it is interesting to apply to aspects of the Old Assyrian situation.[10] White's balance of power, which is a precondition of the Middle Ground model, quite nicely illuminates interactions between Assyrians and Anatolians. Both parties were interested in maintaining and developing their relations, because both benefitted from the exchange of goods. It is obvious that the Anatolian kingdoms had a monopoly of force in the region, and the Assyrians in return monopolized the supply of essential commodities, both strategic goods such as tin and luxury items like textiles, lapis lazuli and exotica of various kinds. In this connection it is also important that the Assyrian traders built up an inner-Anatolian network for trade in copper and wool, where very large quantities of goods were transported between the local states by Assyrian traders. The balance of power was accordingly based on a complex network of interests, contacts and opportunities.

Cultural hybridity or hybridization is a concept that is of particular relevance for studies of material culture – the emphasis on the creation of a new cultural, social and political configuration which borrows, mixes and translates from both groups who are in contact.[11] The concept has been applied in the study of the various seal styles attested in the material, where it is possible to describe the development of mixed styles that include elements from Mesopotamian and Anatolian religious and artistic traditions.[12]

Such general theories may at this stage of our understanding be used in a rather eclectic fashion, where the Middle Ground, trade diaspora and hybridity help to conceptualise aspects of the complexity found here, but theoretical purity itself does not seem to be a meaningful goal when confronted with the evidence.

The examples of cultural encounters offered in this volume should accordingly be understood as cases where the understanding of each historical process has been based on a dialectical interplay between bottom-up analysis of specific encounters and the application of general theoretical models. It is our hope that these cases will contribute to the further development of theoretical frameworks and ensure that these are in fact empirically grounded.

We owe our thanks to a large number of people, and we would first like to thank the speakers at the conference *Cultural Encounters in Near*

---

[10] Lumsden, 'Material Culture and the Middle Ground in the Old Assyrian Period', 2008.
[11] See Burke, *Cultural Hybridity*, 2009, and Ackermann, 'Cultural Hybridity', 2012, for recent discussions of the concept.
[12] Larsen & Lassen, 'Cultural Exchange at Kültepe', 2014.

Eastern History, May 10–11, 2012: Anna Cannavò (Université Lumière, Lyon), Jessica Goldberg (University of Pennsylvania), Joost Kramer (Leiden University), Mogens T. Larsen (University of Copenhagen), Christian E. Loeben (Museum August Kestner, Hannover), Rachel Mairs (Brown University, Rhode Island), Piotr Michalowski (University of Michigan), John P. Nielsen (Loyola University, New Orleans), Cornelius von Pilgrim (Swiss Archaeological Insitute, Cairo), Lauren Ristvet (University of Pennsylvania), Jørgen B. Simonsen (University of Copenhagen), Philipp W. Stockhammer (Heidelberg University), Günter Vittmann (University of Würzburg) and Irene Winter (Harvard University).

The organisation of the conference was a joint effort by numerous people. We owe a special thanks to our colleagues Gojko Barjamovic, Paul John Frandsen and Fredrik Hagen for their support in the planning and execution of the conference, as well as our external board members, John Baines and Piotr Michalowski. We are also extremely grateful to our many dedicated postdoctoral researchers, PhD candidates, students and assistants for their tremendous contribution to the organisation of the conference: Troels Pank Arbøll, Cheresse Burke, Thomas Christiansen, Ole Herslund, Jens Blach Jørgensen, Agnete Lassen, Bjarne Lohdal, Elyse Meaker, Matthias Müller, Seraina Nett, Rune Olsen, Hratch Papazian, Dora Petrova, Rune Rattenborg and Rana Sérida.

Finally, we wish to express our sincere gratitude to the Rector of the University of Copenhagen for supporting the *Center for Canon and Identity Formation in the Earliest Literate Societies*, a five-year research project (2008–2013) financed by the University of Copenhagen Programme of Excellence.

BIBLIOGRAPHY

Ackermann, A. 'Cultural Hybridity: Between Metaphor and Empiricism.' P. W. Stockhammer (ed.), *Conceptualizing Cultural Hybridization – A Transdisciplinary Approach*. Berlin – Heidelberg 2012, pp. 5–25.

Barjamovic, G. *A Historical Geography of Anatolia in the Old Assyrian Colony Period* (CNI Publications 38). Copenhagen, 2011.

Barjamovic, G., T. K. Hertel, and M. T. Larsen *Ups and Down at Kanesh – Observations on Chronology, History and Society in the Old Assyrian Period.* (Old Assyrian Archives Studies 5). Leiden, 2012.

Burke, P. *Cultural Hybridity*. Cambridge, 2009.

Dercksen, J. G. 'Subsistence, Surplus and the Market for Grain and Meat at Ancient Kanesh.' *Altorientalische Forschungen* 35 (2008), pp. 86–102.

Hertel, T. K. *Old Assyrian Legal Practices – Law and Dispute in the Ancient Near East.* (PIHANS 123). Leiden, 2013.

Hertel, T. K. & M. T. Larsen 'Situating Legal Strategies.' S. Dönmez (ed.), *Studies Presented in Honour of Veysel Donbaz*. Istanbul, 2010, pp. 167–182.

Larsen, M. T. 'Individual and Family in Old Assyrian Society.' *Journal of Cuneiform Studies* 59 (2007), pp. 93–106.

Larsen, M. T. & A. K. W. Lassen 'Cultural Exchange at Kültepe.' W. Henkelman, C. Jones, M. Kozuh, and C. Woods (eds.), *Extraction and Control: Studies in Honor of Matthew W. Stolper*. Chicago, 2014, pp. 171–188.

Lassen, A. K. W. *Glyptic Encounters: A Stylistic and Prosopographical Study of Seals in the Old Assyrian Period.* PhD dissertation, University of Copenhagen, 2012.

Lewy, J. 'On Some Institutions of the Old Assyrian Empire.' *Hebrew Union College Annual* 27 (1956), pp. 1–79.

Lumsden, S. 'Material Culture and the Middle Ground in the Old Assyrian Period.' C. Michel (ed.), *Old Assyrian Studies in Memory of Paul Garelli*. Leiden, 2008, pp. 21–43.

Michel, C. 'Considerations on the Assyrian settlement at Kaneš.' L. Atici, F. Kulakoglu, G. Barjamovic, and A. Fairbairn (eds.), *Current Research at Kültepe/Kanesh = Journal of Cuneiform Studies*, Supplemental Series 4 (2014), pp. 69–84.

Polanyi, K., C. M. Arensberg, and H. W. Pearson (eds). *Trade and Market in the Early Empires: Economies in History and Theory*. New York – London, 1957.

Stein, G. 'A Theoretical Model for Political Economy and Social Identity in the Old Assyrian Colonies of Anatolia.' *TÜBA-AR Turkish Academy of Sciences Journal of Archaeology* 11 (2008), pp. 25–40.

Stratford, E. P. *Agents, Archives, and Risk. A Micronarrative Account of Old Assyrian Trade through Salim-ahum's Activities in 1890 B.C.* PhD dissertation, University of Chicago, 2010.

Veenhof, K. R. 'The Old Assyrian Merchants and their Relations with the Native Population of Anatolia.' H. J. Nissen & J. Renger (eds), *Mesopotamien und seine Nachbarn*. Berlin, 1982.

– 'The Old Assyrian Period.' K. R. Veenhof & J. Eidem, *Mesopotamia–The Old Assyrian Period.* (Annäherungen 5, Orbis Biblicus et Orientalis 160/5). Fribourg, 2008, pp. 14–264.

White, R. *The Middle Ground: Indians, Empires, and Republics in the Great Lakes Region, 1650–1815*. Cambridge, 1991.

– 'Creative Misunderstandings and New Understandings.' *William and Mary Quarterly*, 3rd Series, 63 (2006), pp. 9–14.

GREEK AND PHOENICIAN "COLONISATION" IN CYPRUS

Foreign Models vs. Local Practices

ANNA CANNAVÒ

Abstract. The Hellenisation of Cyprus is a highly debated subject in recent studies concerning ancient Cypriot identity formation and ethnicity. If the word "colonisation" is now generally considered inappropriate, there is still no agreement on the approach for interpreting what has been defined as an "invisible migration" of Greek-speaking populations to Cyprus at the end of the Bronze Age. The Phoenician colonisation of Cyprus, some centuries later (at the end of the 9th century BCE) has not received the same theoretical investigation. The major Phoenician site of Cyprus, Kition, is generally presented (by ancient and modern authors) as a Tyrian colony. This has been done without much attention to the local conditions that gave rise to what afterwards was to become, historically, one of the island's most powerful kingdoms. The Greek colonisation model is generally evoked without more appropriate analysis of the specific features of the Cypriot case. The aim of the present contribution is to elucidate these features through a detailed analysis of the textual evidence, frequently evoked in order to support or explain the archaeological data, so as to propose an interpretative approach suitable for both the Hellenisation of Cyprus, and the "Phoenicisation" of Kition.

1. INTRODUCTION

The transition from Late Bronze to Early Iron Age in Cyprus (12th–10th c. BCE) and the evolutionary patterns of the island's civilisation in the Geometric and Archaic periods (11th–early 5th c. BCE) have in recent years become the object of recurrent fruitful methodological debate and theoretical reflection.[1] How did Cyprus – mentioned in the Late Bronze

I wish to thank the anonymous referees for their attentive reading and observations: most of their comments have contributed to strongly improve this paper. Many thanks also go to the editors for their careful and patient revision.

[1] E.g. Iacovou, 'Cultural and Political Configurations in Iron Age Cyprus', 2008 and Voskos & Knapp, 'Cyprus at the End of the Late Bronze Age', 2008.

Near Eastern sources as the kingdom of Alashiya[2] – become that patchwork of Greek- and Phoenician-speaking kingdoms whose existence can be verified with certainty from at least the end of the 8th c. until the end of the 4th c. BCE? With no pretentions of proposing a solution to this problem, I would like to draw attention to some theoretical issues concerning colonisation, migration, Hellenisation and 'Phoenicisation' in Iron Age Cyprus.

The aim of this paper is, however, not to propose a new analysis of the material culture of Early Iron Age Cyprus, neither is its purpose to take up a distinct position within the various debates confronting the traditionalists, the postcolonial theorists and the scholars who adopt a *longue durée* perspective: recent in-depth and detailed studies outline the terms of the discussion in a sufficiently clear and complete manner.[3] The archaeological evidence to be considered is enormous, and a single book would not be enough to study and discuss it in detail.[4] My aim will thus be a modest and precise one: it is my intention to analyse the use that is made of the textual evidence concerning the Hellenisation and "Phoenicisation" of Cyprus in order to check the validity of the colonisation narrative which is currently associated with this evidence. Without explicitly discussing the archaeological evidence, but taking it as the necessary preliminary basis for a complete study of Cypriot Iron Age history, I shall suggest that the textual evidence, if correctly approached, can provide useful elements contributing to a new, Cyprocentric view of the island's history, especially in what concerns the complex migrating phenomena of the Iron Age.

The evidence considered is mainly the expression of royal or elite-constructed ideology. By making reference to legendary motifs, coin iconography, human-size sculpture or fine figure-decorated pottery I am forced to neglect a significant aspect of identity construction, that is, the way political authorities implement their ideological choices in concrete daily life. A bottom-up approach, which would eventually provide evidence of agreement, resistance or alternative identity construction, is

---

[2] Goren *et al.*, 'The Location of Alashiya', 2003.

[3] Iacovou, 'Cyprus: From Migration to Hellenisation', 2008, and Knapp, *Prehistoric and Protohistoric Cyprus*, 2008; see Fourrier, 'Légendes de fondation', 2008, for a historiographic review of the debate.

[4] See the recent books of Satraki, *Κύπριοι Βασιλείς*, 2012, and Papantoniou, *Religion and Social Transformations in Cyprus*, 2012 for important up-to-date analyses of relevant evidence.

by far beyond the purpose of this paper, and generally beyond the limited available evidence for the Archaic and first Classical period in Cyprus.[5]

1.1. The beginning of the Iron Age in Cyprus

During the Late Bronze Age, the kingdom known in the Near Eastern texts as Alashiya displays a consistent and flourishing economic and political activity, all while interacting with contemporary Near Eastern states (Egypt, Ugarit, the Hittite empire). While the Near Eastern texts unanimously speak of a single state – Alashiya – ruled by a king, the archaeological evidence seems to be pointing to a segmented political system, thus implying the existence of more than one political entity organised and acting as independent statelets.[6] Even if the disagreement between the textual and the archaeological evidence is problematic, the political segmentation of Late Bronze Age Cyprus appears as a prelude of the peculiar Iron Age organisation of the island into a number of territorial kingdoms.[7]

According to the written records as well as the archaeological evidence, Alashiya along with many other areas of the Mediterranean appear to have suffered a wide and deep crisis towards the end of the 13th c. BCE. Even if the kingdom of Alashiya still appears in the *Report of Wenamun*, supposedly written between the mid 11th and the mid-10th c. BCE,[8] it is beyond doubt that the transition from the Late Bronze to the Iron Age brought about significant changes among the island's civilisation (topography, language, burial customs).[9] It is within this unclear and somehow vague context that we should set the disappearance of the kingdom of Alashiya.

In Cyprus the transition to the Early Iron Age did not cause the dramatic disruptions that we have otherwise observed in different Mediterranean regions. Even when one stresses the observable innovations on the island it is impossible not to notice a consistent continuity in some fundamental aspects of its civilisation. A major topographical shift appears to have occurred in the 11th century, with

[5] The end of the Classical period and the transition to Hellenism can, on the contrary, be the object of such analysis: the best example is Papantoniou, *Religion and Social Transformations in Cyprus*, 2012.

[6] Iacovou, 'Site Size Estimates and the Diversity Factor', 2007.

[7] The same position has been recently reaffirmed and freshly argued in Iacovou, 'External and Internal Migrations during the 12th Century BC', 2012.

[8] Egberts, 'Hard Times', 1998 and Sass, 'Wenamun and His Levant', 1998.

[9] Iacovou, 'The Topography of Eleventh Century B.C. Cyprus', 1994; Iacovou, 'Cyprus: From Migration to Hellenisation', 2008; Iacovou, 'External and Internal Migrations during the 12th Century BC', 2012.

relocation of settlements and new foundations; two major sites of the island however, Kition and Palaepaphos, appear to have flourished throughout the entirety of this period, and during the 12th century these two sites even came to reinforce the monumental character of their sanctuary sites, thus providing evidence of strong continuity.[10] The Cypriot syllabic script, used during the Late Bronze Age to write an (or perhaps several) unknown local language(s), was adopted during the mid 11th century to write the Greek dialect newly introduced to the island, and during the Iron Age this Cypriot script developed into what became the first-millennium Cypro-syllabic script.[11] When analysing the Early Iron Age material landscape of Cyprus we can moreover observe the complete absence of ethnic boundaries inside the island: the new cultural features (*extra muros* chamber-tombs of Aegean type replacing the intra-mural burial tradition; the adoption of the fast wheel in pottery production) did not spread following ethnic-based patterns, but were adopted all over the island; in a similar manner, the preservation of some well-rooted Cypriot traditions (the script; the use of the open-air type sanctuaries of local cult) was shared by the population of the island irrespective of the possible ethnic origins of its components. The association of external pressure, inter-island migration and regional differentiation has been evoked in order to explain the cultural novelties, the surviving traditions and the homogeneity of Early Iron Age Cypriot material culture.[12] But the archaeological evidence seems to contrast sharply, as we shall see, with the literary tradition, where the latter suggests the arrival of immigrants from the Aegean and the formation of enclaves of indigenous population (Amathus).

For almost a century now, archaeologists have been trying to fit the material evidence of the Cypriot Late Bronze-Iron Age transition into the framework of the literary traditions commonly known as foundation legends, ascribing the creation of the Cypriot Iron Age kingdoms to a handful of Greek and Homeric heroes who arrived on the island after the Trojan War (Teukros, Agapenor, Akamas, Demophon, Praxandros).[13]

---

[10] Iacovou, 'The Topography of Eleventh Century B.C. Cyprus', 1994; see now Iacovou, 'External and Internal Migrations during the 12th Century BC', 2012, pp. 225–228.
[11] Steele, 'The diversity of the Cypro-Minoan corpus', 2012, pp. 542–544.
[12] Iacovou, 'Cyprus: From Migration to Hellenisation', 2008, pp. 248–249; Iacovou, 'External and Internal Migrations during the 12th Century BC', 2012, pp. 222–225.
[13] Fourrier, 'Légendes de fondation', 2008.

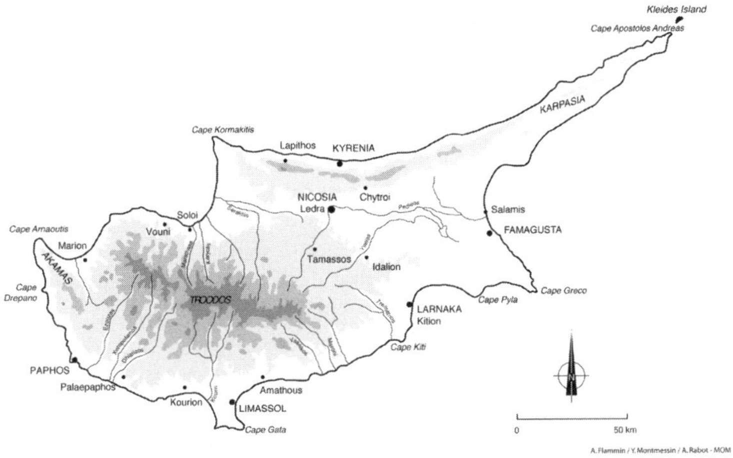

Figure 1. Map of Cyprus with the main Iron Age sites. © A. Flammin, Y. Montessin, A. Rabot, HiSoMA, Lyon.

According to these legends, which are transmitted by a number of Greek and Latin texts ranging from the Classical to the Byzantine period, some of the first-millennium Cypriot kingdoms (Salamis, Paphos, Amathus, Kourion, Lapethos, Chytroi, Soloi) are said to be Greek foundations dating from the period of the *nostoi*: Salamis would have been founded by Teukros, Ajax's brother (Aeschylus, *Persians* 895–896; Pindar, *Nemean* 4, 46–48; Isocrates, *Evagoras* 18, *Nicocles* 28; Lycophron 450–455; etc.); Paphos, by the Arcadian chief Agapenor (Lycophron 479–485; Pausanias 8, 5, 2); Lapethos, by the obscure Laconian Praxandros (Lycophron 486–591; Strabo 14, 682. 20–21); Soloi, by the Athenian Akamas or by his brother Demophon (Lycophron 494–498; Strabo 14, 683. 29–31), and Chytroi, by Akamas' grandson Chytros (Stephanus of Byzantium *s. v.*); Kourion would have been an Argive foundation (Herodotus 5, 113, 1; Strabo 14, 683. 4–5). Amathus, the kingdom related to the Cypriot Kinyras (a local hero already known to Homer), would also be a by-product of this massive Greek expansion movement, since the Greeks would have pushed the indigenous population, ("the companions of Kinyras") to take refuge in Amathus (Theopompus, *FGrHist* 115 F 103).

The historicity of these narratives, which have been interpreted for quite some time as representing the mythical transcriptions of colonial activities – the installation of Mycenaean organised communities in

Cyprus at the end of the Late Bronze Age[14] – is now almost completely discredited.[15] At present, the issue under debate concerns to what extent the movement of Greek-speaking individuals to Cyprus had affected the island's Iron Age civilisation, and whether the notions of "colonisation", "Hellenisation", "migration" or "hybridisation" (to name a few) should be used to understand the complex archaeological situation briefly outlined.[16]

Several criticisms have recently been advanced against the colonisation models and approaches that have guided generations of scholarly research on many ancient societies and people.[17] Such methodological and terminological reassessments are also welcome in what concerns the specific Cypriot case, where the colonisation narrative has appeared to be particularly resistant and long-lasting.[18] However, adopting the term "Hellenisation" in the subsequent pages does not mean any conscious or implicit assent to the colonial-based interpretative framework in which the notion of Hellenisation has developed:[19] this term, as it is also used in some recent studies,[20] is purely descriptive, and as such it seems the best suited for synthetically evoking (without adhering to any artificial, general interpretative model) the migration and settling of Greek-speaking people in Cyprus at the end of the Bronze Age. In the same manner and with the same caution I shall use the uncommon term "Phoenicisation" as a synthetic, useful description of a complex phenomenon that led a Cypriot city – Kition – to become a Cypro-Phoenician kingdom.

The use of this terminology is intended to suggest that a common interpretative framework can be proposed for both cases, the Hellenisation of Cyprus and the Phoenicisation of Kition, once greater attention is paid to the local context and responses to migration phenomena within the peculiar, regional-based Cypriot political landscape.

---

[14] Gjerstad, 'The Colonization of Cyprus', 1944 and Fortin, 'Fondation de villes grecques à Chypre', 1980.

[15] Leriou, 'Constructing an Archaeological narrative', 2002.

[16] Leriou, 'Locating Identities', 2007. This issue is a main concern in Iacovou, 'External and Internal Migrations during the 12th Century BC', 2012.

[17] Dietler, 'The Archaeology of Colonization', 2005.

[18] Fourrier, 'Légendes de fondation', 2008.

[19] As it is supposed, for exemple, in Leriou, 'Constructing an Archaeological Narrative', 2002 and 'Locating Identities', 2007; see also Mairs, 'Hellenization', 2013.

[20] Baurain, *Les Grecs et la Méditerranée orientale*, 1997, pp. 138–146; Iacovou, 'Cyprus: From Migration to Hellenisation', 2008; Iacovou, 'External and Internal Migrations during the 12th Century BC', 2012, p. 222.

2. The Hellenisation of Cyprus and the formation of Cypriot political identities

The historical value of the foundation legends strictly depends upon the approach through which they are studied. Since the beginning of Cypriot studies, they have been taken to the letter as documentary proof of the Greek colonisation of the island that took place at the dawn of the Iron Age. Slightly before the mid 19th century, a reference work such as *Kypros: Eine Monographie*, by the German philologist and historian Wilhelm Heinrich Engel, assembled for the first time the relevant texts.[21] For a long time since then, these texts have constituted the starting point for all research on the topic of the Greek "colonisation" of Cyprus. A little known but remarkable example of this modern tendency has been the object of some recent essays:[22] the French scholar Jean Bérard, who was interested in dating the Trojan War, addressed the archaeological exploration of Paphos in Cyprus precisely because (he thought) that by dating the town founded by the Arcadian chief Agapenor, he would have provided a *terminus ante quem* for the coming of the Greeks to Cyprus, and thus a date for the end of the Trojan War.[23]

In spite of the precocious attempts by Einar Gjerstad to introduce some elements of critical analysis into the study of the foundation legends,[24] most subsequent studies have simply raised the mythological traditions on the Greek colonisation of Cyprus to the rank of historical truth, all while stressing the archaeological evidence that is meant to confirm this view.[25] Yet, Claude Baurain has underlined the theoretical dangers of taking these foundation legends to the letter. It will be sufficient to recall the conclusions of his essay:[26]

> Aussi déchirant sentimentalement que soit le constat, si l'on veut rendre compte en termes de chronologie et surtout d'histoire de la pénétration grecque dans l'île, en bonne méthode, il faut se refuser à exploiter mécaniquement le matériel épique et encore bien davantage les lectures qu'en ont faites les Anciens (à savoir, pour l'essentiel, les légendes de fondation) [...] En définitive, Agapénor, Teukros et les autres offrent autant de sujets d'étude pour le chercheur qui souhaite pénétrer les réactions mentales des anciens Grecs en quête de leur

[21] Engel, *Kypros*, I, 1841, pp. 210–229.
[22] Hermary, 'Dossier Jean Bérard', 2008.
[23] See Bérard, 'La colonisation grecque de Chypre', 2008.
[24] Gjerstad, 'The Colonization of Cyprus', 1944, essentially followed by Vanschoonwinkel, *L'Égée et la Méditerranée orientale*, 1991, pp. 293–312.
[25] Fortin, 'Fondation de villes grecques à Chypre', 1980, and 'Nouvelles découvertes', 1984; Demetriou, *Cypro-Aegean Relations*, 1989, pp. 88–93.
[26] Baurain, 'Passé légendaire, archéologie et réalité historique', 1989, p. 473.

> passé historique, mais les héros fondateurs resteront autant de leurres pour l'archéologue qui cherche à faire parler de vieilles pierres désespérément muettes.

This methodological *caveat*, along with others that reach similar conclusions,[27] seems to have yielded some fruits. The most recent works on the Greek penetration into Cyprus do no longer evoke the foundation legends to corroborate or interpret the archaeological evidence; and the extreme reaction consists in denying any value to these legends, thereby excluding them from the debate.[28]

Bereft of their credibility, the foundation legends have then found themselves relegated to the rank of erudite curiosities. And yet, if they cannot be thought of any longer as historical documents that serve to directly illuminate the complex topic of the Hellenisation of Cyprus, a reason must still be found for their elaboration and exploitation, both of which are apparent in the Classical age. For what, by whom and at what time were these legends created? Can a new approach to this evidence be of some use to the understanding of the Hellenisation of Cyprus?

2.1. The foundation legends: Their historical value

As Irad Malkin has demonstrated in a number of studies,[29] Greek myths – in particular the myths related to the *nostoi* – have played an essential role in the definition of ethnicity throughout the entirety of the Greek colonial enterprise. At the same time, the *nostoi* constituted the key to the Greek interpretation of the colonial reality. These accounts were the basic instrument for the creation of distinctive identities, as well as the main cultural tool the Greeks used in order to communicate and mediate with the local cultures. The extremely flexible Greek mythological system was open to adaptations and modifications to include a potentially infinite number of local genealogies or peoples, and even figures of foreign origin (such was Kinyras, a Cypriot hero).

The charm of this intellectual system – constructed as an open, non-hierarchical and constantly evolving network of mythical relations – is apparent also outside the Greek colonial horizon: the Trojan myth of Rome's origins is the best known example of the insertion of a

---

[27] Maier, 'Kinyras and Agapenor', 1986 and Sherratt, 'Immigration and Archaeology', 1992.

[28] Leriou, 'Locating Identities, 2007, p. 574; Iacovou, 'External and Internal Migrations during the 12th Century BC', 2012, p. 219 ("later etiological myths").

[29] Malkin, *The Returns of Odysseus*, 1998; 'Heroes and the Foundation of Greek Cities', 2001; 'Networks and the Emergence of Greek Identities', 2005; 'Foundations', 2009; *A Small Greek World*, 2011.

"barbarian" city into the Helleno-centric system of the *origines gentium*.[30] The reference to a common mythical heritage allowed groups, cities or communities to legitimate themselves both internally and externally in contrast to others: it was an important political and ideological tool, and a cultural focus for identity formation.

As a means to join the Greek world by sharing a common system of cultural reference, the Cypriots too may also have felt the need to take part in the mythical world of the *nostoi*. I will argue that the Cypriot foundation legends should not exclusively be read as the late creation of Classical authors impelled by etiological curiosity or political urgency: these legends can also be explained as the spontaneous elaboration of the Cypriot kingdoms themselves, wishing by these means to stress their adherence to a common Mediterranean system, wherein the Greek mythical repertoire was constantly open to elaboration and modification for the construction of identities.

From this perspective the different origins of the founders of the Cypriot cities (the Athenian Teukros, the Arcadian Agapenor, the Laconian Praxandros, the Cypriot Kinyras) can be interpreted as the mirror of regional differentiation within the island. Through this differentiation the Cypriot kingdoms claimed their genealogical affinity to different parts of the Greek and non-Greek world, while concurrently stressing their own specificity in regard to their neighbours. For instance, in being the city of the Cypriot hero Kinyras, Amathus could stake a claim to an autochthonism that is one of the most elusive aspects of its Classical history.[31] Nonetheless, this genealogy clearly distinguished it from the neighbouring Phoenician Kition, from the Argive Kourion and still again from the Arcadian Paphos.

It is important to stress that the chronology of the written registration of the legends should not be confused with the chronology of their elaboration – which is extremely obscure, but which could date to the Archaic period in some cases. In a similar manner, the legends should not be confused with the chronology of the elements evoked therein. The Homeric characteristics of some of the mythical figures involved – such as Kinyras – could suggest a long elaboration process dating back to the

---

[30] Ampolo, 'Enea ed Ulisse nel Lazio', 1992.

[31] By saying that the autochthonism of Amathus is "elusive" we do not want to deny the historical reliability of the Eteocypriot language, nor the importance it acquired at the end of the 4th c. BCE (for more about this, see the conclusions of Egetmeyer, 'The Recent Debate', 2009), but simply underline the difficulties we encounter in recognizing a definite identity and a coherent ideological strategy in the limited evidence concerning 5th and 4th-century Amathus.

origins of the Cypriot kingdoms;[32] other cases – such as the traditions concerning the Athenian hero Akamas, the founder of Soloi – are better to be considered as late creations, sometimes even the result of Hellenistic erudite inventiveness.

To summarize, the material at our disposal is not homogeneous: a critical analysis of the elaboration and subsequent transmission of the different mythical kernels – such as the one proposed by Einar Gjerstad[33] – is the necessary premise underlying every later historical usage of the foundation legends. Still, this analysis does not exhaust the interest of this evidence: once aware of the origin and transmission paths of the mythical narratives addressing the origin of the Cypriot kingdoms, we must still illuminate their role in the construction of multiple Cypriot identities as well as how they contribute towards a reasonable understanding of the Hellenisation of Cyprus.

2.2 The heroic pedigree of the Cypriot kingdoms

According to what has been transmitted to us, the foundation legends are a matter of the Classical period. The most ancient texts mentioning the mythical relation existing between the Athenian Salamis and the homonymous Cypriot city are the Aeschylaean tragedy *The Persians* (895–896), and the Fourth Nemean Ode of Pindar (46–48). Both date from slightly before 470 BCE. A few other fifth-century references confirm the existence of a number of traditions of this kind relating the origin of the Cypriot cities to Greek or local peoples and heroes of a mythical age (Herodotus on the Argivian origin of Kourion, 5. 113. 1; a fragment of Hellanicos of Lesbos on the foundation of Karpasia, *FGrHist* 4 F 57).

Nothing invites us to believe that the transmitted legends are the only that existed, nor that they are all particularly ancient or authoritative: if we examine other kinds of evidence (coins, inscriptions, sculptures), we find several references to other myths or heroes. A Classical coin of the kingdom of Marion depicts the legend of the Thessalian Phrixos and his flight on the golden ram, and a monumental representation of the same myth seemed to exist also in the close proximity to the royal palace of Amathus.[34] In a late Classical inscription from Argos (*IG* IV 583), Nikokreon, king of Salamis, claims to be both a descendant of Aeacus and of Argive origin; the latter could be interpreted as a reference to

[32] Baurain, 'Kinyras', 1980.

[33] Gjerstad, 'The Colonization of Cyprus', 1944.

[34] Hermary, 'Les ascendances légendaires des rois chypriotes', 2002.

Perseus (represented in the Archaic Cypriot sculpture as a royal hero)[35] or as an allusion to the strong relations existing between the Salaminian kings and the Zeus of Nemea.[36] But all this evidence dates from the Classical period, and we could then conclude that the practices it documents are in large part a by-product of the Persian Wars, when the Cypriot kingdoms, urged by both the Persians and the Greeks (especially Athens), had to define their identity and to stress their political membership.[37]

But this would be a rushed conclusion, even if the importance of the Persian reality (and of the Greco-Persian conflict) in conditioning and orienting Cypriot identities in the Classical period cannot be overestimated.[38] If not all of the attested legends are of a (relatively) late origin, it is probable that most of them are: not only is the clearly etiologically constructed figure of Chytros, grandson of Akamas and founder of Chytroi, likely to be situated in the context of Hellenistic etiological erudition, but Akamas himself and his role as a founder of Soloi can hardly date from before the 5th century.[39] In a similar way, the stress in the (mostly Athenian) sources on the Attic origin of the kings of Salamis strongly suggests the opportunism underlying the Athenian political agenda of 5th and 4th centuries. The tradition attributing the foundation of Kourion to Kouros, an eponymic unknown son of Kinyras, is probably a late invention of etiological character (Stephanus of Byzantium *s. v.*). Of course, we could multiply the remarks of this kind.

Nevertheless, when broadening the range of the evidence considered in order to include other heroic motifs not mentioned in the foundation legends (and partially exceeding the *nostoi* repertoire), we can observe that the Cypriot exploitation of legendary Greek motifs on behalf of a process of identity formation is a persistent and significant element of the Cypriot royal ideology. Since the dawn of the Iron Age, figure-decorated pottery has alluded to Herakles and the myth of his labours,[40] and significantly the Tyrian god Baal Melqart, identified in the Classical

---

[35] Fourrier, 'La réappropriation du passé', 2007.

[36] Baurain, 'Le *come-back* d'Évagoras de Salamine', 2008. See also Kritzas, 'Επισκόπηση των επιγραφικών μαρτυριών', 1997, and Christodoulou, 'Nicocréon, le dernier roi de Salamine', 2009.

[37] Serghidou, 'Discours ethnographique et quêtes identitaires', 2006.

[38] See about this Mavrojannis, 'L'identité chypriote', 2006 and Serghidou, 'Discours ethnographique et quêtes identitaires', 2006.

[39] On the figure of Akamas as an Athenian oecist see Kron, 'Akamas et Demophon', 1981; if the interpretation proposed for the *pelike* of the Painter of the Birth of Athena (pp. 443–444) is correct, then we should take 450 BCE as the *terminus ante quem* for the elaboration of the foundation legend of Soloi.

[40] Iacovou, *The Pictorial Pottery*, 1988, p. 27 nº 33.

period with the Greek Herakles, is found to be one of the most popular Cypriot royal avatars, provided in the island with a peculiar iconography (a young, bearded man walking, with a lion's skin headdress, the arm raised and waving the club).[41] The several Archaic representations of Geryon, the three-bodied giant killed by Herakles, and sometimes connected to Perseus (another Cypriot royal avatar) confirm the diffusion and the importance of the heroic patterns for Cypriot kingship.[42]

Even if they are less easy to identify, pictorial representations of human figures (warriors) on 11th-century Cypriot pottery seem reminiscent of traditional Aegean symbols, assimilated and newly elaborated to assert a heroic self-representation of the Cypriot elites.[43] Even if the lyre-playing warrior on a kalathos from Palaepaphos-*Xerolimni* cannot reliably be interpreted as representing Kinyras,[44] the iconography of this figure is reminiscent of Aegean motifs suggesting a conscious Cypriot elaboration intended to create a heroic legendary past upon which a new identity could be founded.

It is in this long and insufficiently documented phase, dating from the beginning of the Iron Age to the end of the Archaic period (the foundation and consolidation horizons, in the terms of Maria Iacovou),[45] that we should set the birth and the growth of Cypriot political identities. These were founded on an elite-shaped, heroic ideology of which the foundation legends are mostly a late, weak aftermath.

We can thus say that the Greek, heroic legendary motifs, apparently being a constitutive element of Cypriot elite ideology since the beginning of the Iron Age, are one of the first and less ambiguous signs of the fact that the Greeks have settled on the island. The "invisible migration" left almost no traces of itself in the material record of the 12th c., and it first became visible – although not on ethnic basis – in the mortuary patterns of Early Iron Age.[46] Yet, it gives the first sign of its existence in what seems to be "the earliest manifestations if not of 'Greekness' at least of distinct group identity on what has to become a largely Greek-speaking island in the Archaic and Classical periods".[47] That is, in other words, the

---

[41] Yon, 'À propos de l'Héraklès de Chypre', 1986 and 'Héraclès à Chypre', 1992.
[42] Fourrier, 'La réappropriation du passé', 2007.
[43] Sherratt, 'Immigration and Archaeology', 1992.
[44] Iacovou, *The Pictorial Pottery*, 1988, p. 26 n° 29; Sherratt, 'Immigration and Archaeology', 1992, pp. 336–337.
[45] Iacovou, 'From Ten to Naught', 2002.
[46] Iacovou, 'Cyprus: From Migration to Hellenisation', 2008, pp. 240–243; Iacovou, 'External and Internal Migrations during the 12th Century BC', 2012, pp. 222–225.
[47] Sherratt, 'Immigration and Archaeology', 1992, p. 326.

first manifestation of a typically Cypriot elite-constructed and partially Greek-shaped identity.

2.3 A multicultural royal ideology

The foundation legends have thus turned out to be nothing more than the aftermath of Cyprus' Hellenisation as well as a manifestation of the construction of an elite-defined heroic ideology within the context of the emerging Cypriot kingdoms. But if the Hellenisation of the island seems to be a necessary premise for the subsequent adoption of a Greek system of heroic references, everything in the Cypriot royal ideology is not Greek.

Kinyras, the Cyprus king of the Homeric epic, is a figure of ambiguous and composite origin who had a central role in the definition of royal status in Cyprus. But it is not exactly fortuitous that this non-Hellenic figure is particularly elusive in our mostly Greek-speaking sources. No representation of Kinyras can be safely identified, and the traditions concerning him are a bundle of superimposing narratives, each denoting different attempts to appropriate this highly symbolic hero.[48]

In quite a different way, Herakles / Melqart, the royal avatar *par excellence* in Cyprus, is systematically represented or alluded to on coins and sculptures.[49] He is also venerated in several sanctuaries on the island, but no legend, if not of a late date, puts him in relation to the Hellenisation of Cyprus (in Stephanus of Byzantium, *s. v.* Amathus, Herakles is the father of the otherwise unknown eponymous hero-founder of the city). The Herakles legends have apparently been known from very early on in Cyprus (if we credit the interpretation of the CG I figured plate from Palaepaphos-*Skales*, depicting Herakles and Iolaos killing the Lernaean hydra),[50] and at the latest they made appearances in the Archaic age, during which time they are represented on sculptures, terracottas and seals.[51]

But the heroic figure of Greek origin overlaps with another figure of the lion-skin on Cyprus, whose iconography is fixed in Kition at the end of the Archaic period. This figure has to be interpreted as Baal Melqart, the tutelary god of Tyre and Kition: represented as a smiting god of Oriental type, he is documented throughout a large part of the island and even in the Phoenician Levant throughout the entirety of the Classical

---

48 Baurain, 'Kinyras', 1980.
49 Yon, 'Héraclès à Chypre', 1992. On Melqart see Bonnet, *Melqart*, 1988.
50 Iacovou, *The Pictorial Pottery*, 1988, p. 27 n° 33.
51 Yon, 'Héraclès à Chypre', 1992 and Hermary, 'Quelques remarques', 1992.

period.[52] The royal character of the Herakles / Melqart types probably precedes the overlapping of the two figures, or, to put it another way, most likely contributed to this overlapping. And it is a strong possibility that the place where the assimilation had taken place was Cyprus.[53]

Another figure, of Egyptian origin, also contributed to the definition of the Cypriot Herakles / Melqart type and had a royal connotation in Cyprus (particularly evident in Amathus): Bes, represented as a monster fighting (or mastering) a lion.[54]

The heroic references of Cypriot elites – Kinyras, Herakles / Melqart, Perseus, Teukros, Agapenor, Praxandros, Akamas and possibly others – did not always remain the same. During the long life of some of the Cypriot kingdoms, succeeding dynasties had to change or update their legendary pedigrees in order to adapt them to the evolving world of the Greek myth. If some references (Herakles / Melqart, Kinyras) have appeared very early and have retained their popularity for a long time, others (such as Akamas, or Teukros) are most likely later developments, and bear the marks of particular political contexts through their emergence. But all these legendary figures are the product of the same phenomenon, that is, the elaboration and continuous adaption of Cypriot identities. And this is, despite its ambiguity, one of the most evident and durable effects of the Hellenisation of the island.

3. The Phoenician colonisation in Cyprus: the elements for its definition

The intense debate on the Hellenisation of Cyprus has for a long time overshadowed another crucial phase for Cypriot identity formation and ethnicity: the Phoenician colonial movement. The reason for the scant attention paid to the concrete conditions of the moving and settling of the Phoenicians on Cyprus is mainly that the Phoenician expansion into Cyprus has appeared to be far clearer and less ambiguous to define than the Greek penetration into the island. The Phoenicians can be credited with a main settlement in Cyprus, Kition, which was a Cypro-Phoenician kingdom during the Classical period; even if their presence on the rest of the island has been debated, and their Cypriot settlement of Qarthadasht has not yet been unanimously identified, Kition seems to meet the

[52] Yon, 'Héraclès à Chypre', 1992, pp. 151–154.
[53] Bonnet, 'Héraclès en Orient', 1992, pp. 174–176.
[54] On the importance of the animal mastery motif in Cypriot royal ideology see Counts, 'Divine Symbols and Royal Aspirations', 2010.

requirements for what we expect of a Phoenician colony,[55] and its foundation at the end of the 9th c. BCE fits the first phases of the Phoenician expansion towards the west. The classical sources too, even though of a late date, explicitly say that the Kitians are of Phoenician origin (Cicero, *De finibus* 4, 20. 56: *Citieos e Phoenica profectos*), and Diogenes Laertius, speaking about Kition, resorts to the vocabulary of the Greek colonisation (7, 1: πολίσματος Ἑλληνικοῦ Φοίνικας ἐποίκους ἐσχηκότος).

But as Maria Iacovou has correctly asked, "Phoenician expansion plus Phoenician presence equals Phoenician colonisation"?[56] Do the Phoenician presence in Cyprus and the supposed Phoenician foundations of Kition and Qarthadasht match the theoretical pattern of colonisation? We assume, of course, that the model evoked is not that of the Greek colonisation,[57] but the "non-Greek model of overseas settlement and presence" as defined by Hans-Georg Niemeyer for the Phoenician expansion in the Mediterranean.[58]

3.1. The Cypriot Qarthadasht

Let us recall the archaeological and textual evidence concerning the Phoenician "colonisation" in Cyprus. The epigraphic and archaeological data point to a progressive penetration of Phoenician elements into the island beginning in the 9th c. BCE. This penetration would have concentrated itself on the south-eastern coast, at the site of Kition, where a real Phoenician settlement would have been established at the same place as the Late Bronze Age town. According to the traditional interpretation, supported by Vassos Karageorghis, the excavator of the monumental site of Kition-Kathari, the area, after being founded in the 13th c. and occupied without interruption until the beginning of the first millennium, would have been abandoned during the following century and a half. After that Phoenician colonists would have reoccupied the area in the second half of the 9th c. However, Joanna Smith has recently

---

55 But what is a Phoenician colony? See van Dommelen, 'Colonial Interactions and Hybrid Practices', 2005, for a preliminary discussion on this problem: I wish to express my gratitude to the editors of this volume, Thomas Hertel and Mogens Trolle Larsen, for drawing my attention to this paper.

56 Iacovou, 'Cyprus at the Dawn of the first Millennium BC', 2005, p. 131.

57 On the model of the Greek colonisation see Tsetskhladze, 'Revisiting Ancient Greek Colonisation', 2006.

58 Niemeyer, 'The Phoenicians in the Mediterranean', 2006. On the need to elaborate new, regional-based interpretative approaches of the Phoenician as well as any other colonisation movement, see van Dommelen, 'Colonial Interactions and Hybrid Practices', 2005.

challenged this interpretation, and has particularly denied the existence of a phase of abandonment, supposing that the Phoenician penetration diluted itself throughout a very long space of time[59] – thus sapping the foundations of the "colonial" theory (see below, section 3.2).

Other Cypriot sites show unequivocal signs of Phoenician presence during the Geometric III and Archaic I periods (9th–7th c.). This is the case particularly at Amathus: a Phoenician-type necropolis has been discovered to the southwest of the acropolis,[60] and some extra-urban sanctuaries within the territory of the kingdom seem reserved to the local Phoenician community – a phenomenon otherwise unknown in Cyprus, where no sign of ethnic segregation is documented in this period.[61] The strong Phoenician character of the early phases of the site of Amathus (which has no Late Bronze Age predecessor) has induced several scholars – even very recently[62] – to identify it with the Cypriot Qarthadasht, "New Town", which is mentioned on some Phoenician and Akkadian documents of the 8th and 7th c. BCE first as a Tyrian possession, and then later as an independent kingdom.

The old debate concerning the identification of the Cypriot Qarthadasht is still lively, even if the evidence concerning this town has been well known for a long time. Three documents attest to its existence between the second half of the 8th c. and the first half of the 7th c. BCE: 1) the dedications to the Baal of Lebanon, on two fragmentary bronze bowls found in the countryside of Limassol, by the SKN of Qarthadasht, who declares himself "servant of Hiram, king of the Sidonians" – in all likelihood, this is Hiram II, king of Tyre between 738 and 730 BCE (*CIS* I 5; *KAI* 31; *TSSI* III 17);[63] 2) Esarhaddon's list of ten Cypriot kings and kingdoms, which dates from 673/2 and mentions the kingdom of Qarthadasht with its king Damusi at the 8th position;[64] 3) Assurbanipal's list, dating from after 664 BCE, which gives exactly the same names.[65]

---

[59] Smith, *Art and Society in Cyprus*, 2009.

[60] Christou, 'Cremations in the Western Necropolis of Amathus', 1998.

[61] Fourrier & Petit-Aupert, 'Un sanctuaire phénicien du royaume d'Amathonte', 2007; see the observations of Fourrier, 'La constitution d'identités régionales', 2007, pp. 123–124. For later (Hellenistic and Roman) possible evidence at Paphos, see Raptou, 'Nouvelles pratiques funéraires', 2009.

[62] Hermary, 'Le statut de Kition avant le Ve s. av. J.-C.', 1996 and Smith, 'Cyprus, the Phoenicians and Kition', 2008.

[63] Masson, 'La dédicace à Ba'al du Liban', 1985 and Sznycer, 'Brèves remarques sur l'inscription phénicienne de Chypre', 1985.

[64] Borger, *Die Inschriften Asarhaddons*, 1967, pp. 59-61; Leichty, *The Royal Inscriptions of Esarhaddon*, 2011, p. 23 (1, V 63–72).

[65] Onasch, *Die assyrischen Eroberungen Ägyptens*, 1994, I, pp. 149-150, II, pp. 98–103; Borger, *Beiträge zum Inschriftenwerk Assurbanipals*, 1996, pp. 18–20, 212 (*BIWA* C 14).

The combined evidence from these documents suggests that Qarthadasht, after being a Tyrian possession in the second half of the 8th c BCE, had become an independent Cypriot kingdom some decades later; after that, we find no more trace of it. It is highly improbable that a new, unknown Cypriot site will ever be found to correspond to Qarthadasht. As a result, it is necessary to identify which known, historical Cypriot centre could have been a Tyrian possession before becoming independent and dismissing the Qarthadasht name to adopt a new one – by which it is certainly known to us.

Kition suits this framework particularly well. Known in the later periods as a former Phoenician colony, Kition was certainly under Tyrian control in the last decades of the 8th c. BCE, when according to Menander of Ephesus (*FGrHist* 783 F 4), the Tyrian king Eloulaios had to suppress a local rebellion (*pace* Nadav Na'aman and Karen Radner,[66] we still think that the Eloulaios of Menander and the Lulî of the Neo-Assyrian inscriptions are of one and the same king of Tyre and Sidon during the last three decades of the 8th c. BCE).[67] In 707 the Neo-Assyrian king Sargon II expanded his domination "beyond the Sea of the Setting Sun" and raised a stele somewhere in Kition, most probably within the sacred area of *Bamboula*;[68] this act signals the inclusion of Cyprus into the empire.[69] If the Assyrians could reach Cyprus, it was thanks to the Tyrian fleet, and the erection of the stele in Kition can be read as a sign of the continued Tyrian control on the Cypriot city, since Tyre acted at that time as an important instrument of the Assyrian politics in the West.[70] This did not last long. Under Sargon's successor, Sennacherib, Tyre tried to revolt, but the Assyrian king firmly suppressed the rebellion in 701 BCE and forced Eloulaios / Lulî to flee.[71] It is highly probable that Kition gained its independence from Tyre at this very moment: after Sennacherib's expedition, the Phoenician kingdom lost the greatest part of its territory to the benefit of Sidon, which again became independent; it seems unlikely that Tyre could, at the same time, retain control of the Cypriot city, which had already attempted a revolt a few years earlier.

---

66 Na'aman, 'Eloulaios/Ululaiu', 2006 and Radner, 'The Stele of Sargon II of Assyria at Kition', 2010.

67 See now Boyes, '"The King of the Sidonians"', 2012 (who seems, however, to be ignoring Na'aman's hypothesis), pointing from a different basis to the same conclusion.

68 On the discovery of the stele and its probable place of standing in antiquity see Yon & Malbran-Labat, 'La stèle de Sargon II à Chypre', 1995.

69 Florence Malbran-Labat in Yon, *Kition dans les textes*, 2004, pp. 345–354.

70 Briquel-Chatonnet, *Les relations entre les cités*, 1992, pp. 183–188.

71 Briquel-Chatonnet, *Les relations entre les cités*, 1992, pp. 188–200.

If Kition fits the criteria for being identified as Qarthadasht so well, why is this identification not unanimously accepted? Two arguments are essentially evoked:[72] 1) a well-known 4th c. BCE *ostracon*, found in the sanctuary of Astarte at Kition-*Bamboula* and containing the temple tariff and accounts (*CIS* I 86; *KAI* 37; *TSSI* III 33), mentions both Kition and Qarthadasht. Thus (as is commonly admitted) they are not one and the same place; 2) Kition is not a "New Town": founded in the 13th c. BCE, it was still inhabited at the moment of the arrival of the Tyrians. Moreover, the name Kition is attested since the 11th c. BCE on an inscribed Phoenician arrowhead coming from Lebanon.[73] Also, the name may already be on some Ugaritic documents belonging to the 13th–12th c. BCE.[74]

These two arguments are of differing values, but neither is unquestionable. Let us first deal with the easiest. The temple tariff mentions both Kition (A l. 4: BT ʻŠTRT KT, "the temple of Astarte at Kition") and a person from Qarthadasht, a certain ʻBDʼBST HQRTḤDŠTY, "ʻBDʼBST (Abdubast) the Carthaginian" (B l. 6). It has been asserted that "puisque le nom *Qrthdšt* est attesté à Chypre même, il semble préférable de voir dans ce Carthaginois un Carthaginois de Chypre".[75] But, as mentioned previously, the Cypriot Qarthadasht is documented only for a limited period of time between the mid-8th and the mid-7th c. BCE.[76] In the 4th c. BCE, almost three centuries later, this name can perfectly well be associated with North African Carthage. Also, the name ʻBDʼBST, "servant of Bastet", has no attestation on Cyprus and only late and sporadically in Phoenicia; but it is well attested at Carthage and among the Phoenician community of Elephantine in Egypt.[77]

Thus we can confidently exclude the evidence of the Kition *ostracon* from the debate on the Cypriot Qarthadasht. We can now concentrate on the possible reasons that could have led Kition to change its name temporarily to Qarthadasht, and then later change it back again to its ancient local name. This is not just a simple matter of names: it has to do

---

72 Hermary, 'Le statut de Kition avant le Ve s. av. J.-C.', 1996, with previous references.
73 Sznycer, 'Une possible mention d'un "Kitien"', 1995.
74 Segert, 'Kition and Kittim', 2000, pp. 165–166.
75 Bunnens, *L'expansion phénicienne en Méditerranée*, 1979, p. 353.
76 At any rate, it would be problematic to associate this 4th-century mention of Qarthadasht with Cyprus: the name of Kition is attested in the same document, thus excluding the identification between the two towns; the name of Amathus on the other hand is documented in the same period, on a local inscription (*ICS*² 196), both in its Greek form (Ἀμαθοῦς) and in its Eteocypriot form (which is unknown, but is certainly neither Qarthadasht nor Amathus). It seems highly improbable that the same city had three different names in use at the same time.
77 Benz, *Personal Names*, 1972, pp. 148, 153, 258–259.

with the origin of the town, with the Tyrian colonisation and with the formation of a local identity.

3.2. The birth of the kingdom of Kition

The foundation of Kition dates back to the 13th c. BCE. The town is, along with Palaepaphos, the only Cypriot settlement where continuity has been documented during the crucial phases of the 12th–11th c. BCE, when the topographical shape of the island changed dramatically.[78] The monumental area of Kition-*Kathari*, excavated by the Department of Antiquities of Cyprus between 1959 and 1983, testifies to the flourishing character of the settlement during the transition from the end of the Late Bronze Age to the beginning of the Geometric Period with its temples and ashlar buildings.

As mentioned before, the thesis that there exists a gap in the occupation of this site from the beginning of the Geometric period (CG IB, ca. 1000 BCE) to the end of the Geometric period (end of the 9th c. BCE), when the Phoenician colonists would have reoccupied the site, has recently been challenged by a new study of the ceramic assemblages by Joanna S. Smith.[79] She argues that the Kition-*Kathari* area has been continuously inhabited and never abandoned. She then concludes that the Phoenicians had begun to penetrate the island slowly over the course of time beginning with the 10th c. BCE, and that they had taken political control of the city only near the end of the 8th c. BCE, and only thanks to the support of the Assyrian empire.

The thesis of a continuous occupation of Kition throughout the Geometric period seems to find confirmation in the evidence from the necropolis where no gap is apparent in spite of important changes.[80] Other evidence frequently evoked[81] – the domestic quarter discovered by the French mission on the hill of *Bamboula*, 500 metres to the southeast of *Kathari*, which had been dated to the 10th c. BCE – has proven irrelevant.[82] It is difficult to say when exactly and with which strength the

[78] Iacovou, 'The Topography of Eleventh Century B.C. Cyprus', 1994.
[79] Smith, *Art and Society in Cyprus*, 2009. See now the cautious observations of Georgiadou, 'La production céramique de Kition au Chypro-Géométrique I', 2012, drawing attention to some difficulties in the chronology established by the excavators and suggesting that without a detailed regional-based typology of the pottery of Kition it is impossible to decide on the hypothesis of Joanna S. Smith.
[80] Yon, *Kition de Chypre*, 2006, p. 118.
[81] See Smith, *Art and Society in Cyprus*, 2009, pp. 168–171.
[82] Yon & Caubet, *Le sondage L-N 13*, 1985. See Georgiadou, 'La production céramique de Kition au Chypro-Géométrique I', 2012, pp. 325–326, who demonstrates that the abandonment of the area can be dated from the end of the Late Cypriot IIIB period or the beginning of the Cypro-Geometric I period (first half of the 11th c. BCE).

Tyrian migration affected Kition, but what is sure is that the newcomers did not find a deserted settlement:[83] on the contrary, they came to an inhabited Cypriot town, which they probably knew well beforehand thanks to previous commercial relations.

The Tyrians apparently did not leave the town unchanged when they arrived at Kition in order to settle there. The rearrangement (if not reoccupation) of the sacred and artisanal quarter of Kition-*Kathari* and the establishment of a new sanctuary dedicated to Astarte on the hill of *Bamboula* can tentatively be linked to the newly established Phoenician community. Even if there is no incontestable evidence attributing to the Phoenicians immigrants and the building and rebuilding projects at the end of the 9th c. BCE, it seems fair to put these activities in relation to the appearance of a number of Phoenician documents starting from the end of the 9th c. BCE and increasing in number all along the Archaic Period[84] – especially when we consider that the Cypro-syllabic script in Kition is attested only to a very limited extent during the same period.[85] In brief, the hypothetical arrival and settling of Phoenician people at Kition, even if it "can hardly be supported by a distinct (Phoenician) material package", cannot at the same time be credited, as it has been argued, of a 9th c. BCE inscription alone:[86] the several documents dating from the end of the 9th to the end of the 6th c. BCE suggest, on the contrary, a continuous presence from the Cypro-Geometric III period on. The problem is that in Kition, as in many other Cypriot centres, we are able to observe the result of a process (the Cypro-Phoenician civilisation of Kition), but not its beginnings (its "Phoenicisation"). But when looking for the moment when this process could have started, the end of the 9th c. BCE (or, in archaeological terms, the Cypro-Geometric III period) is the best suited, with its renewal of activities, new installations and rearrangement of previous monumental structures, for admitting the arrival and settling of

---

[83] See Fourrier, 'Compte-rendu de J. S. Smith, Art and Society in Cyprus', 2011, pp. 596–597, who argues for a hiatus in the occupation not only at *Kathari* but also at *Bamboula*, suggesting at the same time the possible existence within the ancient town of topographical shifts still untouched by the well-published but limited archaeological explorations at the sites of *Kathari* and *Bamboula*.

[84] Yon, *Kition dans les textes*, 2004, no. 1100 (end of the 9th c. BCE), no. 1085 (8th c.), no. 1112 (end 8th – beginning 7th c. BCE), nos. 1082, 1083, 1091, 1155 (7th c.), nos. 1096, 1098, 1099, 1113, 1117 (6th c. BCE); Amadasi Guzzo, 'Phoenician inscriptions', 2003, pp. 258–260 nos. 3 and 8 (between 7th and 6th c. BCE).

[85] Egetmeyer, *Le dialecte grec ancien de Chypre*, 2010, 663–664 no. 4 (end of the 8th c. BCE), no. 2–3 (Cypro-Archaic I).

[86] Iacovou, 'Cyprus: From Migration to Hellenisation', 2008, pp. 252–257 (quotation at p. 254).

a group of people supposed to have taken control of the political power in the town.

So the Tyrians settled at Kition, a four-centuries old Cypriot town. But is it possible to deny that what they (re)founded and rearranged there was, from their point of view, their New Town, their Qarthadasht? If the settling of the colonists coincide with the establishment of a political protectorate of Tyre (which I argue in spite of the arguments of Joanna S. Smith,[87] which I find unconvincing in this connection), it would not be surprising if this new name (a kind of nickname) was adopted in the documents in the Phoenician language issued by the local political authorities (the dedications of the SKN of the city). The old name of Kition was probably not eliminated, but simply fell out of use.

When, after at least one failed rebellion (reported by Menander), Kition / Qarthadasht obtained its independence – an event that coincided with the downfall of the Tyrian power under the blows of the Assyrian empire at the very end of the 8th c. BCE – the new Cypriot kingdom possibly readopted the old name of Kition, or perhaps even retained the name of Qarthadasht for some time. But the Assyrian lists of Esarhaddon and Assurbanipal both give the name of Qarthadasht instead of Kition. We would tentatively explain this as the result of Assyrian consistency in scribal practices in the sense that the later scribes retained the name the city had when it was first discovered by the Assyrians; that is, when it was still a Tyrian colony, during the reign of Sargon II, at the moment of the erection of the stele. The name may also testify the Phoenician intermediation in the relations between the Cypriots and the Assyrians, a situation that emerges from the analysis of the Neo-Assyrian documents relating to Cyprus,[88] and where the Phoenicians could have still spoken of their former colony by its "ancient" name. It is also simply possible that the new kingdom did not dismiss outright the name of Qarthadasht, as it did not necessarily coincide with a negative experience in the past.

Be that as it may, sometime between the mid-7th c. and the beginning of the 5th c. BCE the old name of Kition reappeared and became the official name of the kingdom. But why? Once again, it is a matter of identity formation. The construction of the Cypriot political identities is, above all, based on the conscious exploitation of the past: this is what has been shown with the foundation legends – legendary constructions aiming at developing a heroic pedigree for the Cypriot elites. But this passes also through the reoccupation of visible Bronze Age remains for religious purposes towards the end of the Geometric period or the beginning of the

---

[87] Smith, *Art and Society in Cyprus*, 2009.

[88] Cannavò, 'The Role of Cyprus', 2007.

Archaic: the examples are numerous throughout the island, and the reoccupation of the *Kathari* area at Kition is one of these.[89] The name of the city, as a high-symbolic element, could have undergone the same process: recent examples of name changes or recuperations for ideological reasons are not lacking, even if the subject – well documented in modern history (*e.g.* many places in the ex-Soviet Union recovering their pre-revolutionary names after 1991, not to mention more recent and delicate cases) – would require more appropriate investigation for antiquity.

3.3. Constructing a Phoenician civilisation on Cyprus

Assuming that the Cypriot Qarthadasht is Kition, and that Kition / Qarthadasht has been under Tyrian control from its Phoenician (re)foundation at the end of the 9th c. BCE until the end of the 8th c. BCE as argued above, what do we learn about the Phoenician colonisation of Cyprus?

The Phoenicians had, from a formal and political point of view, a possession in Cyprus, Kition / Qarthadasht: for about a century (middle/end 9th – end 8th c. BCE) the town was politically dependent on Tyre, and the Tyrian control over the Cypriot centre could have coincided with some immigration of Phoenician people from the Levantine coast. But it is important to underline that we have no decisive evidence of that, and we only have the progressive increase of Phoenician documents spread over centuries. All similarities with a colonisation movement end here. Arriving at Cyprus, the Tyrians did not occupy an empty land: they decided to rebuild and adapt an existing town, Kition, to their own purposes. This town, already some centuries old, had a history, a civilisation and a population that did not disappear with the arrival of the Phoenicians, but adapted itself to the new incomers, absorbing them to produce a new and original sociocultural configuration, a Phoenician culture of Cyprus. The Phoenician migrants did not segregate in their own customs and civilisation, but let themselves be absorbed by and adjusted to this new Cypriot context: the pottery, funerary habits and religious practices that emerged are distinctively Phoenician but no less distinctively Cypriot.[90] This is the reason why Kition is definitely Cypriot,

---

[89] Fourrier, 'La réappropriation du passé', 2007, pp. 2–3; Papantoniou, 'Cypriot Sanctuaries and Religion', 2012.

[90] On the Phoenician pottery of Kition see Bikai, 'The Phoenician imports', 1981; Bikai, 'Statistical Observations', 2003; Fourrier, 'The Ceramic Repertoire', 2013. On funerary habits see Yon, 'Nécropoles phéniciennes de Kition', 1998; Hadjisavvas, 'The Phoenician Penetration in Cyprus', 2007; Hadjisavvas, *The Phoenician Period Necropolis of Kition*, 2012 and 2013. On religion: Yon, 'Cultes phéniciens à Chypre', 1986 and Caubet, 'Les

while it is impossible to assert that, say, Motya is Sicilian, or Carthage is Libyan.

The ideological practices by which the Kitians constructed their own distinctive identity all throughout the Archaic period are the very same which we can observe on the rest of the island. This includes the recourse to a heroic legendary ascendance, which in Kition takes the forms of Herakles / Melqart, the tutelary god of the town.[91] Kition lacks a Greek foundation legend, such as those we know for the other main Cypriot centres, unless we accept the hypothesis of Claude Baurain. He suggests that the isolated tradition of Philistos of Syracuse (*FGrHist* 556 F 47) on the foundation of Carthage by the heroes Azoros and Carchedon one generation before the Trojan War is in fact meant to relate to Cypriot and not to Libyan Carthage.[92] Even if this is the case, this legend has to be read as an etiological Greek elaboration, and has little to do with the quest for the identity of the Kitians themselves. On the contrary, the various phenomena related to a conscious recuperation of the past (the re-adoption of the name of Kition; the rearrangement or reoccupation of the sacred quarter of Kition-*Kathari*), together with the manifestations of the luxury of the local elites (funerary practices including the sacrifice of horses or donkeys)[93] point to a participation of Kition with the common pan-Cypriot elaboration[94] of a shared kingship model.

4. Conclusions

The model of "colonisation" (both Greek and Phoenician "colonisation") has been found to be maladroit in fixing and describing the phenomena

---

sanctuaires de Kition', 1986, for an overview; Karageorghis, *Excavations at Kition VI*, 1999-2005 with the review of Fourrier, 'Compte-rendu de V. Karageorghis, Excavations at Kition VI', 2007 observing that 'on n'a à aucun moment l'impression d'une implantation extérieure en milieu "indigene", d'une colonie, au sens grec du terme. Le matériel du niveau 3 donne, au contraire, l'image d'une civilisation d'emblée mélangée, cosmopolite' (p. 328).

[91] According to Aubet, *Tiro y las colonias fenicias de Occidente*, 2009, pp. 167–173 Melqart was a specific Tyrian colonial instrument whose presence through the establishment of a sanctuary "convertía automáticamente el establecimiento en una prolongación de la patria de origin, el reino de Tiro" (p. 172). If this can be taken as a plausible explanation for the introduction of the Phoenician god in Cyprus, his assimilation to Herakles and his distinctive Cypriot iconography does not pertain to Tyrian colonisation, but to pan-Cypriot royal ideology.

[92] Baurain & Bonnet, *Les Phéniciens*, 1992, pp. 183–188, arguing that the ancient traditions concerning the foundation of Carthage are in fact a 'téléscopage entre le mythe de fondation de la "Ville Nouvelle" chypriote et celui de sa célèbre homonyme africaine' (p. 186).

[93] Hermary, 'Les équidés à Chypre', 2005, pp. 189-190.

[94] Alternatively defined as a "Cypriot *koine*" (Papantoniou, *Religion and Social Transformations in Cyprus*, 2012, p. 54).

of the Hellenisation and "Phoenicisation" of Cyprus. In both cases, the arrival of external elements has been absorbed and transformed by the existing local civilisation, yielding a new compound as a result.

The Hellenisation of the island is certainly slower and less organised than its "Phoenicisation". No Greek political authority external to Cyprus has ever claimed to exercise any political control on the island or on any part of it, differently from Tyre, which can be credited with having an authentic possession in Cyprus (Kition / Qarthadasht) for more than a century. The Phoenician settlement at Kition could have been an organised enterprise (we have no evidence concerning this point), but this was hardly the case for the Greek arrival and settlement throughout the rest of the island some centuries before.

The essential point is that both the Greeks and the Tyrians did not land upon an empty island. Cyprus was urbanised, had already experienced a form of complex state organisation, had its own (possibly never interrupted) scribal practice and had not yet suffered any major destructions or catastrophes. As Susan Sherratt has vividly said, the Greek migration to Cyprus in the Eastern Mediterranean context of the end of the Late Bronze Age was far from a colonisation, but a movement "from the periphery to the core, from the Provinces to Versailles".[95] The Phoenician expansion responded to different patterns and needs, and the result was, at the beginning, something different: a kind of colonial settlement, politically dependent on the homeland, and possibly serving the interests of Tyre during the struggle with the Assyrians.[96] But after gaining its independence, Kition seems to have developed on the same paths as other Cypriot polities, partaking in the quest for identity and the ideological and theoretical means to attain it.

The development of distinctive political identities is then related, in Cyprus, to ethnicity (or at least to some aspects of it, such as the language), but it is not the mechanical result of their unfolding. Intrinsically composite, the Cypriot civilisation of the Iron Age shows its originality in the way it assimilates and works out the foreign inputs, be they Greek, Phoenician or other. Speaking of "colonisation" in order to describe these external contributions does not help to illuminate the specificity of the Cypriot case, and it merely hinders us from focusing on the regional dynamics that enliven this general model.

---

[95] Sherratt, 'Immigration and Archaeology', 1992, p. 325.

[96] *Contra* Iacovou, 'Cyprus: From Migration to Hellenisation', 2008, pp. 262–263.

BIBLIOGRAPHY

Amadasi Guzzo, M. G. 'Phoenician inscriptions.' V. Karageorghis (ed.). *Excavations at Kition VI. The Phoenician and later levels: Part II.* Nicosia, 2003, pp. 258–264.

Ampolo, C. 'Enea ed Ulisse nel Lazio da Ellanico (FGrHist 4 F 84) a Festo (432 L).' *Parola del Passato* 47 (1992), pp. 321–342.

Aubet, M. E. *Tiro y las colonias fenicias de Occidente.* Barcelona, 2009.

Baurain, C. 'Kinyras. La fin de l'Âge du Bronze à Chypre et la tradition antique.' *Bulletin de Correspondance Hellénique* 104 (1980), pp. 277–308.

– 'Passé légendaire, archéologie et réalité historique: l'hellénisation de Chypre.' *Annales Economies Sociétés Civilisations* 2 (1989), pp. 463–477.

– *Les Grecs et la Méditerranée orientale.* Paris, 1997.

– 'Le *come-back* d'Évagoras de Salamine et l'interprétation des *temple boys* chypriotes.' *Transeuphratène* 37 (2008), pp. 37–55.

Baurain, C. & C. Bonnet. *Les Phéniciens. Marins des trois continents.* Paris, 1992.

Benz, F. L. *Personal Names in the Phoenician and Punic Inscriptions.* Rome, 1972.

Bérard, J. 'La colonisation grecque de Chypre et la date de la guerre de Troie.' *Cahiers du Centre d'Études Chypriotes* 38 (2008), pp. 71–102.

Bikai, P. M. 'The Phoenician imports.' *Excavations at Kition IV. The Non-Cypriote Pottery.* Nicosia, 1981, pp. 23–35.

– 'Statistical observations on the Phoenician pottery of Kition.' V. Karageorghis (ed.). *Excavations at Kition VI. The Phoenician and later levels: Part II.* Nicosia, 2003, pp. 207–257.

Bonnet, C. *Melqart. Cultes et mythes de l'Héraclès tyrien en Méditerranée.* (Studia Phoenicia 8). Leuven, 1988.

– 'Héraclès en Orient: interprétations et syncrétismes.' C. Bonnet & C. Jourdain-Annequin (eds.). *Héracles, d'une rive à l'autre de la Méditerranée.* Bruxelles – Rome, 1992, pp. 165–198.

Borger, R. *Die Inschriften Asarhaddons, Königs von Assyrien.* (Archiv für Orientforschung Beiheft 9.) Osnabrück, 1967.

– *Beiträge zum Inschriftenwerk Assurbanipals.* Wiesbaden, 1996.

Boyes, P. J. '"The King of the Sidonians": Phoenician Ideologies and the Myth of the Kingdom of Tyre-Sidon.' *Bulletin of the American Schools of Oriental Research* 365 (2012), pp. 33–44.

Briquel-Chatonnet, F. *Les relations entre les cités de la côte phénicienne et les royaumes d'Israël et de Juda.* (Studia Phoenicia 12, Orientalia Lovaniensia Analecta 46.) Leuven, 1992.

Bunnens, G. *L'expansion phénicienne en Méditerranée. Essai d'interprétation fondé sur une analyse des traditions littéraires*, Bruxelles – Rome, 1979.

Cannavò, A. 'The Role of Cyprus in the Neo-Assyrian Economic System: Analysis of the Textual Evidence.' *Rivista di Studi Fenici* 35 (2007), pp. 179–190.

Caubet, A. 'Les sanctuaires de Kition à l'époque de la dynastie phénicienne.' C. Bonnet, E. Lipiński & P. Marchetti (eds.). *Religio Phoenicia.* (Studia Phoenicia 4.) Namur, 1986, pp. 153–168.

Christodoulou, P. 'Nicocréon, le dernier roi de Salamine de Chypre. Discours idéologique et pouvoir politique.' *Cahiers du Centre d'Études Chypriotes* 39 (2009), pp. 235–258.

Christou, D. 'Cremations in the Western Necropolis of Amathus.' V. Karageorghis & N. Stampolidis (eds.). *Eastern Mediterranean: Cyprus – Dodecanese – Crete 16th–6th cent. B.C.* Athens, 1998, pp. 207–215.

Counts, D. B. 'Divine Symbols and Royal Aspirations: The Master of Animals in Iron Age Cypriote Religion.' D. B. Counts & B. Arnold (eds.). *The Master of Animals in Old World Iconography*. Budapest, 2010, pp. 135–150.

Demetriou, A. *Cypro-Aegean Relations in the Early Iron Age.* (Studies in Mediterranean Archaeology 83.) Göteborg, 1989.

Dietler, M. 'The Archaeology of Colonization and the Colonization of Archaeology: Theoretical Challenges from an Ancient Mediterranean Colonial Encounter.' G. J. Stein (ed.). *The Archaeology of Colonial Encounters: Comparative Perspectives.* Santa Fe – Oxford, 2005, pp. 33–68.

Egberts, A. 'Hard Times: The Chronology of "The Report of Wenamun" Revised.' *Zeitschrift für Ägyptische Sprache und Altertumskunde* 125 (1998), pp. 93–108.

Egetmeyer, M. 'The Recent Debate on Eteocypriot People and Language.' *Pasiphae* 3 (2009), pp. 69–90.

– *Le dialecte grec ancien de Chypre.* Berlin – New York, 2010.

Engel, W. H. *Kypros. Eine Monographie.* 2 vols. Berlin, 1841.

Fortin, M. 'Fondation de villes grecques à Chypre: légendes et découvertes archéologiques.' J. B. Caron, M. Fortin and G. Maloney (eds.), *Mélanges d'études anciennes offerts à Maurice Lebel.* St-Jean-Chrysostome, 1980, pp. 25–44.

– 'Nouvelles découvertes relatives aux légendes de fondation de villes grecques à Chypre à la fin de l'Âge du Bronze.' *Échos du monde classique / Classical Views* 3 (1984), pp. 133–146.

Fourrier, S. 'La réappropriation du passé: Achéens et autochtones à Chypre à l'Âge du Fer.' S. Müller Celka & J.-C. David (eds.). *Patrimoines culturels en Méditerranée orientale: recherche sciéntifique et enjeux identitaires. 1er atelier (29 novembre 2007): Chypre, une stratigraphie de l'identité.* Lyon, 2007. <http://www.mom.fr/IMG/pdf/Fourrier_ed-2.pdf> (accessed 11 August 2012).

– 'La constitution d'identités régionales à Chypre à l'époque archaïque.' *Pallas* 73 (2007), pp. 115–124.

– 'Compte rendu de V. Karageorghis, *Excavations at Kition VI* (1999–2005).' *Revue archéologique* 44 (2007), pp. 325–328.

– 'Légendes de fondation et hellénisation de Chypre: parcours historiographique.' *Cahiers du Centre d'Études Chypriotes* 38 (2008), pp. 103–118.

– 'Compte rendu de J. S. Smith, *Art and Society in Cyprus* (2009).' *Topoi* 17 (2011), pp. 591–601.

– 'The Ceramic Repertoire of the Classical Period Necropolis of Kition.' S. Hadjisavvas (ed.). *The Phoenician Period Necropolis of Kition. Volume II.* Nicosia, 2014, pp. 135–181.

Fourrier, S. & C. Petit-Aupert. 'Un sanctuaire phénicien du royaume d'Amathonte: Agios Tychonas-*Asvestoton*.' *Cahiers du Centre d'Études Chypriotes* 37 (2007), pp. 251–264.

Georgiadou, A. P. 'La production céramique de Kition au Chypro-Géométrique I.' M. Iacovou (ed.). *Cyprus and the Aegean in the Early Iron Age: The Legacy of Nicolas Coldstream.* Nicosia, 2012, pp. 321–344.

Gjerstad, E. 'The Colonization of Cyprus in Greek Legend.' *Opuscula Archaeologica* 3 (1944), pp. 107–123.

Goren, Y., S. Bunimovitz, I. Finkelstein, and N. Na'aman. 'The Location of Alashiya: New Evidence from Petrographic Investigation of Alashiyan Tablets from El-Amarna and Ugarit.' *American Journal of Archaeology* 107 (2003), pp. 233–255.

Hadjisavvas, S. 'The Phoenician penetration in Cyprus as documented in the necropolis of Kition.' *Cahiers du Centre d'Études Chypriotes* 37 (2007), pp. 185–195.

– *The Phoenician Period Necropolis of Kition. Volume I.* Nicosia, 2012.

– *The Phoenician Period Necropolis of Kition. Volume II.* Nicosia, 2014.

Hermary, A. 'Quelques remarques sur les origines proche-orientales de l'iconographie d'Héraclès.' C. Bonnet & C. Jourdain-Annequin (eds.). *Héracles, d'une rive à l'autre de la Méditerranée.* Bruxelles – Rome, 1992, pp. 129–143.

– 'Le statut de Kition avant le Ve s. av. J.-C.' E. Acquaro (ed.). *Alle soglie della classicità: il Mediterraneo tra tradizione e innovazione. Studi in onore di Sabatino Moscati,* I. Pisa, 1996, pp. 223–229.
– 'Les ascendances légendaires des rois chypriotes. Quelques messages iconographiques.' *Cahiers du Centre d'Études Chypriotes* 32 (2002), pp. 275–288.
– 'Les équidés à Chypre à l'époque des royaumes.' A. Gardeisen (ed.). *Les équidés dans le monde méditerranéen antique.* Lattes, 2005, pp. 183–195.
– 'Dossier Jean Bérard: l'archéologie à Chypre dans les années 1950. Introduction.' *Cahiers du Centre d'Études Chypriotes* 38 (2008), pp. 19–32.

Iacovou, M. *The Pictorial Pottery of Eleventh Century B.C. Cyprus.* (Studies in Mediterranean Archaeology 78.) Göteborg, 1988.
– 'The Topography of Eleventh Century B.C. Cyprus.' V. Karageorghis (ed.). *Proceedings of the International Symposium 'Cyprus in the 11th Century B.C.'* Nicosia, 1994, pp. 149–165.
– 'From Ten to Naught. Formation, Consolidation and Abolition of Cyprus' Iron Age Polities.' *Cahiers du Centre d'Études Chypriotes* 32 (2002), pp. 73–87.
– 'Cyprus at the Dawn of the First Millennium BC: Cultural Homogenisation Versus the Tyranny of Ethnic Identifications.' J. Clarke (ed.). *Archaeological Perspectives on the Transmission and Transformation of Culture in the Eastern Mediterranean.* Oxford, 2005, pp. 125–134.
– 'Site Size Estimates and the Diversity Factor in Late Cypriot Settlement Histories.' *Bulletin of the American Schools of Oriental Research* 348 (2007), pp. 1–23.
– 'Cultural and Political Configurations in Iron Age Cyprus: The Sequel to a Protohistoric Episode.' *American Journal of Archaeology* 112 (2008), pp. 625–657.
– 'Cyprus: From Migration to Hellenisation.' G. R. Tsetskhladze (ed.). *Greek Colonisation: An Account of Greek Colonies and Other Settlements Overseas. Volume 2.* Leiden – Boston, 2008, pp. 219–288.
– 'External and Internal Migrations during the 12th Century BC. Setting the Stage for an Economically Successful Early Iron Age in Cyprus.' M. Iacovou (ed.) *Cyprus and the Aegean in the Early Iron Age: The Legacy of Nicolas Coldstream.* Nicosia, 2012, pp. 217–237.

Karageorghis, V. *Excavations at Kition VI. The Phoenician and Later Levels.* Nicosia, 1999–2005.

Knapp, A. B. *Prehistoric and Protohistoric Cyprus: Identity, Insularity, and Connectivity.* Oxford, 2008.

Kritzas, C. 'Επισκόπηση των επιγραφικών μαρτυριών για σχέσεις Κύπρου και Αργολίδας-Επιδαυρίας.' *Cyprus and the Aegean in Antiquity*. Nicosia, 1997, pp. 311–322.

Kron, U. 'Akamas et Demophon.' *Lexicon Iconographicum Mythologiae Classicae* I. Zürich – München, 1981, pp. 435–446.

Leichty, E. *The Royal Inscriptions of Esarhaddon, King of Assyria (680–669 BC)*. Winona Lake, 2011.

Leriou, A. 'Constructing an Archaeological Narrative: The Hellenization of Cyprus.' *Stanford Journal of Archaeology* 1 (2002). http://www.stanford.edu/dept/archaeology/journal/newdraft/leriou/paper.pdf (accessed 9 January 2013).

– 'Locating identities in the Eastern Mediterranean during the Late Bronze Age-Early Iron Age: The Case of 'Hellenised' Cyprus.' S. Antoniadou & A. Pace (eds.). *Mediterranean Crossroads*. Athens, 2007, pp. 563–591.

Maier, F. G. 'Kinyras and Agapenor.' V. Karageorghis (ed.), *Acts of the International Archaeological Symposium "Cyprus between the Orient and the Occident."* Nicosia, 1986, pp. 311–320.

Mairs, R. 'Hellenization.' R. S. Bagnall, K. Brodersen, C. B. Champion, A. Erskine and S. R. Huebner (eds.). *The Encyclopedia of Ancient History*. Oxford, 2012.

Malkin, I. *The Returns of Odysseus: Colonization and Ethnicity*, Berkeley, 1998.

– 'Heroes and the Foundation of Greek Cities.' P. Azara, R. Mar and E. Subías (eds.). *Mites de fundació de ciutats al món antic (Mesopotàmia, Grècia i Roma)*. Barcelona, 2001, pp. 123–129.

– 'Networks and the Emergence of Greek Identity.' I. Malkin (ed.). *Mediterranean Paradigms and Classical Antiquity*. New York, 2005, pp. 56–74.

– 'Foundations.' K. A. Raaflaub & H. van Wees (eds.), *A Companion to Archaic Greece*. Oxford, 2009, pp. 373–394.

– *A Small Greek World: Networks in the Ancient Mediterranean*. New York, 2011.

Masson, O. 'La dédicace a Ba'al du Liban (CIS I, 5) et sa provenance probable de la région de Limassol.' *Semitica* 35 (1985), pp. 33–46.

Mavrojannis, T. 'L'identité chypriote de la révolte ionienne à Évagoras Ier (499–374 avant J.-C.).' S. Fourrier & G. Grivaud (eds.). *Identités croisées en un milieu méditerranéen: le cas de Chypre (Antiquité - Moyen Âge)*. Rouen, 2006, pp. 153–163.

Na'aman, N. 'Eloulaios/Ululaiu in Josephus, *Antiquities* IX, 284.' *Nouvelles Assyriologiques Brèves et Utilitaires* 6 (2006).

Niemeyer, H. G. 'The Phoenicians in the Mediterranean. Between Expansion and Colonisation: A Non-Greek Model of Overseas Settlement and Presence.' G. R. Tsetskhladze (ed.). *Greek Colonisation: An Account of Greek Colonies and Other Settlements Overseas. Volume 1*. Leiden, 2006, pp. 143–168.

Onasch, H. U. *Die assyrischen Eroberungen Ägyptens*. (Ägypten und Altes Testament 27.) Wiesbaden, 1994.

Papantoniou, G. 'Cypriot Sanctuaries and Religion in the Early Iron Age: Views from Before and After.' M. Iacovou (ed.). *Cyprus and the Aegean in the Early Iron Age: The Legacy of Nicolas Coldstream*. Nicosia, 2012, pp. 285–319.

– *Religion and Social Transformations in Cyprus*. (Mnemosyne Supplements 347.) Leiden, 2012.

Radner, K. 'The Stele of Sargon II of Assyria at Kition: A Focus for an Emerging Cypriot Identity?' R. Rollinger, B. Gufler, M. Lang & I. Madreiter (eds.). *Interkulturalität in der Alten Welt: Vorderasien, Hellas, Ägypten und die vielfältigen Ebenen des Kontakts*. Wiesbaden, 2010, pp. 429–449.

Raptou, E. 'Nouvelles pratiques funéraires à Paphos hellénistique et romaine.' *Cahiers du Centre d'Études Chypriotes* 39 (2009), pp. 89–112.

Sass, B. 'Wenamun and His Levant 1075 BC or 925 BC?' *Ägypten und Levante* 12 (1998), pp. 247–255.

Satraki, A. *Κύπριοι Βασιλείς από τον Κόσμασο στο Νικοκρέοντα*. (Αρχαιογνωσία 9). Athens, 2012.

Segert, S. 'Kition & Kittim.' P. Åström & D. Surenhagen (eds.). *Periplus. Festschrift für Hans-Gunter Buchholz*. (Studies in Mediterranean Archaeology 127.) Jonsered, 2000, pp. 165–172.

Serghidou, A. 'Discours ethnographique et quêtes identitaires en Chypre ancienne.' S. Fourrier & G. Grivaud (eds.). *Identités croisées en un milieu méditerranéen: le cas de Chypre (Antiquité - Moyen Âge)*. Rouen, 2006, pp. 165–186.

Sherratt, S. 'Immigration and Archaeology: Some Indirect Reflections.' P. Åström (ed.), *Acta Cypria 2*. Jonsered, 1992, pp. 316–347.

Smith, J. S. 'Cyprus, the Phoenicians and Kition.' C. Sagona (ed.). *Beyond the Homeland: Markers in Phoenician Chronology*. Leuven, 2008, pp. 261–303.

– *Art and Society in Cyprus from the Bronze Age into the Iron Age*. New York, 2009.

Steele, P. M. 'The Diversity of the Cypro-Minoan Corpus.' P. Carlier, C. D. Lamberterie, M. Egetmeyer, N. Guilleux, F. Rougemont & J.

Zurbach (eds.). *Études mycéniennes 2010.* Pisa – Roma, 2012, pp. 537–544.

Sznycer, M. 'Brèves remarques sur l'inscription phénicienne de Chypre, CIS, I, 5.' *Semitica* 35 (1985), pp. 47–50.

– 'Une possible mention d'un 'Kitien' (KTY) au XIe s. av. J.-C.' *Cahiers du Centre d'Études Chypriotes* 24 (1995), pp. 3–5.

Tsetskhladze, G. R. 'Revisiting Ancient Greek Colonisation.' G. R. Tsetskhladze (ed.). *Greek Colonisation: An Account of Greek Colonies and Other Settlements Overseas. Volume 1.* (Mnemosyne Supplements 193.) Leiden, 2006, pp. xxiii–lxxxiii.

van Dommelen, P. 'Colonial Interactions and Hybrid Practices: Phoenician and Cartaginian Settlement in the Ancient Mediterranean.' G. J. Stein (ed.). *The Archaeology of Colonial Encounters: Comparative Perspectives.* Santa Fe – Oxford, 2005, pp. 109–141.

Vanschoonwinkel, J. *L'Egée et la Méditerranée orientale à la fin du IIe millénaire. Témoignages archéologiques et sources écrites.* Louvain-la-Neuve – Providence, 1991.

Voskos, I., & A. B. Knapp. 'Cyprus at the End of the Late Bronze Age: Crisis and Colonization or Continuity and Hybridization?' *American Journal of Archaeology* 112 (2008), pp. 659–684.

Yon, M. 'À propos de l'Héraklès de Chypre.' L. Kahil, C. Augé & P. Linant de Bellefonds (eds.). *Iconographie classique et identités régionales.* (Bulletin de Correspondance Hellénique, Supplement 14.) Athènes, 1986, pp. 287–297.

– 'Cultes phéniciens à Chypre: l'interprétation chypriote'. C. Bonnet, E. Lipiński & P. Marchetti (eds.). *Religio Phoenicia.* (Studia Phoenicia 4.) Namur, 1986, pp. 153–168.

– 'Héraclès à Chypre.' C. Bonnet & C. Jourdain-Annequin (eds.). *Héracles, d'une rive à l'autre de la Méditerranée.* Bruxelles – Rome, 1992, pp. 145–163.

– 'Nécropoles phéniciennes de Kition.' S. Marchegay, M. T. Le Dinahet & J. F. Salles (eds.). *Nécropoles et pouvoir. Idéologies, pratiques et interprétations*, Lyon, 1998, pp. 217–227.

– *Kition dans les textes.* (Kition-Bamboula V). Paris, 2004.

– *Kition de Chypre.* Paris, 2006.

Yon, M. & A. Caubet. *Le sondage L-N 13.* (Kition-Bamboula III). Paris, 1985.

Yon, M. & F. Malbran-Labat. 'La stèle de Sargon II à Chypre.' A. Caubet (ed.). *Khorsabad, le palais de Sargon II, roi d'Assyrie.* Paris, 1995, pp. 159–179.

WRESTLING WITH THE PAST

The Appropriation of Pharaonic History in Medieval Egypt*

JOOST KRAMER

Abstract. This paper focuses on how medieval Islamic historians appropriated Egypt's pre-Islamic history and used it to distinguish Egypt among the other regions of the Islamic Empire. An important approach applied in this paper is that medieval historians did not necessarily present historical facts but rather used their narratives to convey contemporary issues. One of these issues was that historians needed to address Egypt's dubious role in the Quran, e.g. in the story of Moses. By presenting a narrative that emphasized Egypt's merits mentioned in the Quran, historians incorporated pre-Islamic Egypt into Islam. Now this pre-Islamic history could be used to present a distinct Egypt raised above the other regions of Islam. In doing so, this history could serve as a source for early Arab Muslims, who settled in Egypt immediately after the conquest, as well as converted Copts in shaping their identities.

1. INTRODUCTION

When the Arab Muslims conquered Egypt in 642 AD, they were immediately confronted with Egypt's pre-Islamic past, which was most visible in the immense monuments that were still standing such as the pyramids and the temples. To the Arabs the history of ancient Egypt was mainly known through the stories of the Quran. The most common example may be the story of the exodus of Moses and the Israelites from Egypt. In this episode the Egyptian pharaoh was depicted as a ruthless tyrant and Egypt's pre-Islamic history was associated with his reign of terror and violence. This did not mean that its history was neglected. From as early as the eighth century AD Islamic scholars started to describe pharaonic history and its monuments resulting in historical narratives that were still transmitted in the seventeenth century. Surely, the

* I would like to thank prof. dr. Jan Just Witkam, Daniel Soliman, Marieke van Werven, and Jurgen van Oostenrijk for reading my article and providing me with their comments. I am indebted to Tina Loo for correcting my English. Finally I would like to thank prof. dr. Petra Sijpesteijn for supervising my master's thesis on which this paper is based.

impressiveness of the monuments must have been among the reasons for historians to include pharaonic chronology in their works, but there was more to it than just that. They presented Egypt as a land where Islamic prophets roamed, where science was first brought and protected, and where just and wise kings ruled. Medieval historical writings on ancient Egypt suggest that the Egypt of their days could benefit from this meritorious past. So in short in the Islamic Middle Ages there was an ambiguity in perception of ancient Egypt; on the one hand pharaonic Egypt was a place of debauchery where Pharaoh ruled as a vicious tyrant, while on the other hand Egypt was the cradle of scientific knowledge and had brought forth awe-inspiring monuments.

In this paper I will describe the encounter between two different cultural entities, namely the pharaonic heritage and the newly arriving Muslim elite, and I will examine how this new elite appropriated this heritage and whether they used it to construct a new Islamic Egyptian identity. This paper is based on texts preserved in manuscripts and will focus on the early period in which Islamic narratives on pharaonic Egypt were developed, i.e. the eighth to tenth century AD. However, since these narratives were hardly altered in subsequent centuries some later examples will be given as well.

2. Theoretical framework

This section will discuss the theoretical framework of the research. First it will shed some light on the theory of cultural appropriation, which will be applied to the material. Second, a methodological outline will be given on the approach of this material since it is believed that medieval Islamic historians did not necessarily present their view of historical reality but implicitly told the story of their contemporary values and problems.

2.1. Cultural appropriation

Cultural appropriation has been defined as 'the taking – from a culture that is not one's own – of intellectual property, cultural expressions or artefacts, history and ways of knowledge.'[1] This definition is adopted in this paper.

When medieval Islamic historians started to describe the pharaonic past, the culture of the 'other', they made it consistent with their own accepted views of Islamic religion and Arab culture. In this sense they appropriated pharaonic culture, changed it to some degree and formed their own version of Egyptian pre-Islamic history. The Muslims of early

[1] Ziff & Rao, 'Introduction to Cultural Appropriation', 1997, p. 1.

Islamic Egypt formed the local elite and were as such the dominant social group. Did they have political motives to appropriate the pharaonic heritage? The Muslims saw the Copts as the heirs of pharaonic culture, but did the Copts see themselves as such and how did they interact with this pre-Christian heritage – if at all? Finally, did the Islamic appropriation of pharaonic Egypt lead to a shared history of both Muslims and Copts? Applying the theory of cultural appropriation to historical accounts written in the medieval Islamic world allows us to more sharply define these questions, which this paper intends to answer.

2.2. Describing historical reality?

In this paper I assume that medieval Islamic historians did not necessarily present a narrative, which they deemed historically factual. In fact, I argue that more often than not these historians wished to convey contemporary issues, be they political, social, moral, etc., instead of presenting historical reality.[2]

In Arabic studies there have been several approaches to medieval chronicles and histories.[3] One of these approaches, which Fred Donner calls the sceptical approach, denies that there is a kernel of historical fact distinguishable in Islamic historical works. He believes that whatever factual essence remained was either redacted out of existence or flooded with additions making it impossible to identify.[4] A good example of this approach is Konrad Hirschler's study of the works of the chroniclers Abū Shāma (d. 1268) and Ibn Wāsil (d. 1298), in which Hirschler draws heavily on Hayden White's theories.[5] Hirschler has applied relevant emplotments – ways of structuring material within a context to give meaning to the material – to the works of the two chroniclers in order to show that their complex narratives have to be understood in view of 'the author's positions in social and intellectual terms.'[6] Although the authors were writing history, they discussed in the same text several issues of their own time and place, notably the matter of ideal rule.[7] Hirschler's work is an example of a study that emphasises the difference between the presentation of historical reality and the presentation of contemporary

[2] This is for example argued by the American historian Hayden White, according to whom annals and chronicle forms do not necessarily conform to the discourse that the modern history form is supposed to embody, but that they are alternative conceptions of history (White, 'The Value of Narrativity in the Representation of Reality', 1980, p. 10).

[3] Cf. Donner, *Narratives of Islamic Origins*, 1998, pp. 5–25.

[4] Donner, *Narratives of Islamic Origins*, 1998, p. 23.

[5] Hirschler, *Medieval Arabic Historiography*, 2006, pp. 63f.

[6] Hirschler, *Medieval Arabic Historiography*, 2006, p. 122.

[7] Hirschler, *Medieval Arabic Historiography*, 2006, p. 122.

issues within Islamic historical writing, and further cautions that modern scholars should be aware of this difference in their approaches.

This paper will take an approach similar to Hirschler's, which corresponds to what Donner has called the sceptical approach. This means that I will consider the accounts of medieval Islamic historians on pharaonic history as mirrors of contemporary society, not as a representation of what these medieval historians saw as factual history of ancient Egypt. This approach is legitimate because in some instances as described below, it is possible to prove that medieval historians had access to factual information regarding pharaonic history but that they chose to ignore it.

One example is the story of the Alexandrian lighthouse, which, according to an often-transmitted narrative, possessed several fantastic statues and an incredibly powerful mirror that could set ships on fire using the rays of the sun. However, when the traveller Yāqūt (d. 1229) ascended the lighthouse he did not find any trace of mirrors, but later Islamic historians never referred to his account.[8] Another example is the king list of the Central Asian polymath al-Bīrūnī (d. 1048). He translated the king list of the Ptolemaic priest Manetho via a Syriac intermediary and added a new dynasty to the already existing pharaonic chronology as it was seen by Islamic historians.[9] Al-Bīrūnī's historically accurate list, which was widely available in the medieval Near East, was copied only by al-Maqrīzī (d. 1442) who used it as an addendum to the traditional Muslim king list of pharaonic Egypt.[10] Apparently no other Islamic historian felt obligated to incorporate this slice of truth. These two examples suggest that medieval scholars were selective in their presentation of pharaonic history and although they had access to at least some historically accurate sources, they chose a different narrative. The question I will ask is what is this narrative and why did historians choose a particular one? Since a sceptical approach addresses these problems, I will apply it in this paper.

3. Historical Setting

In this section the historical background will be presented starting with the advent of Islam in Egypt up until Egypt's Ṭūlūnid dynasty. The reason for this demarcation is that in this period the foundations were laid for Islamic views on pharaonic Egypt. The focus will be placed on shifts in power, social groups, religion, and ethnicity.

---

[8] Yāqūt, *Muʿjam al-buldān*, 1984, V, p. 188.
[9] al-Bīrūnī, *al-Athār al-bāqiya*, 1923, pp. 90f.
[10] al-Maqrīzī, *Khiṭaṭ*, 2002, I, pp. 390f.

3.1. Egypt before Islam

Already long before the Islamic conquest of Egypt, the country was ruled by foreign sovereigns. The last native Egyptian pharaoh Nectanebo II (r. 360–343 BC) was defeated by the Persian Artaxerxes III in 343 BC. The Persians in turn were defeated by Alexander the Great, who entered Egypt in 332 BC. After the death of Alexander, his general Ptolemy usurped the throne of Egypt, first as satrap and, from 305 BC, as an independent king. The recently founded Alexandria became Egypt's brand new capital and Greek was adopted as the language of the administration. However, in order to legitimize their reign, the new rulers still commissioned temples in native Egyptian style where the gods of the traditional Egyptian pantheon were appeased.[11] During the last two centuries BC, the Ptolemaic dynasty started to decline and was characterised by civil war, blood feuds, and loss of foreign territory to the emerging Roman Empire. The last Ptolemaic ruler was Cleopatra VII, who sided with Marc Antony but was defeated by Octavian. Octavian added Egypt to the Roman Empire on August 1, 30 BC.

From 30 BC until the Arab Conquest in 642 AD, Egypt was a province of the Roman Empire. Although there was strong segregation in which Romans and Greeks were exempt from certain taxes, chores and punishments, the first two centuries of Roman rule were relatively peaceful.[12] Perhaps one of the most important developments of this era was the rise of Christianity and the subsequent Christianisation. Christianity first appeared in Jewish communities in the first and second centuries AD and remained low-key. The Roman emperors forbade the religion as they saw it as a politically dangerous sect, whose intentions were to protest against Rome. The intolerance culminated in violent actions against Christians of which the most gruesome purge took place during the reign of Diocletian in 302 AD. However, a decade later in 313 the Edict of Milan was signed under emperor Constantine I, which called for religious tolerance in the Eastern Roman Empire. Under emperor Theodosius Christianity became the state religion in 391 AD.

Now that Christianity had become an accepted religion, its dogmas, canon, and hierarchy were established during several synods. The question of the nature of Christ caused a schism in the Eastern Church between the Egyptian and Byzantine patriarchs. This theological dispute had far reaching political consequences. The Egyptian Coptic church was well organised by now, and the Byzantine emperor needed to control the Egyptian church in order to control Egypt. Almost as a rule, the Egyptians

---

[11] Bagnall & Rathbone (eds.), *Egypt. From Alexander to the Copts*, 2004, p. 14.

[12] Ritner, 'Egypt under Roman Rule', 1998, p. 11.

did not accept the imperial Byzantine patriarchs sent to Egypt. Gradually the emperor lost power over Egypt and internal problems at the imperial palace contributed to his political fall. Meanwhile Christians were strongly opposed to the few remaining cult centres of ancient Egyptian religion and Hellenistic polytheism. The pressure of the Christianisation of Egypt meant the definitive closure of Egyptian temples.

Rejection – or better, neglect – of the pharaonic past by the Copts is also visible in their historiographic traditions. The best-known Coptic historical work is the *History of the Patriarchs of Alexandria*, a cycle to which many Alexandrian patriarchs contributed covering the first to the thirteenth century, but leaving out pharaonic Egypt.[13] In a different historical work simply entitled *Chronicle*, bishop John of Nikiu (d. seventh century) described not only the Arab conquest to which he was a near contemporary, but also aimed to cover the history of mankind from Adam up until the Roman emperors including a few passages on pharaonic chronology. His work is heavily influenced by Greek authors, for example Herodotus.[14] A subsequent author Ibn al-Rāhib (d. between 1282 and 1295) presented in his *Kitāb al-tawārīkh* (*Book of the Historical Tracts*) a chronology from Adam up until his own day including Jewish, Persian, and Greek dynasties, but strangely enough excluding pharaonic history.[15] Finally, the topographical work of the twelfth century bishop Abū ‘l-Makārim did include several narratives on ancient Egypt.[16] However, Abū ‘l-Makārim's work was based on the fully developed Islamic historical tradition on pharaonic history rather than a Coptic tradition.[17] Omitting pharaonic history may be explained by the absence of and inaccessibility to sources concerning pharaonic history, but that did not restrain later Islamic historians from presenting detailed accounts on ancient Egypt, as we will see. Rather, an explanation should be sought in the rejection Copts felt for the pharaonic past.

3.2. The Arab Conquest

[13] Evetts, *History of the Patriarchs of the Coptic Church of Alexandria*, 1947–1953.

[14] Cf. John of Nikiu, *Chronicle*, 1916, p. 21; John relates how the pyramids of Giza were built by a king called Rampsinitus, a Greek version of Kheops, who forced his daughter to sleep with every man willing to contribute a stone to the construction. The same story can be found in Herodotus (*Historiae*, Book II, 124).

[15] Ibn al-Rāhib, *Kitāb al-tawārīkh*, 1903.

[16] The editor and translator of this work erroneously attributed this work to a certain Abū Ṣāliḥ al-Armānī, who appeared to be the owner of one of the manuscripts and possibly ordered the worked but was not the author.

[17] His sources include Ibn ᶜAbd al-Ḥakam (d. 871) and Ibn al-Kindī (act. second half tenth century); cf. Abū ’l-Makārim, *Ta’rīkh al-kanā’is*, 1895, pp. 54, 69, 93, and 97.

On the eve of the Arab conquest, Byzantine control over Egypt was weakened. Moreover, the Egyptians were disgusted by the involvement of Constantinople in religious matters. So when ᶜAmr b. al-ᶜĀṣ (d. 664), a prominent member of the Umayyad clan, entered Egypt in late 639 or early 640, his army was met with little resistance. His first objective was the fortress of Babylon, just north of the ancient capital of Memphis. When the fortress fell in April 641, the Muslim forces marched on to Alexandria, Egypt's Byzantine capital. A treaty was signed at the end of that year stipulating that the last Roman forces were to leave Alexandria in September 642. Apart from Babylon and Alexandria, the Muslims did not meet with much resistance.

3.3. The first centuries of Islamic rule

The Islamic troops settled in a newly founded city called al-Fusṭāṭ, which was located just north of the fortress of Babylon. Parcels of land, called *khiṭaṭ*, were divided among several of the Arab tribes coming mainly from southern Arabia and Yemen. The centre of the administration was transferred from Alexandria to al-Fusṭāṭ. The Muslims did not intermingle much with the native Egyptians as long as taxes were paid. During the first century of Islamic rule the Egyptians remained cooperative towards the new rulers since the Muslims were less oppressive than the Byzantines, who had interfered in their religious activities.[18] Non-Muslims who belonged to the *ahl al-kitāb* (the people of the Book, meaning Christians, Jews and in some cases Zoroastrians) were allowed to practice their respective religions as long as they paid the *jizya*, a poll-tax, by which one would become a *dhimmī*, one who is protected through a covenant.[19] Apart from the *dhimma* Copts also had *raḥim*, meaning a kinship relation, with the Arabs and thus they were recommended for good treatment.[20] Due to their favourable status as *dhimmī* and *raḥim*, Copts did not convert *en masse* to Islam. Only later did it become more interesting and in some cases necessary for Copts to learn Arabic and to convert to Islam, e.g. when it was decided in 706 that the government administration was only to be compiled in Arabic.[21] However, converting to Islam was not necessarily enough to advance socially. Native Egyptians also needed to be part of an Arab tribe. They could do so by becoming a client, a *mawlā*, of one such tribe.

[18] Kennedy, 'Egypt as a Province in the Islamic Caliphate, 641–868', 1998, p. 67.
[19] Crone, *God's Rule*, 2004, p. 358.
[20] Bashear, *Arabs and Others in Islam*, 1997, p. 69.
[21] Kennedy, 'Egypt as a Province in the Islamic Caliphate', 1998, p. 67.

In the seventh to ninth century, Egypt was neither the political nor cultural centre of the Islamic Empire. This position was reserved for Damascus and from around 750 AD for Baghdad. Egypt was ruled through the governor (*wālī*), who was appointed by the caliph. He was responsible for the Friday prayer and collection of taxes. Next came the commander of the police forces (*ṣāḥib al-shurṭa*) and the judge (*qāḍī*), who were drafted from the ranks of the local Egyptian Muslim elite, the *wujūh*. After the ᶜAbbāsid revolt in 750 al-Fusṭāṭ became the scene of a struggle between the *wujūh* and the *wālī*, who now often came from the Khurāsānī military elite from Persia. In the first decade of the ninth century caliph Hārūn al-Rashīd (r. 786–809) decided to dispatch Khurāsānī to Egypt in order to restore balance. Only during the reign of his successor al-Ma'mūn (r. 813–833), who installed 'super-governors' in Egypt often of Turkish descent, did the Egyptian province become more stable. These newcomers were of different ethnic origin than the Egyptians and the Muslims already living in Egypt.

3.4. The Ṭūlūnids

The unrest of the first half of the ninth dynasty gave way to the rise of the governor Ibn Ṭūlūn (d. 884), who raised a private slave army and established the Ṭūlūnid dynasty in Egypt, which lasted until 969 AD. During their reign al-Fusṭāṭ became an important centre for Islamic and Arab culture, especially for historical writing.[22] This position endured through the ages.

3.5. Shuᶜūbiyya: An anti-Arab sentiment

The first centuries after the conquests witnessed the rise of the *shuᶜūbiyya*-movement. *Shuᶜūbiyya*, which is derived from *shuᶜūb*, peoples, denotes the movement of the various peoples who lived in the Islamic Empire and had converted to Islam, but who did not belong to an Arab tribe. The central idea of the *shuᶜūbiyya* is that in Islam all Muslims are equal and that Arabs do not have any exclusive rights.[23] The movement started in Persia in the eighth and ninth century as a reaction to Arab arrogance. It is not merely coincidence that the movement started in Persia. Persian Muslims of non-Arab descent became increasingly powerful after the ᶜAbbāsid revolution in 750 AD, and it was only logical that this led to a national sentiment based on the inheritance of their

---

[22] Bianquis, 'Autonomous Egypt from Ibn Ṭūlūn to Kāfūr, 868–969', 1998, p. 98.
[23] Goldziher, *Muslim Studies*, I, 1967, p. 137.

ancient empire.[24] In other words, Islam lost its Arab identity.[25] Persian poets and scholars wrote works in praise of the age-old Persian national culture, e.g. the *Shahnameh* (*The Book of Kings*) by Firdawsī (d. 1020). Ibn Waḥshiyya (d. 930/931) contributed to this process with his *Filāḥa al-Nabaṭiyya* (*Nabatean Agriculture*) and *Kitāb shawq al-mustahām fī maᶜrifat rumūz al-aqlām* (*The Book of the Yearning for the Love of Knowing the Symbols of the Scripts*), both alleged translations of old Syrian texts in which Ibn Waḥshiyya emphasized the rural roots of the Arabs versus the developed culture of ancient Babylonia and Mesopotamia.

Like Mesopotamia and Persia, Egypt possessed its share of ancient monuments and from the Ṭūlūnid dynasty onwards, Egypt was either semi-autonomous or the centre of a larger Islamic Empire, such as the Fāṭimid Empire. But in contrast to Mesopotamia and Persia, Egyptian Islam did not loose its Arab identity, or at least lost it at a much slower pace. This may be explained by the slow rate of Islamisation in the first centuries of Islamic Egypt due to the favourable status awarded to the indigenous Copts by their Islamic rulers. Nonetheless, according to Ignaz Goldziher, there was a Coptic sentiment of the old nation against Arabism, which was expressed in Coptic books.[26] Unfortunately Goldziher does not name them.

A certain sense of the old nation against Arabism was reflected in the late antique *Cambyses Story*,[27] which presents Egyptian national pride.[28] The Persian king threatens the Egyptian people, but they stand behind king and country. The message is that Egypt is the greatest nation in the world. However, I was not able to ascertain the popularity of this story in early Islamic Egypt. The sense of national pride based on the pharaonic heritage should not be overestimated. In Egypt we do not see a Firdawsī, who imbibed Persian medieval literature with a pre-Islamic awareness. Nor was there an Egyptian Ibn Waḥshiyya. Egypt had lost its identification with the past as was pointed out by Michael Cook.[29] Nonetheless we should not forget that Egypt was an ancient civilization with a rich history confined to the same geographical borders at the

---

[24] Hämeen-Anttila, *The Last Pagans of Iraq*, 2006, pp. 33f.
[25] Hämeen-Anttila, *The Last Pagans of Iraq*, 2006, p. 34.
[26] Goldziher, *Muslim Studies*, I, 1967, p. 147.
[27] Jansen, *The Coptic Story of Cambyses' Invasion of Egypt*, 1950, pp. 59-70.
[28] The terms 'nation' and 'national' are generally seen as modern notions. However, Anthony Smith has examined the roots of nation formation in ancient societies and concluded that ancient Egypt possessed elements of nation formation (Smith, *The Antiquity of Nations*, 2004, p. 146).
[29] Cook, 'Pharaonic History in Medieval Egypt', 1983, p. 100.

beginning of the second millennium AD as it was in pharaonic times. This may have given rise to a form of regional sentiment.[30]

3.6. Islamic historiography and pharaonic history

More than a century after the Arab Conquest of Egypt its pre-Islamic past was described by the Egyptian Muslim Ibn Lahīᶜa (d. 790). Although his work is lost – we know that he wrote on Egyptian history from Ibn ᶜAbd al-Ḥakam (d. 871), who quotes Ibn Lahīᶜa extensively[31] – he seems to be the first Islamic scholar to have written on the subject. When Ibn Ṭūlūn rose to power and established his own dynasty in Egypt gaining more independence from the Islamic caliphate in Baghdad, Ibn ᶜAbd al-Ḥakam wrote his extensive work on Egyptian history. Interest in pre-Islamic Egypt remained and the next century was witness to writers such as Ibn Zūlāq, al-Kindī, his son Ibn al-Kindī. The former and the latter employed the genre of *faḍā'il* (virtues) for the Egypt, which will be discussed below.

4. The transmitters of the tradition

This section will deal with several historians who introduced and/or developed the Islamic tradition of pharaonic chronology. A discussion of the background of these historians is important because it puts the narratives on ancient Egypt in context, which affects the conclusions we can derive from the material.

4.1. Ibn ᶜAbd al-Ḥakam (d. 871)

The earliest author to have written works on ancient Egypt, which are still preserved, is Ibn ᶜAbd al-Ḥakam, who was born around 798/799 AD in al-Fusṭāṭ and died there in 871. Although he was a member of an influential family of legal scholars and historians from ninth-century Egypt, not much is known about his life.[32] He is primarily known for his *Futūḥ Miṣr wa akhbāruhā* (*The Conquests of Egypt and its Reports*).[33] The main part consists of a historical narrative on Egypt from its earliest mythological beginnings until the event of the death of ᶜAmr b. al-ᶜĀṣ (d. 664), i.e. the period of the actual conquest. He also pays attention to the division of land (*khiṭaṭ*) of al-Fusṭāṭ, where the first Muslims settled in Egypt. As he was a traditionist – meaning he followed the traditions of Muhammad – the work is written through the eyes of a legal scholar,

---

[30] Haarmann, 'Regional Sentiment in Medieval Islamic Egypt', 1980.
[31] Ibn ᶜAbd al-Ḥakam, *Futūḥ Miṣr*, 1922, p. 6*.
[32] Rosenthal, 'Ibn ᶜAbd al-Ḥakam', 1971, III, p. 674.
[33] Ibn ᶜAbd al-Ḥakam, *Futūḥ Miṣr*, 1922.

rather than a historian.[34] For example, his writings deal with the companions of the Prophet who came to Egypt and the *aḥādīth* (sayings of the Prophet, s. *ḥadīth*) they transmitted there on their authority. The relevant chapters for the present study deal with the pharaonic kings after the Flood and the monuments they erected. Ibn ᶜAbd al-Ḥakam mainly used traditionist sources, which he cited in his chains of transmission (*isnād*, pl. *asānīd*). One such scholar was the Egyptian Ibn Lahīᶜa, who has already been mentioned. Ibn ᶜAbd al-Ḥakam's authority was widely recognised during the Middle Ages given the many quotations in the works of later authors.[35]

4.2. al-Masᶜūdī (d. 956)

Abū 'l-Ḥasan ᶜAlī b. al-Ḥusayn al-Masᶜūdī was born in 896 in Baghdad where he spent his youth.[36] From his two major works, *Murūj al-dhahab wa maᶜādin al-jawhar* (*The Meadows of Gold and the Mines of Gems*) and *Kitāb al-tanbīh wa-'l-ishrāf* (*Book of Notification and Control*), we can deduce that al-Masᶜūdī made many travels and spent part of his life in Egypt and Syria.[37] He spent his last years in al-Fusṭāṭ where he finished *al-Tanbīh* just before his death in 956.[38]

In both *Murūj al-dhahab* and *Kitāb al-tanbīh* al-Masᶜūdī comes to deal with Egypt's pre-Islamic history. The *Murūj al-dhahab* contains two parts. The first part deals with the history of the prophets up until Muḥammad and with geographical data of many countries such as Egypt, India, China and Greece. This part includes a description of pharaonic history and several monuments, such as the pyramids of Giza. The second part is a history of the Islamic empire from Muḥammad up until his own day and is currently of less concern. *Kitāb al-tanbīh* is of similar character as *Murūj al-dhahab*, though it is not an abridgement. It gives a description of astronomical and meteorological phenomena, divisions of the earth, the seas and ancient nations. Like Ibn ᶜAbd al-Ḥakam, al-Masᶜūdī remained popular and especially his *Murūj al-dhahab* was still available in the later Middle Ages.

4.3. Ibn Zūlāq (d. 996)

[34] Ibn ᶜAbd al-Ḥakam, *Futūḥ Miṣr*, 1922, p. 1*.
[35] Yāqūt, *Muᶜjam al-buldān*, 1984, V, p. 401; al-Idrīsī, *Kitāb anwār*, 1991, pp. 90f.; al-Maqrīzī, *Khiṭaṭ*, 2002, I, pp. 319, 428; al-Suyūṭī, *Ḥusn al-muḥāḍara*, 1967, I, p. 70.
[36] Pellat, 'al-Masᶜūdī', 1991, VI, p. 784.
[37] al-Masᶜūdī, *Murūj*, 1966, II, p. 126; al-Masᶜūdī, *Murūj*, 1965, I, pp. 114f.; al-Masᶜūdī, *Tanbīh*, 1894, p. 401.
[38] al-Masᶜūdī, *Tanbīh*, 1894, p. 401.

Abū Ḥasan b. Ibrāhīm al-Laythī b. Zūlāq was born in 919 and died in 996.[39] Not much is known about this individual. He was an Egyptian author who wrote bibliographical, topographical, and historical works on Egypt. Although many of those works are now unfortunately lost, his *Faḍā'il Miṣr wa akhbāruhā wa khawāṣṣuhā* (*The Virtues of Egypt and its Reports and Characteristics*) has survived. It treats the pharaonic monuments in the wider context of Egypt's merits including Egypt in the Quran and sayings of the Prophet and his companions. For his accounts on the pyramids, Ibn Ẓahīra refers to 'some of the *ᶜulamā'* [scholars of religious sciences] of Egypt',[40] which suggests that he was using oral sources. He does not name written sources, Islamic or otherwise. Ibn Zūlāq is quoted by several later historians, including Yāqūt, al-Idrīsī (d. 1251) and al-Maqrīzī.

4.4. Ibn al-Kindī (act. second half tenth century)

The Egyptian ᶜUmar b. al-Kindī was the son of the more famous historian Abū ᶜUmar al-Kindī (d. 961), who wrote on early Islamic Egypt, though not its pre-Islamic past.[41] Ibn al-Kindī compiled his *Faḍā'il Miṣr* (*The Virtues of Egypt*) in the third quarter of the tenth century.[42] This work, similar in content to that of Ibn Zūlāq, is a compilation of Egypt's virtues. Next to its monuments it also deals with Quranic references to Egypt, Egyptian sages and the prophets, who visited the land. Later authors did not refer so much to Ibn al-Kindī as they did to Ibn ᶜAbd al-Ḥakam and al-Masᶜūdī, but he is quoted by al-Maqrīzī and the Christian bishop Abū 'l-Makārim.

4.5. Ibrāhīm b. Waṣīf Shāh (act. second part tenth century)

The last author who will be discussed here is believed to be the writer of a work on ancient Egyptian history, which is known under various titles including *Kitāb al-ᶜajā'ib* (*Book of Wonders*) and *Akhbār al-zamān* (*Reports of the Past*). The work specifically treats ancient Egyptian history from its earliest roots until the events of the exodus of Moses, introducing what has been called Egypt's antediluvian dynasty. According to the title pages of several manuscripts of this text, the authorship is attributed to al-Masᶜūdī.[43] Bernard Carra de Vaux, who edited several manuscripts in 1899 under the title *L'Abrégé des*

---

39 Bearman *et al.*, 'Ibn Zūlāq', 1971, III, p. 979.
40 Ibn Zūlāq, *Faḍā'il Miṣr wa akhbāruhā wa khawāṣṣuhā*, 1999, p. 70.
41 Cf. al-Kindī, *Ta'rīkh wulāt Miṣr wa yalīhi kitāb tasmiyat quḍātihā*, 1987.
42 Rosenthal, 'al-Kindī', 1986, V, 121. See Ibn al-Kindī, *Faḍā'il Miṣr*, 1971.
43 E.g. MSS Paris 1470 and 1471.

Merveilles, was not convinced, because both style and content deviated from al-Masᶜūdī's usual works. He proposed attributing the work to the little known author Ibrāhīm b. Waṣīf Shāh instead.[44] But the question remains who that person is.

Opinions as to the value of the work and the identification of the author are varied. Michael Cook does not see it as a pharaonic history, which was transmitted in early Islamic Egypt, but as a Hermetic history and argues that the name Ibrāhīm b. Waṣīf Shāh is merely a fancy version of al-Waṣīfī.[45] According to Ursula Sezgin, it is likely that Ibn Waṣīf Shāh had a Ṣābian origin given his interests in Egypt and she identifies him with the ophthalmologist Aḥmad(?) Ibn Waṣīf al-Ṣābi' (act. second half tenth century (970 AD at the latest))[46] who had spent some time in Egypt where he visited the temple of Akhmim.[47] If he was a Ṣābian indeed, he originated from the city of Ḥarrān, a place where pagan deities were worshipped well into the Islamic era. More importantly, (pseudo-)scientific traditions from Hellenistic Egypt and the eastern Mediterranean prevailed here – mostly in Syriac – and were introduced into the Islamic world.

Ibn Waṣīf Shāh mainly used anonymous Coptic sources, which were transmitted orally as well as in written form. He was quoted by many authors such as al-Bakrī (d. 1094), al-Idrīsī, al-Nuwayrī (d. 1333), and al-Maqrīzī. An anonymous work written by Murtaḍā b. al-ᶜAfīf (d. 1237) was heavily influenced by Ibn Waṣīf Shāh.[48]

4.6. Concluding remarks

Although all of these authors shared a strong relation to Egypt – most were Egyptians, others stayed there for years – they differed in their approach to describing the pharaonic past. While Ibn ᶜAbd al-Ḥakam's work is still firmly based on Quranic exegesis and narratives connecting Egypt to the Arabian Peninsula, al-Masᶜūdī emphasized geographical data, and Ibn Zūlāq and Ibn al-Kindī used Egypt's pharaonic heritage to promote the country. Finally, if Ibn Waṣīf Shāh was indeed a Ṣābian, his work may well have been influenced by Hellenistic traditions from the

---

44 Ibn Waṣīf Shāh, *Akhbār al-zamān*, 1898, p. xxxiii.

45 Cook, 'Pharaonic History', 1983, p. 76.

46 Sezgin, 'Pharaonische Wunderwerke bei Ibn Waṣīf aṣ-Ṣābi' und al-Masᶜūdī', 1994, pp. 229f. Cf. Chwolsohn, *Die Ssabier und die Ssabismus*, 1856, I, pp. 618f. For a more detailed account on the Ṣābians see below.

47 Sezgin, 'Wunderwerke', 1994, p. 231.

48 Unfortunately we only possess a seventeenth-century translation of this text for the original Arabic MS was lost in a fire (Murtaḍā b. al-ᶜAfīf, *L'Égypte de Murtadi, fils du Gaphiphe*, 1666).

Eastern Mediterranean, adding new elements to Egyptian history, as it was known in the Islamic Middle Ages. The various approaches are reflected in the variety of the narratives, as we will see now.

5. Medieval Islamic narratives on ancient Egypt

The Islamic scholars discussed above gave rise to several historical narratives presenting pharaonic history. These narratives were developed during the last centuries of the first millennium AD and remained mostly unchanged until the sixteenth and seventeenth centuries when written records of the narratives died out. It is also important to note that a historian could very well include different, contending stories in his account on pharaonic history, without favouring one over the other.

Here I will discuss the narratives of the Arab king Shaddād, queen Dalūka, the prophet Joseph, the sage Hermes, and the Egyptian king Sūrīd. For every narrative it is important to decide its origin, since it is important to determine whether Islamic scholars copied their stories from older colleagues or whether they invented a new and distinct narrative of pharaonic history.

5.1. The narrative of Shaddād b. ᶜĀd

The first narrative I will discuss is that of Shaddād b. ᶜĀd. The earliest preserved source we have is the *Futūḥ Miṣr* by Ibn ᶜAbd al-Ḥakam, but since one of his sources for this narrative is his fellow Egyptian Ibn Lahīᶜa this story was at least a century older, i.e. eighth century AD. King Shaddād allegedly built the pyramids of Giza[49] and the city of Alexandria.[50] According to later authors he ordered the construction of the pyramids because he had seen a vision of an eschatological flood.[51]

Throughout the Quran there are passages concerning an Arabian tribe called ᶜĀd (primarily Q7:69–72). Here the tribe of ᶜĀd, originating from what is Yemen today, was visited by the prophet Hūd, who was sent by God to preach to the members of the tribe. They did not heed the call of the prophet and thereupon were destroyed by God. Quranic exegetes add that the wrath of God was caused by the fact that their king Shaddād built his capital Iram to rival paradise.[52] Islamic historians also incorporated Shaddād and the ᶜĀdites in their histories on the pre-Islamic Arab kings.

---

[49] Ibn ᶜAbd al-Ḥakam, *Futūḥ*, 1922, p. 43. Cf. Yāqūt, *Muᶜjam*, 1984, V, p. 401; al-Idrīsī, *Anwār*, 1991, pp. 23, 93, 110; al-Maqrīzī, *Khiṭaṭ*, 2002, I, p. 318; al-Suyūṭī, *Ḥusn al-muḥāḍara*, 1967, I, pp. 70, 77.

[50] Ibn ᶜAbd al-Ḥakam, *Futūḥ*, 1922, p. 43.

[51] al-Idrīsī, *Kitāb anwār*, 1991, p. 104; al-Maqrīzī, *Khiṭaṭ*, 2002, I, p. 322.

[52] Cobb, 'Iram', 2002, II, p. 559.

According to them ᶜĀd was the first ruler to form a kingdom after Noah and the Flood.[53] His son Shaddād ruled for 900 years[54] and conquered Syria, Iraq, India and Egypt.[55]

This narrative presents a distinctively Islamic story in which the hero Shaddād is an Arab king, who conquers many lands and who builds amazing structures. In this latter aspect he was well suited as the creator of the pyramids.

5.2. Queen Dalūka

A second narrative, which can also be found in Ibn ᶜAbd al-Ḥakam's *Futūḥ* features the old queen Dalūka bint Zabbā.' Her account became very popular and was transmitted throughout the Middle Ages. According to Islamic historians, the old and wise queen Dalūka was responsible for the construction of the lighthouse of Alexandria,[56] the temples of Upper Egypt,[57] and the Old Lady's Wall,[58] which was named after her. We learn that she had these structures built as a defence system against Egypt's enemies after the pharaoh Muṣᶜab b. Walīd chased Moses and the Israelites through the Red Sea and drowned with his men. As there were only women and slaves left in Egypt Dalūka married them so that they could repopulate Egypt.

The story of Dalūka forms the aftermath to the Biblical and Quranic story of the Exodus. The story of Dalūka itself appears to have been newly created since there is no pre-Islamic account of a queen ruling Egypt after the Exodus.[59] Although Islamic historians attributed this narrative to Coptic sources, it seems that it was an Islamic invention. Why would this story appear in Islamic histories of pharaonic Egypt? According to Petra Sijpesteijn, these accounts do not describe history, as it would not be logical that Dalūka's constructions served as a defence.[60] Enclosing the entire country with a wall would have been impossible and moreover unnecessary because of Egypt's isolated geography. Rather we must see this narrative as an explanation of the remaining pharaonic monuments in a way that made them part of the Quranic discourse of history. In this sense the purpose of the story of Dalūka resembles that of Shaddād as

---

53 al-Masᶜūdī, *Murūj*, 1966, II, p. 153.
54 al-Masᶜūdī, *Murūj*, 1966, II, p. 154.
55 al-Qalqashandī, *Ṣubḥ*, 1914, V, p. 18.
56 Ibn ᶜAbd al-Ḥakam, *Futūḥ*, 1922, p. 40; al-Masᶜūdī, *Murūj*, 1966, II, p. 104; al-Gharnāṭī, *Tuḥfat*, 1925, pp. 226f.; al-Maqrīzī, *Khiṭaṭ*, 2002, I, pp. 422f.
57 Ibn Zūlāq, *Faḍā'il*, 1999, p. 70; Yāqūt, *Muᶜjam*, 1979, I, p. 124.
58 Ibn Zūlāq, *Faḍā'il*, 1999, p. 70.
59 Sijpesteijn, 'Building an Egyptian Identity', 2011, p. 99.
60 Sijpesteijn, 'Building an Egyptian Identity', 2011, p. 99.

they both place pre-Islamic Egypt in the context of the Quran. I will further develop this idea in the next section.

5.3. The granaries of Joseph the prophet

The third narrative I will discuss evolves around the well known Biblical and Quranic story of Joseph.[61] When Joseph was released from prison by the pharaoh he was appointed as overseer of the storage of food surplus for the seven meagre years he predicted. The pyramids of Giza were identified as the granaries of Joseph.

This identification was already forged in late antique Byzantium. The eighth-century patriarch of Antioch Dionysius of Tell Maḥrē (d. after 775) refers to the Byzantine archbishop Gregory of Nazianzus (d. 389 or 390), also known as Gregory the Theologian, as follows:

> Nous avons vu en Égypte ces pyramides dont parle le Théologien [Gregory of Nazianzus] dans ses chants. Ce ne sont pas les greniers de Joseph, comme quelques-uns l'ont pensé, mais admirables édifices bâtis au-dessus des tombeaux des anciens rois.[62]

Although Dionysius himself refuted the notion that the pyramids were built by Joseph, this was apparently a view held in late Antiquity.[63] This view was repeated by Michael the Syrian (d. 1199), patriarch of the Syrian church,[64] and by the Syrian church father and historian Bar Hebraeus (d. 1286), who wrote in Arabic.[65] In a different context, the Spanish Jew Benjamin of Tudela (act. second half twelfth century) wrote in his travelogue *Sefer ha-massaᶜot* (*The Book of Travels*) that either the pyramids of Giza or the ruins of Memphis were built by Joseph.[66] According to the French Franciscan priest André Thevet (d. 1590) in his travelogue *Cosmographie du Levant*, many Jewish chroniclers identified the pyramids of Giza as the granaries of Joseph.[67] Thevet himself did not think it was credible but rather said that the pyramids were sepulchres.

In the Arabic tradition, the identification of the pyramids of Giza as the granaries of Joseph is only rarely attested. According to al-Masᶜūdī Joseph built the pyramids, but he does not mention that the prophet used

[61] Gen. 12:42f. and Q12.
[62] Dionysius of Tell Maḥrē, *Chronique*, 1895, IV, p. xxv.
[63] Cf. Silvestre de Sacy, 'Observations sur l'origine du nom donné par les Grecs et les Arabes aux Pyramides d'Ægypte', 1905, p. 225.
[64] Michael the Syrian, *Chronique*, 1905, III, p. 82.
[65] al-Baghdādī, *al-Ifāda*, 1810, p. 504.
[66] Benjamin of Tudela, *Sefer ha-massaᶜot*, 1907, p. 73.
[67] Thevet, *Cosmographie du Levant*, 1985, p. 154.

them as storage facilities.[68] Both al-Muqaddasī (d. 990) and Abū Manṣūr al-Thaᶜālibī (d. 1038) claim that Joseph indeed built the pyramids as granaries.[69] Ibn Ḥawqal (d. after 973) goes a bit further in stating that 'some pretend that the pyramids are tombs. That is utterly wrong … some more recent kings made these two pyramids [of Kheops and Khefren] into their granaries and stored grain in them.'[70]

The Joseph narrative is clearly of Judeo-Christian origin in which episodes of the Old Testament were associated with physical features of the Egyptian landscape such as pharaonic monuments. The inspiration for the Joseph tradition in late Antiquity and in Jewish chronicles can be found in the book of Genesis. Similarly, in Islam Joseph is an important prophet and it is therefore not surprising that in Islamic histories the pyramids and other monuments were connected with him. This was, however, not widely adopted and no fixed Joseph-narrative was developed. I have not been able to find any link between Islamic traditions and Jewish and Christian traditions, but we may assume that especially later Islamic historians were familiar with the Christian tradition since for example al-Maqrīzī (d. 1442) clearly had read Bar Hebraeus, whom he quotes on several occasions. Thus, Islamic historians did not merely copy older traditions with which they were familiar despite the fact that some of these traditions, such as the attribution of the pyramids to Joseph, could be beneficial to Egypt. An explanation may be that the Judeo-Christian origins of this story were too alien for Islamic historians.

5.4. The sage Hermes Trismegistos

The fourth narrative is that of the prophet Hermes Trismegistos. According to Islamic historians Hermes built the pyramids and the temples of Upper Egypt because he had a dream in which the earth would be destroyed.[71] As he feared that this would mean the loss of all knowledge of crafts and sciences, he had them recorded on the walls of the pyramids and the temples. Hermes was buried in one of the two great pyramids of Giza. The prophet Agathodaimon, who is sometimes seen as the master of Hermes and sometimes as his pupil, was buried in the other pyramid.[72] Medieval Islamic historians transmitted this information on

---

[68] al-Masᶜūdī, *Murūj*, 1966, II, p. 80.
[69] al-Muqaddasī, *Aḥsan al-taqālīm*, 1903, p. 210; al-Thaᶜālibī, *Thimār al-qulūb*, 1908, p. 414.
[70] Ibn Ḥawqal, *Ṣūrat al-arḍ*, 1938, p. 152.
[71] Cf. Yāqūt, *Muᶜjam*, 1984, V, p. 410; al-Nuwayrī, *Nihayāt al-arab*, 1923, I, p. 388; al-Idrīsī, *Kitāb anwār*, 1991, pp. 96f.; al-Maqrīzī, *Khiṭaṭ*, 2002, I, p. 322.
[72] Yāqūt, *Muᶜjam*, 1984, V, p. 410; al-Idrīsī, *Anwār*, 1991, p. 22; al-Maqrīzī, *Khiṭaṭ*, 2002, I, p. 327; al-Suyūṭī, *Ḥusn al-muḥāḍara*, 1967, I, p. 94.

authority of the Ṣābians from the Mesopotamian city of Ḥarrān, discussed more fully below. The story of Hermes as part of pharaonic chronology can first be found in the works of al-Mas^cūdī, i.e. the first half of the tenth century. It remained popular ever since and was transmitted by many scholars working on ancient Egypt.

Hermes is by origin not an Arabic personage but found his way into Arabic and Islamic thought and literature from elsewhere. The discipline of hermeneutics was derived from Hermes Trismegistos (*Τρισμέγιστος*, the Thrice Greatest), who was the Greek equivalent of the ancient Egyptian deity of wisdom, Thoth. This is appropriate because hermeneutics is the result of a mix of scientific traditions of ancient Egypt on the one hand and Greek or Hellenistic traditions on the other, which took place in Alexandria in the first century AD.[73] As Kevin van Bladel puts it, native Egyptian sages in Roman Egypt wrote treatises on science and philosophy in Greek, but they remained part of a distinctive Egyptian tradition.[74] Among these sciences were fields like astrology, cosmology, and medicine. In subsequent centuries, hermeneutics found its way into the Coptic language, for example in the Naj^c Ḥammādī codices of the fourth century AD.[75]

In late Antiquity hermeneutics had spread across the eastern Mediterranean and was also known to Christian scholars in Syria.[76] For example Ibn Waḥshiyya, mentioned above, rewrote antique scientific and pseudo-scientific works of the Hellenistic world.[77] His *Kitāb shawq al-mustahām* is an Arabic translation of a Chaldean original, which had accumulated over ninety ancient scripts and provided a key. One of those scripts is called 'the script of the philosopher Hermes the Greatest, which is the script written on the temples, the pyramids, the sarcophagi, the stones, and ancient shrines.'[78] Apart from the fact that this work shows that there was a degree of interest and knowledge in hermeneutics in late antique and early Islamic Syria, it can also be seen as part of the *shu^cūbiyya* showing the richness of recorded scripts in the pre-Islamic Near East.

In Islamic times hermeneutics was regarded as ancient knowledge from before the revelation of Islam.[79] The influential Baghdadi astrologer Abū Ma^cshar (d. 886) was the first to describe Hermes as a prophet who

[73] Fowden, *The Egyptian Hermes*, 1986, p. 161.
[74] Van Bladel, *The Arabic Hermes*, 2009, p. 4.
[75] Van Bladel, *The Arabic Hermes*, 2009, p. 12.
[76] Van Bladel, *The Arabic Hermes*, 2009, p. 12.
[77] Fahd, 'Ibn Waḥshiyya', 1971, III, p. 964.
[78] Ibn Waḥshiyya, *Shawq al-mustahām*, 1806, p. 81.
[79] Van Bladel, *The Arabic Hermes*, 2009, p. 16.

resided in Upper Egypt, where he built the temples and filled their walls with depictions of the sciences and crafts known to mankind.[80] This was later acknowledged by other astronomers and physicians such as Ibn Juljul (d. 994).[81] Abū Maᶜshar and Ibn Juljul can be placed in what is called the translation movement. In ᶜAbbāsid Baghdad there was an interest in scientific knowledge in such areas as astronomy, geography, alchemy, and medicine. Arab scholars derived their knowledge primarily from Greek, Persian, and Indian works, which were translated into Arabic. Abū Maᶜshar and Ibn Juljul were part of this tradition and it is here that the Arabic Hermes, which was based on the Egyptian/Hellenistic Hermes of pharaonic history, was born.

I have already spoken of the Ṣābians from the city of Ḥarrān. A discussion of their origins is required because they appear to be an authoritative source on the legend of Hermes in pharaonic history. Islamic travellers and geographers mention the Ṣābians performing pilgrimages to the pyramids where they offered roosters and perfume.[82]

A most striking characteristic of the Ṣābians is that they adhered to their pagan cult despite the Christianisation and subsequent Islamisation of the region. Hermes and Agathodaimon were important prophets in Ḥarrānian belief. They adopted the name 'Ṣābian' only later in accordance with the Quran, which mentions the Ṣābians favourably next to Muslims, Christians, and Jews.[83] Islamic scholars became better acquainted with Ṣābian religion when the influential Ṣābian family of the philosopher Thābit b. Qurra (d. 901) broke with Ḥarrān and relocated to Baghdad.

Several Ṣābian scholars have busied themselves with ancient Egyptian history. One of them is Ibn Waḥshiyya, whom I already mentioned. Ibn Waṣīf Shāh also wrote on pharaonic history but mostly on the Sūrīd narrative, which will be discussed below. It has been suggested that Ibn Waṣīf Shāh was a Ṣābian as well.[84]

To rephrase, the character of Hermes can be traced back to Hellenistic Egypt. The narrative of Hermes, as used by Islamic historians, is of Islamic provenance and should be placed within the context of the translation movement. However the spirit in which this narrative was written, is entirely in line with the Hellenistic tradition, which was preserved in the writings of the Ṣābians of Ḥarrān and presumably other

---

[80] Pingree, *The Thousands of Abū Maᶜshar*, 1968, p. 14.

[81] Ibn Juljul, *Ṭabaqāt al-aṭibbā'*, 1955, pp. 5–10; Ibn al-Qifṭī, *Ta'rīkh al-ḥukamā'*, 1903, pp. 5f.; Ibn Abī Usaybiᶜa, *ᶜUyūn al-anbā'*, 1998, pp. 24f.

[82] al-Gharnāṭī, *Tuḥfat al-albāb*, 1925, p. 227; al-Idrīsī, *Anwār*, 1991, p. 22.

[83] Q 2:62; 5:69; 22:17.

[84] Sezgin, 'al-Masᶜūdī, Ibrāhīm b. Waṣīfšāh und das *Kitāb al-ᶜağā'ib*', 1993, p. 10.

peoples in the eastern Mediterranean. It seems that Islamic historians recognised the importance of ancient knowledge. In the case of pharaonic Egypt, this knowledge could not have served any practical purpose since medieval historians were not able to read the ancient Egyptian hieroglyphs – Ibn Waḥshiyya's key for pharaonic script is incorrect – and thus pharaonic scientific corpora remained inaccessible to them. But ancient knowledge did serve an ideological purpose. Especially during the translation movement pre-Islamic sciences were valued and several Muslim writers of non-Arab descent, such as Ibn Waḥshiyya, used it as an example in their anti-Arab polemic. For Egypt Thoth/Hermes was most suitable to fulfil the role of protagonist in this tradition.

5.5. The Egyptian king Sūrīd and the dynasty before the Flood

The fifth and last narrative is the story of the Egyptian king Sūrīd, who was one of the mythological rulers of the antediluvian dynasty, that is, the dynasty which reigned before the Flood of Noah. This story can first be found in the *Akhbār al-zamān* of Ibn Waṣīf Shāh, i.e. in the second part of the tenth century.[85] The narratives of the antediluvian dynasty in general and of king Sūrīd in particular became widespread and remained ever popular in the medieval Near East. This narrative was still transmitted in the seventeenth century by the Turkish traveller Evliya Çelebi.[86]

Medieval Islamic historians recognise nineteen to twenty antediluvian kings, but most often only their names are mentioned.[87] Sūrīd is an exception as several historians have presented a fairly detailed account of his rule. He was a priest king, who had two dreams in which the earth was destroyed by water and by fire.[88] He was distressed by this and he sent for the counsel of the high priests of Egypt. One of the priests, Philemon, said he had had a similar dream and he therefore interpreted Sūrīd dreams literally; the earth would be destroyed. Thus Sūrīd ordered the pyramids and the temples to be built and hid his treasures, the bodies of the kings, and knowledge of the sciences inside the monuments. The aftermath took place 300 years later during the rule of king Firᶜawn (Pharaoh), who was warned by Noah and a priest, again called Philemon, of an impending disaster.[89] Of course the king did not listen. When the Flood came, the

---

[85] Ibn Waṣīf Shāh, *Akhbār al-zamān*, 1938.

[86] Evliya Çelebi, *Book of Travels*, 2010, p. 403.

[87] Ibn Waṣīf Shāh, *Akhbār al-zamān*, 1938, pp. 157–203; al-Maqrīzī, *Khiṭaṭ*, 2002, I, pp. 350–363.

[88] Ibn Waṣīf Shāh, *Akhbār al-zamān*, 1938, p. 182; al-Maqrīzī, *Khiṭaṭ*, 2002, I, pp. 360f.

[89] Ibn Waṣīf Shāh, *Akhbār al-zamān*, 1938, pp. 200–203; al-Maqrīzī, *Khiṭaṭ*, 2002, I, pp. 362f.

king tried to reach the pyramids, but as he was inebriated he tripped and drowned.

Islamic historians always refer to Coptic sources concerning this history, no doubt because Islamic historians saw the Copts as the heirs of the pharaonic legacy. But what is more relevant here is whether Islamic historians consulted Coptic historical data. If we take Islamic historians at their word then they were indeed aware of Coptic traditions of pharaonic Egypt. The Egyptian scholar Ibn al-Dawādārī (d. after 1335) wrote that he got his information from a Coptic book, which was given to him in the White Monastery of Sohag.[90] Al-Suyūṭī (d. 1505), also an Egyptian scholar, had trouble finding a Copt who was able to read a work on pharaonic history.[91] Historians also consulted oral sources. Thus al-Masᶜūdī presents an interview between the Egyptian governor Ibn Ṭūlūn and an aged Copt who informs the official among other things of the pyramids.[92] However, if we want to further identify these Coptic sources we face the problem of their anonymity. Islamic scholars did not mention their sources by name, not even the authors of the Coptic books they consulted. Conversely, Coptic historiographical works only rarely include pharaonic history. When Coptic historians include pharaonic history, it is usually borrowed from Greek material, which presents completely different narratives than the Islamic traditions.

Contrary to Coptic and Greek sources, we have evidence that Sūrīd was known in late antique Syria and Mesopotamia and that he was associated with ancient Egypt. Similar to Hermes, Sūrīd was known to Ibn Waḥshiyya, who incorporated the 'temple script' (*qalam al-birbāwī*, from the word *birbā*, which was specifically used to designate pharaonic temples), which was attributed to king Sūrīd.[93]

From a linguistic assessment we can conclude that the Arabic accounts of the legend of Sūrīd have Coptic or pharaonic origins as well as Syriac sources. Alexander Fodor has argued that the Greek version of the name of Sūrīd, Σουρίδ, is a corruption of Σουφίς (Souphis), which is a Greek name of Kheops.[94] His conclusion is that medieval historians had at least some knowledge about the builder of the great pyramid. As for the Syriac sources, Van Reeth has identified several Syriac loanwords, which were used in medieval Arabic accounts on pharaonic history. One of them is *ḥīd al-maghyār* (the cave of treasure), which is of Syriac origin and is

[90] Ibn al-Dawādārī, *Kanz al-durar*, 1981, III, p. 214.
[91] al-Suyūṭī, *Ḥusn al-muḥāḍara*, 1967, I, p. 72.
[92] al-Masᶜūdī, *Murūj*, 1966, II, pp. 73–83.
[93] Ibn Waḥshiyya, *Shawq al-mustahām*, 1806, p. 24.
[94] Fodor, 'The Origins of the Arabic Legends of the Pyramids', 1973, p. 357.

often attested to describe a room underneath the pyramids allegedly filled with treasure.[95]

There is also a thematic continuity discernable between the ancient and the Islamic Near East. First, the interpretation of dreams takes an important role in the narrative of Sūrīd, who had several dreams himself. In ancient Egypt, indeed in the whole ancient Near East, as well as in the Islamic Middle Ages this practice was very popular. Second, there is a similarity between Sūrīd, who hid knowledge of the sciences on the walls inside of the pyramids and temples, and the Demotic story of Setna Khaemwase, who sets out to find the Book of Thoth, filled with ancient wisdom. Third, I would like to point out the theme of an eschatological Flood, which was a well-known story in Babylonian literature. There are also ancient Egyptian examples such as the primeval ocean, which technically existed before creation, but expresses a contrary situation to Life as did the Flood. This thematic consistency is found not only in the narrative of Sūrīd but also in those of Shaddād and Hermes as we have seen above.

In short, medieval Islamic scholars saw the narrative of king Sūrīd, indeed of his entire dynasty, as genuinely Egyptian. They attributed their sources to Coptic authorities. The name Sūrīd also appears in Arabic translations of late antique texts originally written in Syriac. Although it is difficult to ascertain the degree of continuity in the Sūrīd narrative between pharaonic Egypt and Islamic Egypt, it certainly seems that medieval scholars had at least some knowledge of ancient Egypt via Syriac and Coptic sources.

5.6. Conclusions: A deliberate history?

I began this section emphasising the importance of determining whether Islamic historians took their material from older traditions or whether they invented their own histories of pharaonic Egypt. For several different historical narratives the latter seems to be the case. The stories of Shaddād and Dalūka had no precedents in pre-Islamic historiography that we know of, while others, for example the narratives of Joseph, Hermes and Sūrīd, show that Islamic scholars had some knowledge of ancient Near Eastern themes. The overall historical compilation though remained of Islamic provenance and the product of deliberate discourse. This is illustrated by the story of Joseph and the granaries. If Islamic historians invented their own traditions then the question arises why they invented these specific traditions. This will be addressed in the next section.

[95] Van Reeth, 'Caliph al-Ma'mūn and the Treasure of the Pyramids', 1994, p. 227.

6. MAKING PRE-ISLAMIC EGYPT COMPATIBLE WITH ISLAMIC EGYPT

It was already mentioned in the introduction that pre-Islamic Egypt was at first glance not compatible with Islamic doctrine, which denounced polytheism, the use of images of man and animal, and tyranny, most visible in the story of Moses. This section explains how Islamic historians dealt with the paradox between pre-Islamic past and Islamic present by describing three examples. To better comprehend medieval adaptation of pharaonic history it is important to understand the mechanisms through which it occurred.

6.1. The cleansing of Egypt

We have seen in the previous section that several historical narratives of pharaonic Egypt reserve a key position for the theme of an eschatological Flood, in which almost all human life is destroyed. Similarly in the story of Dalūka, or rather preceding Dalūka, the pharaoh of Moses is drowned in the Red Sea together with all Egyptian males when they chase the Israelites. Both themes, the Flood and the episode of the Red Sea, constitute the cleansing of Egypt's evil elements.

6.1.1. *The Flood*

The Flood as a historical event in Egypt is described from the tenth century onwards by al-Masᶜūdī and Ibn Wāṣīf Shāh.[96] There are several different narratives, which describe the precedents to the Flood. Hermes built the pyramids and the temples after he had a dream of the Flood. Sūrīd had a similar dream and acted upon it. Finally, it is said that Shaddād built the pyramids after he had a dream. Although no reference is made to the Flood, it is a clear allusion. The only narrative to go into the event of the Flood itself is that of the antediluvian chronology of Ibn Waṣīf Shāh. The families of both Noah and Philemon were saved. When the water retreated, Noah's great grandson Miṣra'īm ascended the throne of Egypt and married the daughter of Philemon, thus connecting himself, if not to antediluvian royalty, at least to its ruling class. This detailed story can only be found in the works of certain historians such as Ibn Waṣīf Shāh and al-Maqrīzī,[97] but is missing in most. The devastating Flood cleansing the earth is a common narrative however, and it can already be read in Ibn ᶜAbd al-Ḥakam's ninth century *Futūḥ* who in turn refers to older sources, such as Ibn Lahīᶜa (i.e. eighth century).

[96] al-Masᶜūdī, *Murūj*, 1966, II, 89-90; Ibn Waṣīf Shāh, *Akhbār al-zamān*, 1938, p. 149f.
[97] Ibn Waṣīf Shāh, *Akhbār al-zamān*, 1938, p. 152; al-Maqrīzī, *Khiṭaṭ*, 2002, I, p. 363.

6.1.2. *The pharaoh of Moses and the Israelites*

This story, which is taken almost directly from the Old Testament and the Quran, concerns the pharaoh of Moses. It can already be read in Ibn ᶜAbd al-Ḥakam's *Futūḥ*, and it is included in several Arab histories of ancient Egypt.[98] This pharaoh, whose name is al-Walīd b. Muṣᶜab, but who is also called the seventh pharaoh or Ẓalmā (perhaps from *ẓulm*, 'tyrant'), is allegedly the last king of the ᶜAmālīqite overlords of Egypt. In line with the Bible and Quran, al-Walīd b. Muṣᶜab chased Moses and the Israelites into the Red Sea, which God separated for the prophet. When the sea closed over al-Walīd and his men, the king converted to the faith of Moses. Nevertheless, the men of Egypt died, leaving the slaves and the women as Egypt's only inhabitants. The Arab historians contributed mainly to the epilogue, adding the story of Dalūka. It seems that Dalūka is not related to the ᶜAmālīqites in any way but rather founded a new dynasty. The name of her father, Zabbā', does not appear anywhere but in the name of Dalūka. The ᶜAmālīqite kings were foreign oppressors originating from Syria as some historians tell us,[99] and their status as foreigners and oppressors was cause for their divine destruction. For Dalūka Egypt's slate was cleaned.

6.1.3. *Comparison: The narratives of cleansing and the role of the monuments*

These two stories have a similar pattern. The old rulers have become corrupted. The antediluvian Firᶜawn is a murderer and so is the Syrian al-Walīd b. Muṣᶜab. Both neglect the warnings of prophets (Noah and Moses), an act that can be seen as rejecting the words of God. Both rulers drown together with the (male) population of Egypt. Afterwards, a new period starts and Egypt is again reigned by just rulers.

The cleansing of Egypt had to be incorporated in Egyptian history because they were Biblical and Quranic events. But the historians did make an Egyptian version of this history, for in the story of the Flood the pyramids have a special role. Like Noah's ark they were built out of fear for the Flood and eventually were the only structures left unaffected. Furthermore, the pyramids, and according to some historians the temples as well, were built by king Sūrīd, who was considered to be a just ruler, or by Hermes, who is identified with the Quranic prophet Idrīs, as

[98] Ibn ᶜAbd al-Ḥakam, *Futūḥ*, 1922, pp. 26f.; al-Masᶜūdī, *Murūj*, 1966, II, p. 87; Ibn Waṣīf Shāh, *Akhbār al-zamān*, 1938, pp. 242f.; al-Maqrīzī, *Khiṭaṭ*, 2002, I, p. 387.

[99] Ibn ᶜAbd al-Ḥakam, *Futūḥ*, 1922, pp. 19f.; al-Masᶜūdī, *Murūj*, 1966, II, p. 86; Ibn Waṣīf Shāh, *Akhbār al-zamān*, 1938, p. 112; al-Nuwayrī, *Nihāyat al-arab*, XV, p. 114; al-Maqrīzī, *Khiṭaṭ*, 2002, I, p. 383.

discussed below. As the Flood cleansed the earth of Egypt, so were the pyramids cleansed in their turn. Similarly, the construction of the lighthouse of Alexandria as well as the temples was attributed to the wise queen Dalūka and hence they were not corrupted by the wickedness of the pharaohs.

Contrary to the view that Muslims have always looked at pre-Islamic eras with disinterest or even disdain, it seems that at least these scholars were selective in their discussion while writing on pre-Islamic Egypt. There were some rotten apples in the pharaonic basket. Following the Old Testament and the Quran Fir^cawn and most of the ^cAmālīqite dynasty, notably Moses' pharaoh, were horrific rulers. But the historians also followed the Old Testament and Quran when it came to the pharaoh of Joseph, who recognised the gift of the prophet.[100] Furthermore, Sūrīd, Hermes, and Dalūkā were wise and just rulers who were inextricably linked to ancient Egypt as we have seen. In short, one could say that medieval historians peeled off the polluted layer of pharaonic history and showed that Fir^cawn and Moses' pharaoh were only a small part of Egyptian history, which in its totality had a lot to offer.

6.2. Hermes and Idrīs

Hermes has already been discussed in some detail above. However, his significance in this chapter lies in his identification with the prophet Idrīs/Enoch. It appears that part of the Arabic character of Hermes Trismegistos was based on the Quranic prophet Idrīs and the Biblical prophet Enoch. For example, Ibn Juljul (d. 994) already equates Hermes to Idrīs and Enoch, saying that 'Hermes, whom the Hebrews call Enoch, he is Idrīs, peace be upon him.'[101] Many subsequent authors have followed this example. The identification was established in the early Islamic period during the translation movement and was acknowledged by Islamic historians writing on ancient Egypt. The identification was based on a theological debate in which passages from the Old Testament and the Quran were compared. In his *Kitāb al-tarbī^c wa-'l-tadwīr* (*Book of the Square and the Circle*) the Iraqi litterateur al-Jāḥiẓ (d. 868/869) already raised the question of whether Hermes was Idrīs.[102] Shortly afterwards, though, the identification of Hermes with Idrīs became established with Abū Ma^cshar's *Kitāb al-ulūf* (*The Book of Thousands*).[103]

---

[100] Gen. 41:1–57 and Q12:50–57. Instead of *fir^cawn* the pharaoh of Joseph is designated with *malik*, king.
[101] Ibn Juljul, *Ṭabaqāt al-aṭibbā' wa-'l-hukamā'*, 1955, pp. 5f.
[102] al-Jāḥiẓ, *Kitāb al-tarbī^c*, 1955, p. 26, § 40.
[103] Van Bladel, *The Arabic Hermes*, 2009, p. 168.

The discussion revolved around the celestial ascent of Enoch, who was brought to heaven by the archangel Michael and was instructed in all the secrets.[104] Idrīs, a prophet in Islam, is mentioned twice in the Quran, namely in verses 19:56–57 and 21:85–86. In Q19:57, Idrīs is raised to a high place, associated with heaven where Enoch was instructed. Enoch and Idrīs became interchangeable, which becomes clear from e.g. *Kitāb al-bad' wa-'l-ta'rīkh* (*The Book of Creation and History*) by al-Maqdisī (act. tenth century). Here the name of Idrīs is used instead of Enoch in the genealogy of Adam.[105] With the identification of Hermes with Enoch and Idrīs, Hermes was also eligible to make an ascent to heaven.[106] Here he received knowledge of astrology, medicine and other sciences, which he brought back to earth.

This line of thought is important and is a clear example of medieval adaptation of pharaonic Egypt, combining pharaonic history, Islamic theology and contemporary issues. Hermes was a prophet and a sage, who possessed ancient, that is pre-Islamic, knowledge on fields, which was deemed important during the translation movement of the late eighth and ninth century. At the same time Hermes was associated with Enoch/Idrīs and was accordingly placed within the context of monotheistic theology. As the protagonist of one of the prominent narratives on pharaonic history it was important that he could be referred to as an Islamic prophet. Again we see that the pyramids and the temples, the remaining and tangible heritage of ancient Egypt, were created by a person who had his place within Islam.

6.3. The narrative of Shaddād b. ᶜĀd

The same line of thought may be applied to the narrative of the Arab king Shaddād b. ᶜĀd, who was already discussed above. The origins of this narrative were clearly Islamic. The tribe of ᶜĀd is mentioned at length in the Quran[107] and in Quranic exegesis.[108] As the builder of the pyramids, Shaddād brought them, and by extension the whole of pre-Islamic Egypt, under the patronage of Islam. Also, Muslim historians could claim ancient ties between Arabia, the cradle of Islam, and the land of Egypt.

---

[104] Van Bladel, *The Arabic Hermes*, 2009, p. 168. The story of Enoch's ascent is told in the Ethiopian apocryphon 1 Enoch 71:3–5.

[105] al-Maqdisī, *Kitāb al-bad' wa-'l-ta'rīkh*, 1903, III, pp. 11–13.

[106] Van Bladel, *The Arabic Hermes*, 2009, p. 169.

[107] Q11:60–61; 26:123–139; 46:24.

[108] Tottoli, 'ᶜĀd', 2001, I, p. 21.

6.4. Concluding remarks

The purpose of the previous section was to examine how Islamic historians dealt with the apparent ambiguity in the perception of pre-Islamic Egypt. Historians placed pharaonic chronology in context with the Quran as much as possible. This was a necessity mainly because the Quran was also seen as a historically accurate document, but it also inevitably resulted in inextricable links between pre-Islamic and Islamic Egypt. Following Quranic discourse, the Flood submerged Egypt and the pharaoh of Moses drowned in the Red Sea. Thus Egypt was cleansed. The Quran and the Old Testament remained silent when it came to pharaonic chronology as a whole and the monuments in particular. Here the historians were free to look for positive alternatives to Ẓalmā and Walīd b. Muṣᶜab. Hermes was particularly appropriate since he was also associated with an Islamic prophet. In general historians differentiated sharply between good and bad; bad was destroyed while good was the source of the greatness of Egypt's pharaonic past and its still visible monuments.

7. Using Egypt's pharaonic past

Now that pharaonic history was legitimized in Islamic thought, it could be used. This section describes how the ancient Egyptian past was used to create a distinctive Egyptian Islam.

7.1. The faḍā'il

One of the genres in Arabic literature is the *faḍā'il*, which enumerated the virtues of a group of people, an individual, a city or province or something as simple as coffee.[109] The earliest examples date to the late eighth century AD, but the oldest preserved *faḍā'il* works on Egypt are those written by Ibn al-Kindī and Ibn Zūlāq, respectively called simply *Faḍā'il Miṣr* and *Faḍā'il Miṣr wa akhbārihā wa khawāṣṣuhā*. These works are a collection of certain topics placing Egypt in a favourable light. For example, the prophets are discussed[110] as well as the companions of the Prophet,[111] who visited Egypt. Most relevant is their treatment of the *ᶜajā'ib* (marvels) of Egypt. Ibn al-Kindī places both Biblical references, such as Moses separating the Red Sea, as well as ancient monuments among these

[109] Sellheim, 'Faḍīla', 1965, II, p. 728.
[110] Ibn al-Kindī, *Faḍā'il*, 1971, pp. 28f.; Ibn Zūlāq, *Faḍā'il*, 1999, 9-10; cf. Ibn Ẓahīra, *Faḍā'il*, 1969, pp. 78–80.
[111] Ibn al-Kindī, *Faḍā'il*, 1971, pp. 38–40; Ibn Zūlāq, *Faḍā'il*, 1999, pp. 27.

marvels.[112] Ibn Zūlāq wrote that certain sages reported that twenty of the thirty wonders of the world were located in Egypt.[113] Many monuments, such as the pyramids, the temple of Akhmim and the lighthouse of Alexandria, are included in their discussions. Ibn Ẓahīra lists the same twenty wonders of Egypt.[114] Al-Suyūṭī presents yet again the same list on the much older authority of al-Jāḥiẓ.[115]

Clearly, these works stressed that Egypt had its share of famous visitors and favourable Quranic references and in this sense the *faḍā'il* placed Egypt above other regions of the Islamic Empire. This is implied by the authors who make a comparison between Egypt's twenty wonders and the remaining ten in the rest of the world. It is interesting to note that all authors of the *faḍā'il* works (Ibn al-Kindī, Ibn Zūlāq, and Ibn Ẓahīra) or of works with elements of the *faḍā'il* (al-Suyūṭī) are of Egyptian origin. Although the *faḍā'il* aimed at establishing a self-evident, distinct Muslim realm, it did not indicate national or regional pride per se, since al-Suyūṭī transmitted his list of thirty wonders on the authority of the Baghdadi al-Jāḥiẓ. It could very well represent the dominant view of the ninth century.

7.2. Egypt as the cradle and the guardian of science and knowledge

Throughout Islamic histories of pharaonic Egypt, focus is placed on Egypt's role in the development of science and knowledge, and the land was seen both as the cradle as well as the guardian of science and knowledge. The best example is the story of Hermes, who was raised to heaven where he received knowledge of sciences such as astronomy and medicine, but also the production of clothes. Since Hermes was well versed in astronomy he was able to read in the stars of an impending disaster and he built the pyramids and the temples engraving all crafts and all craftsmen on the walls. The same is said of king Sūrīd, who placed the knowledge of science together with the bodies of the Egyptian kings and other treasures inside the pyramids.

Egypt held a vital position in the scientific tradition. As mentioned before, Islamic historians did not see the pursuit of knowledge merely as a theme pertaining to ancient societies, but it materialized out of the Iraqi translation movement of the late eighth and ninth century. Pharaonic Egypt was given an active place in this discourse. It was regarded as a useful source in a contemporary discussion.

---

112 Ibn al-Kindī, *Faḍā'il*, 1971, pp. 65–70.
113 Ibn Zūlāq, *Faḍā'il*, 1999, pp. 69-73.
114 Ibn Ẓahīra, *Faḍā'il*, 1969, pp. 150–157.
115 al-Suyūṭī, *Ḥusn al-muḥāḍara*, 1967, I, p. 65.

8. Conclusions

I started this article with the question of whether Muslims used pharaonic history in constructing an Egyptian Muslim identity, and if so, how it was done. The theory of cultural appropriation was applied to historical narratives of the ninth and tenth century.

First of all, the narratives that were written down by Islamic historians were indeed of Islamic origin. There may have been a kernel of historical truth present in their accounts, but in general these narratives were developed in the ninth and tenth century by Muslim scholars. At certain points Islamic scholars possessed historically factual records, such as the king list of Manetho, but they chose to ignore them. In other instances questionable narrative content is not disputed despite evidence in the form of eyewitness accounts to the contrary. An example is Yāqūt's account in search of traces of the mirror of the lighthouse of Alexandria, which he did not find. From this we can conclude that not only were Islamic narratives of pharaonic Egypt of Islamic provenance, they also did not necessarily express historical fact and instead were conceived to support contemporary Islamic thought. In other words, pharaonic history was used for present day issues, such as political and moral discussions. In this sense the pharaonic heritage was appropriated. Not so much from the Copts, who at least in their written records did not seem to care too much about the pharaonic heritage. Islamic historians rather appropriated pharaonic history from that very history itself.

As was explained in the introduction, Islam and pharaonic history did not go well together at first sight, which becomes especially clear from the story of the Exodus. Historians had to make ancient Egyptian history and chronology compatible with Islam. In other words, Egypt's negative image, the image of the tyrant suppressing the Israelites and the Egyptian people in general came to be seen from an Islamic perspective as 'the other.' The historians wanted to change this 'otherness', which they did by placing Egyptian history into a historical chronology compatible with that of the Quran and by extension the Old Testament. They isolated the elements making up Egypt's negative image by destroying pharaohs Ẓalmā and Muṣᶜab b. al-Walīd in the Flood and the Red Sea.

Now Egypt's history was ready to be used to make Egypt a distinct region from yet another 'other', namely the rest of the Islamic Empire. Egyptian historians used the genre of *faḍā'il* to make the Egyptian landscape, including its pharaonic heritage, sacred. The genre illustrated Egypt's unique heritage and this was emphasised by different themes such as Egypt's role as the cradle and guardian of knowledge.

If we place this in a historical context we see two groups. First, there was the Muslim elite who settled in al-Fusṭāṭ after the conquest. They started integrating in Egypt in the late eighth and ninth centuries. From the 830s onwards they lost their fiscal privileges to the newly arrived Turkish and Persian military elite and this provided the impetus for their absorption into the Egyptian landscape. This also meant that the Muslim Arabs from al-Fusṭāṭ absorbed pharaonic history into the Islamic narrative. Ibn ᶜAbd al-Ḥakam, who wrote in this period, did not give the Copts a place of authority as later authors would, but instead presented the narrative of Shaddād more prominently, Arabizing pre-Islamic Egypt. Second, there were the Copts. Although they were the heirs to pharaonic culture, they did not express a strong national sentiment based on their inheritance. However, more and more Copts converted to Islam and were in need of an Egyptian version of Islam. In the late ninth and tenth centuries we see that the narratives of Hermes and Sūrīd were developed, the latter giving a prominent place to the Copts.

In the early centuries of Islamic Egypt, pharaonic history was used to create a communal source for early Arab Muslims and converted Copts. Pharaonic history was Islamicised but not necessarily Arabized, which explains why the narratives of Hermes and Sūrīd were much more popular than Shaddād's. This is also consistent with the anti-Arab sentiments of the *shuᶜūbiyya*. It was a way for early Arab Muslims and converted Copts to make their own Egypt special and distinctive from the rest of the Muslim world.

BIBLIOGRAPHY

Abū 'l-Makārim (= pseudo-Abū Ṣāliḥ al-Armānī). *Ta'rīkh al-kanā'is*. Oxford, 1895.

al-Baghdādī. *Kitāb al-ifāda wa-'l-iᶜtibār fī 'l-umūr al-mushāhada wa-'l-ḥawādith al-muᶜāyanna bi-arḍ Miṣr*. Paris, 1810.

Bagnall, R. S., and D. W. Rathbone (eds.). *Egypt. From Alexander to the Copts. An Archaeological and Historical Guide*. London, 2004.

Bashear, S. *Arabs and Others in Early Islam*. (Studies in Late Antiquity and Early Islam 8.) Princeton, 1997.

Bearman, P., Th. Bianquis, E. Bosworth, E. J. van Donzel, and W. Heinrichs, 'Ibn Zūlāq.' *Encyclopaedia of Islam, Second Edition*, 1971, III, p. 979.

Benjamin of Tudela. *Sefer ha-massaᶜot*. Oxford, 1907.

Bianquis, Th. 'Autonomous Egypt from Ibn Ṭūlūn to Kāfūr, 868–969.' C. F. Petry (ed.) *The Cambridge History of Egypt. Volume 1. Islamic Egypt, 640–1517*. Cambridge, 1998, pp. 86–119.

al-Bīrūnī. *al-Athār al-bāqiya* ^c^*an al-qurūn al-khāliya*. Leipzig, 1923.
Chwolsohn, D. *Die Ssabier und die Ssabismus*. 2 Vols. St. Petersburg, 1856.
Cobb, P. 'Iram.' *Encyclopaedia of the Qur'ān*, 2002, II, p. 559.
Cook, M. 'Pharaonic History in Medieval Egypt.' *Studia Islamica* 57 (1983), pp. 67–103.
Crone, P. *God's Rule. Government and Islam. Six Centuries of Medieval Islamic Political Thought*. New York, 2004.
Dionysius of Tell Maḥrē. *Chronique*. Paris, 1895.
Donner, F. M. *Narratives of Islamic Origins. The Beginnings of Islamic Historical Writing*. (Studies in Late Antiquity and Early Islam 14.) Princeton, 1998.
Evetts, B. T. A. *History of the Patriarchs of the Coptic Church of Alexandria*. Paris, 1947–1959.
Evliya Çelebi. *Book of Travels*. London, 2010.
Fahd, T. 'Ibn Waḥshiyya.' *Encyclopaedia of Islam, Second Edition*, 1971, III, pp. 963–965.
Fodor, A. 'The Origins of the Arabic Legends of the Pyramids.' *Acta Orientalia Hungaricae* 23 (1970), pp. 335–363.
Fowden, G. *The Egyptian Hermes*. Cambridge, 1986.
al-Gharnāṭī. *Tuḥfat al-albāb*. Paris, 1925.
Goldziher, I. *Muslim Studies. Volume 1*. Tr. by C. R. Barber and S. M. Stern. London, 1967.
Haarmann, U. 'Regional Sentiment in Medieval Islamic Egypt.' *Bulletin of the School of Oriental and African Studies* 43 (1980), pp. 55–66.
Hämeen-Anttila, J. *The Last Pagans of Iraq. Ibn Waḥshiyya and his* Nabatean Agriculture. Leiden, 2006.
Hirschler, K. *Medieval Arabic Historiography. Authors as Actors*. London, 2006.
Ibn ^c^Abd al-Ḥakam. *Futūḥ Miṣr wa akhbāruhā*. New Haven, 1922.
Ibn Abī Uṣaybi^c^a. ^c^*Uyūn al-anbā' fī ṭabaqāt al-aṭibbā.'* Beirut, 1998.
Ibn Dawādārī. *Kanz al-durar wa jāmi*^c^ *al-ghurar*. 3 Vols. Cairo, 1981.
Ibn Ḥawqal. *Kitāb ṣūrat al-arḍ*. Leiden, 1938.
Ibn Juljul. *Ṭabaqāt al-aṭībbā' wa-'l-ḥukamā'*. Cairo, 1955.
Ibn al-Kindī. *Faḍā'il Miṣr*. Cairo, 1971.
Ibn al-Qifṭī. *Ta'rīkh al-ḥukamā'*. Leipzig, 1903.
Ibn Rāhib *Kitāb al-tawārīkh*. Wiesbaden, 1903.
Ibn Waḥshiyya. *Shawq al-mustahām fī ma*^c^*rifat rumūz al-aqlām*. London, 1806.
Ibn Waṣīf Shāh (= pseudo-al-Mas^c^ūdī). *Akhbār al-zamān wa man abādahu 'l-ḥidhthān wa* ^c^*ajā'ib al-buldān wa ghāmir bi-'l-mā' wa-'l-*^c^*umrān*. Paris, 1898.

Ibn Waṣīf Shāh (= pseudo-al-Mas^{c}ūdī). *Akhbār al-zamān wa man abādahu 'l-ḥidhthān wa ^{c}ajā'ib al-buldān wa ghāmir bi-'l-mā' wa-'l-^{c}umrān*. Cairo, 1938.

Ibn Ẓahīra. *al-Faḍā'il al-bāhira fī maḥāsin Miṣr wa-'l-Qāhira*. Cairo, 1969.

Ibn Zūlāq. *Faḍā'il Miṣr wa akhbāruhā wa khawāṣuhā*. Alexandria, 1999.

al-Idrīsī *Kitāb. anwār al-^{c}ulūw al-ajrām fī 'l-kashf ^{c}an asrār al-ahrām*. Beirut, 1991.

al-Jāḥiẓ. *Kitāb al-tarbī^{c} wa-'l-tadwīr*. Damascus, 1955.

Jansen, H. L. *The Coptic Story of Cambyses' Invasion of Egypt: A Critical Analysis of its Literary Form and its Historical Purpose*. Oslo, 1950.

John of Nikiu, *The Chronicle of John of Nikiu. Translated from Zotenberg's Ethiopic Text by R. H. Charles*. Oxford, 1916.

Kennedy, H. 'Egypt as a Province in the Islamic Caliphate.' C. F. Petry, *The Cambridge History of Egypt. Volume 1. Islamic Egypt, 640–1517*. Cambridge, 1998, pp. 62–85.

al-Kindī. *Kitāb wulāt Miṣr wa yalīhi kitāb tasmiyat quḍātihā*. Beirut, 1987.

al-Maqdisī. *Kitāb al-bad' wa-'l-ta'rīkh*. 6 Vols. Paris, 1899–1919.

al-Maqrīzī. *al-Mawā^{c}iẓ wa-'l-i^{c}tibār fī dhikr al-khiṭaṭ wa-'l-athār*. 5 Vols. (Ed. by A. F. Sayyid). London, 2002.

al-Mas^{c}ūdī. *Kitāb al-Tanbīh wa-'l-ishrāf*. (Bibliotheca Geographicorum Arabicorum 8.) Leiden, 1894.

al-Mas^{c}ūdī. *Murūj al-dhahab wa ma^{c}ādin al-jawhar*. 5 Vols. Beirut, 1966–1979.

Michael the Syrian. *Chronique*. 4 Vols. Paris, 1899–1910.

al-Muqaddasī. *Kitāb aḥsan al-taqālīm fī mu^{c}arifa al-aqlīm*. Leiden, 1903.

Murtaḍā b. al-^{c}Afīf *L'Égypte de Murtadi, fils du Gaphiphe*. Paris, 1666.

al-Nuwayrī. *Nihāyat al-arab fī funūn al-ādab*. 33 Vols. Cairo, 1923–1997.

Pellat, Ch. 'al-Mas^{c}ūdī.' *Encyclopaedia of Islam, Second Edition*, 1991, VI, pp. 784–789.

Pingree, D. *The Thousands of Abū Ma^{c}shar*. (Studies of the Warburg Institute 30.) London, 1968.

al-Qalqashandī. *Ṣubḥ al-a^{c}shā*. 14 Vols. Cairo, 1913–1919.

Ritner, R. K. 'Egypt under Roman Rule: The Legacy of Ancient Egypt.' C. F. Petry (ed.). *The Cambridge History of Egypt. Volume 1. Islamic Egypt, 640–1517*. Cambridge, 1998, pp. 1–33.

Rosenthal, F. 'Ibn ^{c}Abd al-Ḥakam.' *Encyclopaedia of Islam*, 1971, III, pp. 674–675.

Rosenthal, F. 'al-Kindī.' *Encyclopaedia of Islam*, 1986, V, p. 121–122.

Sellheim, R. 'Faḍīla.' *Encyclopaedia of Islam, Second Edition*, 1965, II, pp. 728–729.
Sezgin, U. 'al-Mas^cūdī, Ibrāhīm b. Waṣīfšāh und das *Kitāb al-^cağā'ib*. Aigyptiaka in arabischen Texten des 10. Jahrhunderts n. Chr.' *Zeitschrift für Geschichte der Arabisch-Islamischen Wissenschaften* 8 (1993), pp. 1–70.
Sezgin, U. 'Pharaonische Wunderwerke bei Ibn Waṣīf aṣ-Ṣābi' und al-Mas^cūdī. Einige Reminiszenzen an Ägyptens vergangene Grösse und an Meisterwerke der alexandrinischen Geleherten in arabischen Texten des 10. Jahrhunderts n. Chr.' *Zeitschrift für Geschichte der Arabisch-Islamischen Wissenschaften* 9 (1994), pp. 229–287.
Sijpesteijn, P. M. 'Building an Egyptian Identity.' A. Q. Ahmed, *The Islamic Scholarly Tradition. Studies in History, Law, and Thought in Honor of Professor Michael Allen Cook.* (Islamic History and Civilization 83). Leiden, 2011, pp. 85–105.
Silvestre de Sacy, A. I. 'Observations sur l'origine de nom donné par les Grecs et les Arabes aux pyramides d'Ægypte, et sur quelques autres objects relatifs aux antiquités ægyptiennes.' *Bibliothèque des Arabisants Français* 1. Cairo, 1905, pp. 223–264.
Smith, A. D. *The Antiquity of Nations*. Cambridge, 2004.
al-Suyūṭī. *Ḥusn al-muḥāḍara fī ta'rīkh Miṣr wa-'l-Qāhira*. 2 Vols. Cairo, 1967–1968.
al-Tha^cālibī. *Thimār al-qulūb fī 'l-muḍāf wa-'l-manṣūb*. Cairo, 1908.
Thevet, A. *Cosmographie du Levant*. Geneva, 1985.
Tottoli, R. '^cĀd.' *Encyclopaedia of the Qur'ān*, 2001, I, p. 21.
Van Bladel, K. *The Arabic Hermes*. Oxford, 2009.
Van Reeth, J. M. F. 'Caliph al-Ma'mūn and the Treasure of the Pyramids.' *Orientalia Loveniensa Periodica* 25 (1994), pp. 221–236.
White, H. 'The Value of Narrativity in the Representation of Reality.' *Critical Inquiry* 7:1 (1980), pp. 5–27.
Yāqūt al-Rūmī. *Mu^cjam al-buldān*. 5 Vols. Beirut, 1979–1984.
Ziff, B., and P. V. Rao. *Borrowed Power. Essays on Cultural Appropriation*. New Brunswick, 1997.

HELIODOTOS AND HELIODOROS

Identity and Ambiguity in Two Inscriptions from the Hellenistic Far East

RACHEL MAIRS

Abstract. In the late fourth century BC, Alexander the Great set up a network of garrisons across Central Asia and north-western India. Over the following three hundred years, the descendants of the Greek and Macedonian soldiers left in these settlements established a series of autonomous Hellenistic states. This article will explore topics of cultural interaction, identity formation and external diplomacy in the Graeco-Bactrian and Indo-Greek kingdoms through the lives and careers of two men. Heliodotos, around the turn of the third-second centuries BC, commissioned a Greek inscription somewhere in southern Tajikistan or north-eastern Afghanistan (the stone is unprovenanced), in which he offers an altar to Hestia in a 'grove of Zeus' for the sake of king Euthydemos and his son Demetrios. Around ninety years later – after the conquests which this same Demetrios had made in north-western India – a man named Heliodoros, a Greek ambassador to the court of an Indian king, Bhāgabhadra, dedicated a Prākrit inscription in which he is described as a devotee of Vishnu. It is argued that the cultural reference points in both inscriptions could be understood in different ways by different audiences, and that this polysemy was more generally characteristic of forms of public display in the Hellenistic Far East.

1. THE HELLENISTIC FAR EAST

The areas of Greek settlement in Central Asia and north-western India once enjoyed a somewhat dubious reputation as the 'Siberia of the Hellenistic world';[1] they are now more generously – but no less exotically – known as the 'Hellenistic Far East'.[2] Bactria, Sogdiana, Arachosia, Gandhāra and the Indus valley were geographically distant from the centres of the various Near Eastern empires which asserted control over them at different periods: the Persian empire, under the Achaemenid

---

[1] Rawlinson, *Bactria*, 1909, p. 23.

[2] The term and its history is discussed in Mairs, *The Archaeology of the Hellenistic Far East*, 2011, p. 9.

dynasty, and later the empire of Alexander the Great and his Seleucid successors. But Bactria, the basin of the upper river Oxus, in particular, was neither economically nor politically peripheral. It possessed considerable natural resources – notably its agricultural potential, and sources of precious stones and minerals such as lapis lazuli – and it occupied a strategic position between the Near East, South Asia, and the world of the Eurasian steppe. The resources which made Bactria attractive to the Persians and then to the Greeks also meant that it could be used as a power base, whether as a springboard for a satrap's imperial ambitions, or for the secession of an independent regional state. In the period with which I shall be concerned in the following discussion – from the late fourth century BC through to the late second century BC – such regional autonomy was the rule, although there were occasional attempts by outside powers to reintegrate the Hellenistic Far East into their empires. The Hellenistic Far East itself was also prone to internal division and civil war, and the material which I shall discuss comes from two very different regions within it: north-eastern Bactria, inside the boundaries of the Graeco-Bactrian state, and central India, in an independent kingdom with which Indo-Greek kings were in diplomatic contact.

In the 320s BC, Alexander the Great entered Central Asia in pursuit of Bessos, the pretender to the Persian throne. Alexander's Central Asian campaigns were perhaps the most difficult of his whole expedition.[3] His armies were faced with hostile territory and climate and hostile local populations. Like many an invader of Afghanistan before and since, Alexander found himself helpless to fight a conventional war using heavily-armed ground troops against an enemy who could retreat to fortified hilltops and remain there practically indefinitely. Alexander spent three years in Central Asia, and when the mass of his army did move on to India, he left behind large numbers of demobilised Greek and Macedonian troops in garrisons and settlements which he often, with typical modesty, named 'Alexandria'.[4]

The settlers left in these garrisons were less than content. This is a matter upon which the Greek historical sources are unusually eloquent for the region and the period. Following a rumour of Alexander's death in India, they attempted to revolt and return to Greece.[5] Upon news of Alexander's actual death in Babylon, in 323 BC, there was a second uprising, and armies were sent to keep the settlers in Central Asia. These

---

[3] Holt, *Alexander the Great and Bactria*, 1988 and Holt, *Into the Land of Bones*, 2005.

[4] The Alexander foundations in the 'Far East' is discussed by Cohen, *The Hellenistic Settlements in the East from Armenia and Mesopotamia to Bactria and India*, 2013.

[5] The settler revolts have been discussed most recently by Iliakis, 'Greek Mercenary Revolts in Bactria', 2013.

men – I place deliberate emphasis upon their gender – were the founding fathers of the Greek kingdoms of the Hellenistic Far East. Alexander's settlements were, by definition, almost entirely male on the Greek side. Unlike more attractive, Mediterranean destinations, such as Egypt, Bactria is highly unlikely to have received a significant additional influx of new Greek immigrants during the course of the Hellenistic period. In the new Alexandrias, and garrisoned old cities such as Samarkand and Bactra, intermarriage between Greek men and local women must have been the rule from the very earliest days of the settlements.[6] In the absence of a substantial documentary record, such as the papyri of Graeco-Roman Egypt, we cannot trace intersections of gender and ethnicity in Bactria much further.[7] But I reiterate the point that the Greek settlements of the Hellenistic Far East were ethnically, linguistically and culturally mixed from their very foundation.

There are few surviving documentary sources from the Hellenistic Far East.[8] There are also very few traditional historical sources – the Greek kingdoms of Bactria and India appear only very rarely in the extant works of Greek and Roman historians.[9] One of the lengthiest such passages is Polybios' account of the siege of Bactra by the Seleucid king Antiochos III in the final years of the third century BC. Bactria had been effectively independent under local Greek kings for some time, but Antiochos attempted to reassert Seleucid control. There followed a protracted siege of the capital city, Bactra, in which Antiochos was finally offered the opportunity to save face by coming to an agreement with king Euthydemos which played upon their common Greekness. Euthydemos appealed to Antiochos to join forces, with a fellow Greek king, against barbarian nomadic hordes which were apparently menacing the Greek civilisation of Bactria:

> For Euthydemos was himself a Magnesian and, defending himself to Teleas [Antiochos' envoy], alleged that it was unjust for Antiochos to demand his removal from power, since he himself had not rebelled against the king. Rather, when others had revolted, he had destroyed their descendants and thus gained possession of the Bactrian throne.

---

[6] Intermarriage and the formation of ethnic identities in the Hellenistic Far East is discussed by Mairs, 'The Places in Between', 2011, pp. 179-182, and more generally in Mairs, 'Greek Identity and the Settler Community in Hellenistic Bactria and Arachosia', 2008.

[7] On similar questions in Egypt, see e.g. Rowlandson, 'Gender and Cultural Identity in Roman Egypt', 2004.

[8] There are currently three known Greek documentary texts on perishable materials of the Hellenistic period, all of which came from the antiquities market and not from excavated contexts: Bernard & Rapin, 'Un parchemin gréco-bactrien d'une collection privée', 1994 and Clarysse & Thompson, 'Two Greek Texts on Skin from Hellenistic Bactria', 2007.

[9] These passages are collected in Holt, *Thundering Zeus*, 1999, Appendix D.

> After further discussing this matter along these same lines, he begged Teleas to mediate peace in a kindly manner, exhorting Antiochos not to begrudge him his royal name and state. For if Antiochos did not make these concessions, neither of them would be safe: not far away were great numbers of nomads who not only posed a danger to them both but also threatened to barbarise the whole area if they attacked. After saying these things, Euthydemos sent Teleas to Antiochos. The king had long been looking for a way out of the situation, so hearing these things from Teleas he readily accepted peace for the aforementioned reasons.[10]

This was, for both kings, a convenient fiction. But in one of the three documentary texts on leather preserved from Hellenistic Bactria, we find another side to this story:

> *Βασιλεύοντος Ἀντιμάχου ἔτους τριακοστοῦ [μηνὸς - -]*
> *ἐν Ἀμφιπόλει τῆι πρὸς K.αρελοτηι εἰσηγειτα[ι - - τῶν]*
> *ξένων μαν.ηερχολλ.μηνον..... τῶν τεσσαρά[κοντα - - -]*
> *Σκυθῶν ἀργυρίου ἐπισήμου δραχμῶν ἑκατὸν [ι]*
> *[.....τοῦ ..].ε..μενου πλήθους τοῦ ἀργυρίου [- - -]*
> *[.]αρε. [ ] traces of ink*
>
> In the reign of Antimachos in year 30 [month + day] in Amphipolis near K.arelote has introduced [NN of the] mercenaries (?) [] NN of the for[ty - - -] Scythians, of one hundred drachmas of coined silver [- - -].[ ] of [the above mentioned (?)] sum of money [*traces*].[11]

This document dates to the decades around the turn of the third to the second centuries BC, and is thus broadly contemporary to the events described by Polybios. It is a fragmentary contract, relating to a purchase or loan, and the remaining legible text suggests that it is between two military men, in charge of detachments of mercenaries, one of which is composed of 'Scythians', nomadic horsemen of the Central Asian steppes. Evidence from archaeological excavations and field survey throughout Central Asia indicates that there was no clear geographical or socio-economic divide between sedentary 'civilisations' such as the Graeco-Bactrian state and nomadic and the mobile pastoralist groups they referred to as 'Scythians', 'Sakas' or the like, and that relations between nomadic and settled populations were more often symbiotic than antagonistic.[12] This document further suggests that Graeco-Bactrian kings were using Scythian mercenaries. There is little enough material

---

[10] Polybios 11.34 6–14, trans. after Holt, *Thundering Zeus*, 1999, pp. 181–182.
[11] Text, translation and commentary: Clarysse & Thompson, 'Two Greek Texts on Skin from Hellenistic Bactria', 2007, pp. 273–279.
[12] See e.g. Stride, 'Regions and Territories in Southern Central Asia', 2007.

here to work with, but the implications are clear: the Greek settler community of the Hellenistic Far East did not live in isolation but in close interaction both with the local sedentary population, in the cities and villages of Bactria, and the very 'nomad hordes' which Polybios claims were a threat to Graeco-Bactrian 'civilisation'.

In addition to the dearth of documentary and historical sources, there is only a limited amount of archaeological material available from the Hellenistic Far East. This is a topic which I shall discuss at greater length below. Coins have traditionally been one of the most important sources of evidence on the Graeco-Bactrian and Indo-Greek states and their rulers: far more names of these kings are known from their coins than from historical or documentary sources.[13] In Bactria, kings with Greek names minted coins on the Attic standard with Greek legends and iconography. Around the turn of the third-second centuries BC, after the Greek kings of Bactria invaded north-western India, the many competing Indo-Greek statelets established there began to mint new, additional series of coins, on Indian weight standards and with bilingual legends, and Greek and Indian iconography. On these, in a striking juxtaposition, we find the same Greek-named kings identified as both Greek *basileus* and Indian *mahārājah*.

The cultural affinities of these Graeco-Bactrian and Indo-Greek states, and the ethnic identities of their populations, have naturally been a matter of some controversy. Two of the major scholars in the field in the mid-twentieth century – Wiliam Woodthorpe Tarn and A. K. Narain – took rather different stances on this question. In Tarn's view, Bactria should be treated alongside other successor kingdoms to Alexander's conquests in the eastern Mediterranean, as a 'lost chapter of Hellenistic history'.[14] Narain, on the other hand, argued, very quotably, that 'the Greeks came, they saw but India conquered'.[15] There does not, in fact, have to be any fundamental contradiction between these positions.[16] Tarn is correct that the political and cultural roots of the states of the Hellenistic Far East are Hellenistic. Narain is also correct that, in north-western India in the first century BC, there ceases to be much about the material culture and political and religious iconography of the Indo-Greek kingdoms which is identifiably Greek.

Given the scarcity of biographical information on the kings of the Hellenistic Far East, it might appear that the prospects for research on the

[13] For an introduction, see Holt, *Thundering Zeus*, 1999, pp. 67–86.
[14] Tarn, *The Greeks in Bactria and India*, 1951 [1938], p. xiii.
[15] Narain, *The Indo-Greeks*, 1957, p. 18.
[16] As argued in Mairs, 'Hellenistic India', 2006.

biographies, social lives and ethnic identities of the wider population are not good. But some individuals named in our extant sources do offer the opportunity for research of this sort. In economic texts, written on jars, in the treasury of the city of Ai Khanoum, in eastern Bactria, we find the names of officials involved in processing and measuring commodities.[17] There are also a few names written on burial urns from a mausoleum outside the city walls: Isidora, Lysanias, Kosmas, and 'the two little ones'.[18] A shrine inside the walls contained the tomb of a man named Kineas, who may be the city's founder, with an inscription from Delphi copied by one Klearchos, and an inscription in the gymnasium was dedicated by 'Triballos and Straton, sons of Straton'.[19] With the exception of a few of the treasury officials, all these names are Greek, and all of the texts themselves are written in Greek. Greek inscriptions from Kandahar, in southern Afghanistan, ancient Arachosia, name two third- or second-century BC inhabitants of the city: a man with the patronymic Aristonax who dedicates a thank-offering – his own name is not preserved in the inscription – and one Sōphytos, the son of Naratos, whose acrostich epitaph, composed in elegant Hellenistic literary Greek, was purchased on the antiquities market.[20]

Sōphytos, with his Greek education and non-Greek name, has become something of a celebrity in studies of the Hellenistic Far East, inasmuch as the field has celebrities.[21] A person who has received less attention – his story tucked away in the latter part of the same article in the *Journal des Savants* in which Sōphytos was made known to the scholarly community – is a man named Heliodotos, who also set up a Greek inscription somewhere in the Hellenistic Far East, probably in what is now southern Tajikistan, around the turn of the third to second centuries BC. Heliodotos is the first subject of my paper. My second subject is Heliodoros son of Dion, another member of the easternmost Hellenistic Greek diaspora communities. Heliodoros dedicated not a Greek, but a

[17] Rapin, 'Les inscriptions économiques', 1983; Grenet, 'L'onomastique iranienne à Aï Khanoum', 1983.

[18] Canali De Rossi, *Iscrizioni dello Estremo Oriente Greco*, 2004, nos. 360–362.

[19] Canali De Rossi, *Iscrizioni dello Estremo Oriente Greco*, 2004, nos 381 and 382; Robert, 'De Delphes à l'Oxus', 1968.

[20] The 'son of Aristonax': Canali De Rossi, *Iscrizioni dello Estremo Oriente Greco*, 2004, no. 293; Fraser, 'The Son of Aristonax at Kandahar', 1979. Sōphytos son of Naratos: Bernard, Pinault and Rougemont, 'Deux nouvelles inscriptions grecques de l'Asie Centrale', 2004, pp. 227–332.

[21] He is discussed, at greater or lesser length, by Bernard, 'Hellenistic Arachosia', 2005; Sartre, *Histoires grecques*, 2009; Hollis, 'Greek Letters in Hellenistic Bactria', 2011; and Mairs, '*Sopha Grammata*', 2012, inter alia.

Prākrit inscription in a city outside Greek-controlled territories, Vidiśā in central India, not quite a hundred years later, in the 120s-110s BC.

I do not propose that we can reconstruct full biographies for either man. I would like to use their stories – what we know of them – as starting points for exploring the political and cultural landscape of the Hellenistic states of Central Asia and India, their internal dynamics, and their relations with neighbouring states and peoples. The reader may find it tiresome to constantly differentiate between Heliodotos and Heliodoros. For the purposes of the present study, the coincidence of the names may be rhetorically neat, but I will further suggest in my concluding remarks that there may be good reasons why two such theophoric names of the Greek sun-god Helios appear among our very restricted repertoire of Greek names from the Hellenistic Far East.

2. HELIODOTOS

Τόνδε σοι βωμὸν θυώδη, πρέσβα κυδίστη θεῶν
Ἑστία, Διος κ(α)τ' ἄλσος καλλίδενδρον ἔκτισεν
καὶ κλυταῖς ἤσκησε λοιβαῖς ἐμπύροις Ἡλιόδοτος,
ὄφρα τὸμ πάντων μέγιστον Εὐθύδημον βασιλέων
τοῦ τε παῖδα καλλίνικον ἐκπρεπῆ Δημήτριον
πρευμενὴς σώιζῃς ἀκηδεῖ(ς) σὺν Τύχαι θεόφρον[ι][22]

This fragrant altar to you, Hestia, most honoured among the gods, Heliodotos established in the grove of Zeus with its fair trees, furnishing it with libations and burnt-offerings, so that you may graciously preserve free from care, together with divine good fortune, Euthydemos, greatest of all kings, and his outstanding son Demetrios, renowned for fine victories.[23]

The pillar inscription of Heliodoros, which I shall discuss in the following section, has been known to scholarship for over a hundred years and stands to this day at the temple site in central India where it was originally erected in the late second century BC. The inscription of Heliodotos, in contrast, was first published in the *Journal des Savants* in 2004, and neither the circumstances of its discovery, nor its current location, are a matter of public record.[24] The editors' sources indicated that it came from Kuliab, a city in southern Tajikistan. Kuliab's location, less than fifty kilometres by road from the border with Afghanistan, as well as the fact

[22] Text: Bernard, Pinault and Rougemont, 'Deux nouvelles inscriptions grecques de l'Asie Centrale', 2004, p. 333.
[23] Trans. Hollis, 'Greek Letters in Hellenistic Bactria', 2011, p. 110.
[24] Bernard, Pinault and Rougemont, 'Deux nouvelles inscriptions grecques de l'Asie Centrale', 2004, pp. 333–356.

that even in the late nineteenth century the city supported a market in ancient coins,[25] suggests to me that we should keep an open mind as to the actual archaeological provenance of the inscription, and include the whole of southern Tajikistan and north-eastern Afghanistan within the realm of possibility. Internal evidence, as I shall discuss, allows the inscription to be dated to within a few years of the turn of the third to second centuries BC.

In antiquity, the river Oxus/Amu-darya – the present-day border between Afghanistan and the former Soviet Central Asian Republics – seldom represented any kind of political or cultural boundary. Ancient Bactria is best defined as the basin of the upper river Oxus, encompassing most of northern Afghanistan and southern Tajikistan and Uzbekistan. In comparison to neighbouring regions, the archaeological landscape of southern Tajikistan remains relatively poorly known, but there are a number of small excavated sites of the Hellenistic or Kushan periods, as well as one, partially-excavated, larger settlement site, Takht-i Sangin, with its 'Temple of the Oxus'.[26] The most important excavated Hellenistic-period site in Central Asia, however, is also nearby. This is the city of Ai Khanoum, on the south bank of the Oxus in north-eastern Afghanistan.[27] Ai Khanoum was excavated by the Délégation archéologique française en Afghanistan (DAFA) in the 1960s and 1970s. From 1974 to 1978, an extensive archaeological field survey was also undertaken in the city's hinterland. Political circumstances meant that excavations ceased in 1978 and were never resumed, and the city's remains have never been fully published.[28]

Ai Khanoum – the ancient name of the city is unknown – was situated at the junction of the river Oxus with a southern tributary, the Kokcha, and controlled a large agricultural plain as well as access to mineral resources upstream in the Badakshan mountains. Although there was some earlier and later occupation on the site, the Graeco-Bactrian city had a fairly brief period of occupation, from the immediate aftermath of Alexander's conquests in the late fourth century BC, through to the fall of the Graeco-Bactrian kingdom in the mid-second century BC. The city comprised an elevated triangular plateau – the 'acropolis' or upper city – and a lower city at the confluence itself. The city had formidable natural

[25] Gorshenina, *The Private Collections of Russian Turkestan*, 2004, p. 29.

[26] Mairs, *The Archaeology of the Hellenistic Far East*, 2011, pp. 24–26.

[27] Full references to the published reports on the site of Ai Khanoum and the Eastern Bactriane survey are collected in Mairs, *The Archaeology of the Hellenistic Far East*, 2011, pp. 26–29.

[28] On the site's excavation and publication history, see Fussman, 'Southern Bactria and Northern India before Islam', 1996.

and man-made fortifications and was laid out on a massive scale, with a grand central quarter of public buildings, and a 'main street' which ran for over a kilometre along the foot of the acropolis. The city's public and domestic architecture was eclectic in its range of influences from the Classical Mediterranean world, Near East and Central Asia. Its dominant written language, however, was Greek.[29] A handful of public inscriptions, fragments of literary texts and a small collection of economic documents from the city's treasury testify to the language's dominance and its vitality. I have already noted the presence of both Greek and Iranian personal names in these.

Given Ai Khanoum's status as the only extensively excavated Graeco-Bactrian settlement site, it is important not to use its remains to generate arguments about, and structural and theoretical models for, the culture and society of the Graeco-Bactrian kingdom more generally. Unlike, for example, the capital city at Bactra, Ai Khanoum was a new colonial foundation, and the ethnic balance among its inhabitants may well have been very different to that of most of the rest of the region. It was also, to some extent, a 'planned city': in the first part of the second century BC, a large swath of the lower city was razed and rebuilt, and it can be difficult to trace the outlines of earlier buildings underneath this grand new architectural programme. Nor did the residential districts of the city grow 'organically': the southern quarter of the lower city is composed of blocks of mansions of identical size and format. Finally, in the period after the city's destruction in around the 140s BC, it was looted and reoccupied by people the excavators refer to as 'squatters', who moved around goods and building materials, and repurposed many official buildings as domestic residences. Any study of Ai Khanoum must therefore take account of these factors, and recognise that the city must be analysed on its own terms, and not used as a false basis for any wider generalisations about Graeco-Bactrian culture and society.

Ai Khanoum – where its regional context has been considered at all – has tended to be discussed in relation to lowland north-eastern Afghanistan, but as more becomes known of the archaeology of southern Tajikistan, the interconnectivity of regions on either side of the river become clearer. The site of Saksanokhur, a mere 35 km as the crow flies north-east of Ai Khanoum, had some chronological overlap with the active life of the city.[30] It too yielded analogous 'Classical' column

[29] There are two exceptions: an ostrakon in Aramaic script, and a silver ingot with a runic inscription in an unknown language. See Mairs, *The Archaeology of the Hellenistic Far East*, 2011, p. 42.

[30] Mairs, *The Archaeology of the Hellenistic Far East*, 2011, p. 26.

capitals, and the layout of the central complex bears some similarities to the traditions of Graeco-Bactrian architecture attested at Ai Khanoum.

Although the inscription of Heliodotos is without archaeological context, it is therefore possible to suggest several known archaeological sites from which it may have come, and to situate it more broadly within a cultural and political milieu of north-eastern Bactria in the third and second centuries BC. It is worth at least considering that the inscription of Heliodotos may have come from Ai Khanoum itself. Certainly, other looted items from the city have passed onto the international antiquities market, although these appear to have come via Afghanistan and Pakistan rather than Tajikistan.[31] Within this region, both Ai Khanoum and Takht-i Sangin have already yielded Greek inscriptions, and there is no reason why the occasional Greek dedication should not also be found at smaller sites. A Greek funerary inscription of a man named Diogenes, for example, was found at Zhiga-tepe in the Bactra oasis, a possible cult site, but not a major centre of population.[32]

The internal evidence of the inscription of Heliodotos itself offers only the broadest clues to its provenance and original architectural and cultural context. It states that it was set up in a wooded grove of Zeus, on an altar dedicated to Hestia. The divine names used are Greek, but in Hellenistic Bactria Greek gods can appear in some rather unexpected contexts. At Ai Khanoum, a Greek inscription in the gymnasium is dedicated to Hermes and Herakles, the typical gods associated with the gymnasium in the Greek world,[33] but elsewhere in the city we find a Greek-style cult statue, possibly of a Zeus, within a temple building whose architectural style owes more to the Near East than to Greece.[34] Downstream, at the Temple of the Oxus at Takht-i Sangin, on the north bank of the river, a man named Atrosokes – an Iranian name – dedicates a Greek inscription to the deified river Oxus.[35] The temples at Takht-i Sangin and Ai Khanoum, and their sanctuaries, were catholic in their outlook, loci for diverse forms of activity, directed at diverse divine forces, worshipped, most probably, under a multiplicity of names. What Heliodotos refers to as a grove of Zeus might quite possibly have been thought of and identified as

---

[31] See e.g. Bopearachchi, 'Contribution of Greeks to the Art and Culture of Bactria and India', 2005, and Bopearachchi & Bernard, 'Deux bracelets grecs avec inscriptions grecques trouvés dans l'Asie centrale hellénisée', 2002.

[32] Mairs, *The Archaeology of the Hellenistic Far East*, 2011, pp. 30, 39.

[33] Robert, 'De Delphes à l'Oxus', 1968, pp. 417–421; Canali De Rossi, *Iscrizioni dello Estremo Oriente Greco*, 2004, no. 381.

[34] See e.g. Martinez-Sève, 'À propos du temple aux niches indentées d'Aï Khanoum', 2010; Mairs, 'The "Temple with Indented Niches" at Ai Khanoum', 2013.

[35] Litvinskii, Vinogradov and Pichikyan, 'Вотив Атросока из Храма Окса в Северной Бактрии', 1985; Canali De Rossi, *Iscrizioni dello Estremo Oriente Greco*, 2004, no. 311.

something else, in another language, by other people engaged in religious practices within the same space. 'Zeus' and 'Hestia', too, were quite likely known by names other than these by other people or in other contexts. These are questions upon which I shall expand in my conclusion.

Heliodotos' dedication was also a political act, not simply an expression of religious piety. The figures for whose sake he dedicates, Euthydemos and his son Demetrios, are among the very few Graeco-Bactrian kings to make an appearance in Classical historical sources. As I have already discussed, the Seleucid king Antiochos III besieged Euthydemos at his capital, Bactra, in 208–206 BC, and finally withdrew after negotiations in which the king's son Demetrios, while still a young man, played a key role (Polybios 11.34.6–14). Demetrios was responsible for spear-heading the Graeco-Bactrian expansion across the Hindu Kush into north-western India only a few years later. Strabo (11.11.1) records Demetrios as one of the most important Graeco-Bactrian conquerors of India. In the inscription of Heliodotos, Demetrios is honoured alongside his father and is given the epithet *kallinikos* – 'renowed for fine victories' – indicating that he has already had military success during his father's reign. As well as gaining renown for Demetrios and his forces, the conquests in north-western India had economic and even cultural implications back home in Bactria. At Ai Khanoum, the treasury contained Indian luxury goods, and large numbers of Indian coins.[36] Heliodotos' inscription is therefore testimony to a period of Graeco-Bactrian confidence and prosperity, in which territorial gains in India reflected glory back onto the Bactrian kings who made them, and allowed the city of Ai Khanoum to undergo major renovations to its urban fabric, funded by Indian tribute and booty.

3. Heliodoros

*[de]vadevasa v[ā][*sude]vasa garuḍadhvaje ayaṃ*
kārit[e] i[a?] heliodoreṇa bhāga-
vatena diyasa putreṇa ta[khkha]silākena
yonadūtena āgatena mahārājasa
aṃtalikitasa upa[ṃ]tā sakāsaṃ raño
kāsīput[r]asa bhāgabhadrasa trātārasa
vasena ca[tu]dasena rājena vadhamānasa

[36] Rapin, *Indian Art from Afghanistan*, 1996; Audouin & Bernard, 'Trésor de monnaies indiennes et indo-grecques d'Aï Khanoum (Afghanistan). I. Les monnaies indiennes', 1973.

> This Garuḍa-pillar of Vāsudeva, the god of gods, was constructed here by Heliodora [Hēliodōros], the Bhāgavata, son of Diya [Diōn], of Takhkhasilā [Taxila], the Greek ambassador who came from the Great King Aṃtalikita [Antialkidas] to King Kāsīputra [Kāśīputra] Bhāgabhadra, the Savior, prospering in (his) fourteenth regnal year.
>
> *trini amutapād[ā]ni [i][me?] [su]anuṭhitāni*
> *neyaṃti sva[gaṃ] dam[e] cāga apramād*
>
> (These?) three steps to immortality, when correctly followed, lead to heaven: control, generosity, and attention.[37]

We take up the story of Heliodoros around eighty or ninety years later, in a rather different political and cultural context. Demetrios' conquests resulted in lasting Greek dominance in north-western India, but Bactria itself fell to Central Asian and Parthian invaders in the 140s BC. The Indian conquests gave ambitious generals and junior royals the military power and wealth to carve out their own fiefdoms, and the Indo-Greek domain was politically fragmented for much of its existence, until the demise of the last Greek-named king to mint coins in northern India, Strato II, in the very early first century AD.[38]

The city of Taxila, around 30 kilometres north-west of modern Islamabad in Pakistan, became one of the most important Indo-Greek metropoleis.[39] Unlike Ai Khanoum, it was not a completely new foundation: there had been settlement at the site for hundreds of years, and Alexander the Great had received the submission of the local king in 326 BC. Under Indo-Greek rule, however, a new city site was established adjacent to the earlier one. This was a common pattern followed by successive waves of invaders in the Taxila valley. Bhir Mound, the Achaemenid and Mauryan settlement, was succeeded by Sirkap, the Indo-Greek city, and then by Sirsukh, founded under the Kushans. Heliodoros' king, Antialkidas (fl. c. 115–95 BC), who controlled Taxila, is known from his bilingual coinage – upon which he bears the epithet *nikephoros*, 'victorious' – but is not mentioned in any historical sources (Fig. 1). The Heliodoros inscription is therefore important evidence for his rule at Taxila and diplomatic contact with other kings in the Indian subcontinent.

The Heliodoros inscription, which is in the local Prākrit, comes from outside the Indo-Greek domains, from Besnagar, in the modern Indian

---

[37] Text and translation: Salomon, *Indian Epigraphy*, 1998, pp. 265–266. The two parts of the inscription appear at different places on the same pillar.

[38] See e.g. Bopearachchi, 'Les derniers souverains indo-grecs', 1991 and Senior & MacDonald, *The Decline of the Indo-Greeks*, 1998.

[39] Mairs, *The Archaeology of the Hellenistic Far East*, 2011, pp. 36–37.

state of Madhya Pradesh, the site of an ancient city named Vidiśā.[40] In contrast to the inscription of Heliodotos, the pillar upon which Heliodoros left his inscription not only has an archaeological context, but remains in situ. It was 'discovered' – in the sense of being recorded and reported by a European – in the late nineteenth century. The first report of the pillar (but not the inscription) was published by Sir Alexander Cunningham of the Archaeological Survey of India in 1880.[41] Cunningham was not able to examine the pillar closely, because it remained an object of devotion, and pilgrims had smeared it with a thick coat of vermillion paint, but he accepted the reports of locals that it was uninscribed. The first European to inspect the pillar more thoroughly was Sir John Marshall, later excavator of Taxila, and a transcription and translation by Theodor Bloch was included in his report of 1909.[42] Following the discovery of the inscription, the entire pillar was cleaned under the orders of the local Maharaja, Madho Rao Scindia, but no further writing was found.

Figure 1. Coin of Antialkidas with bilingual Greek-Prākrit legend.
© Trustees of the British Museum.

In the late nineteenth century, when the pillar was first described by Cunningham, ruins were preserved in the vicinity, but these had not yet been subject to serious archaeological investigation. The most extensive

[40] On the archaeology of Besnagar/Vidiśā see (concisely) Khare, 'Besnagar', 1989, Chakrabarti, *The Archaeology of Ancient Indian Cities*, 1995, pp. 221–222; and (full study of the wider region) Tripathi, *Archaeology of Vidiśā (Daśārṇa) Region*, 2002. Summaries of the excavation history of the site surrounding the pillar of Heliodoros: Khare, 'Discovery of a Vishṇu Temple near the Heliodoros Pillar, Besnagar, Dist. Vidisha (M.P.)', 1966, p. 21; Irwin, 'The Heliodorus Pillar at Besnagar', 1975–76, pp. 168–170.
[41] Cunningham, *Archaeological Survey of India Vol 10*, 1880, pp. 41–42.
[42] Marshall, 'Notes on Archaeological Exploration in India, 1908–9', 1909.

excavations, in the 1960s, revealed an elliptical shaped temple, dating back to the fourth century BC. This early temple was destroyed at some point and rebuilt on a raised platform, with rubble retaining walls, which are preserved. The internal chronology of the building and these constructions are not known clearly, but there was a temple of some kind on the site at the time of the pillar dedication – which would be evident in any case from its contents.[43]

Like Heliodotos in Bactria, Heliodoros includes references to divine figures and to local religious sites and practices in his inscription, but at Besnagar something of the archaeological context of these is preserved. Broadly speaking, the temple, pillar and inscription are dedicated to the cult of the god Vishnu. The 'Vāsudeva' of the inscription is a patronymic indicating Krishna, an avatar of Vishnu, and the mythical bird Garuda was Vishnu's mount. Heliodoros is referred to as a *bhāgavata*, a term used for a devotee of a vaishnavite cult. Heliodoros' dedication of a pillar – described as a *garuḍadhvaja* or 'standard of Garuda' – was a typical form of devotion at the site, for prominent people, or those who could afford it. The remains of several additional pillars are preserved, along with traces of pits to hold the foundations of others, set out at uniform intervals in a line outside the temple retaining wall.

Another point which the inscriptions of Heliodotos in Bactria and Heliodoros in India have in common is their appeal to secular as well as to divine authorities. Heliodoros son of Dion is described as a *yonadūta*, a 'Greek ambassador', on a mission from Antialkidas at Taxila. Little is, unfortunately, known about the local king, Bhāgabhadra, to whom Heliodoros came as emissary, nor do we have any further information on the nature or duration of his mission. Given his official position, as the representative of a foreign king, one might question whether Heliodoros' display of devotion to a local god, at a local cult site, was a diplomatic rather than a personal act. But an element of personal piety is not automatically to be excluded. At Heliodoros' home city of Taxila, there is evidence for considerable diversity in religious practice, including the worship of gods under names and images typical of the Indian subcontinent rather than of the Classical Mediterranean world.[44] Although Heliodoros is expressly marked out as a foreigner – a 'Greek ambassador' – it is possible that the culture and society which he experienced at Vidiśā was not dissimilar to that with which he was already familiar from within the Indo-Greek domains.

---

[43] Khare, 'Discovery of a Vishṇu Temple near the Heliodoros Pillar, Besnagar, Dist. Vidisha (M.P.)', 1966.

[44] See e.g. Dar, 'A Fresh Study of Four Unique Temples at Takshasila (Taxila)', 1980 and Rapin, 'Hinduism in the Indo-Greek Area', 1995.

4. Authorship, Identities and Polysemic Readings

Despite the absence of much supporting historical or archaeological evidence, these two inscriptions in fact tell us rather a lot about Heliodotos and Heliodoros and their worlds. As I have already indicated, they also have a certain amount in common. Both inscriptions were commissioned, in some sense, as political acts. They mention, and in the case of Heliodotos, dedicate for the sake of reigning monarchs. The arena for this political act, in each case, was a religious precinct. The various descriptors used to mark Heliodotos and Heliodoros are not some private expressions of social identity (under which I subsume ethnic identity). These descriptions are very context-specific, and we do not know whether either man authored his inscription himself, or what input, if any, he would have had in its wording.

Much ink has been spilt over whether one ought to call Heliodoros an Indian or a Greek.[45] Given its more recent publication, and exclusively Greek cultural referents, little has yet been said on this account about Heliodotos, but doubtless it shall. The question of authorship is crucial to how we approach and interpret these inscriptions, and it is important to separate out emic and etic perspectives from one another: is 'Greek ambassador', for example, an ethnic and a professional title Heliodoros claims for himself, or is it how he was described by the people around him at Bhāgabhadra's court in Vidiśā? Would he have chosen to refer to himself in the same way in a Greek inscription in his home city?

A crucial difference between the two inscriptions is that Heliodoros is given an explicit ethnic label and Heliodotos is not. It is only in the inscription of Heliodoros – in a language other than Greek, and outside Greek-controlled territories – that his identity as a 'Greek' became salient, something which served to identify him both professionally, and as someone of different ethnicity to those around him. For Heliodotos, in a Greek inscription, within a Greek-ruled kingdom, such a statement of his ethnicity was unnecessary and irrelevant.

What matters above all, in ascribing an 'identity' to a past individual, is their self-definition and their contemporary definition by others in the milieux in which they functioned. If Heliodoros is described as a 'Greek', then a Greek he is. What is naturally more complex is establishing what

[45] Various different views have been expressed by, for example: Khare, 'Discovery of a Vishṇu Temple near the Heliodoros Pillar, Besnagar, Dist. Vidisha (M.P.)', 1966, p. 24: 'foreign convert'; Harmatta, 'Languages and Scripts in Graeco-Bactria and the Saka Kingdoms', 1994, p. 397: 'half-Indianized Greek'; Karttunen, *India and the Hellenistic World*, 1997: 'a Greek (or at least someone using a Greek name even in an Indian inscription)'.

range of social behaviours and cultural indicia were permitted to be displayed as part of contemporary, local ‘Greek’ identity, and how far these differed from those of other ‘Greek’ communities.[46] The statements of a written text may sometimes seem to stand in contrast, or opposition, to matters such as iconography, language choice, dress, or other forms of externally observable cultural behaviour, but, in the construction and articulation of an ethnic identity, what people understand to have ethnic resonance, and what is innocent of such resonance, is not universal across cultures. Being named as a devotee of an Indian god in an Indian inscription does not make Heliodoros not-Greek. But equally, all the Greek cultural and political references in his inscription do not serve to make Heliodotos a Greek. In Bactria, it is hoped that future discoveries – from scientific excavation rather than from the antiquities market – will supply more details about Heliodotos’ social and cultural milieu, and the different identities, forms of cultural expression and religious devotion which he and his contemporaries may have displayed in other circumstances.

I would like to conclude by arguing that in the terminology used by, and used to describe, Heliodotos and Heliodoros there is sufficient (I would suggest, deliberate) ambiguity to permit a range of readings. Polysemy can be socially and politically convenient. Double meanings may exist not just in the names for gods and locales used in the two inscriptions, but in the names of the men themselves.

I have already suggested that the similarity in these two men’s names may be something more than simple coincidence. Both mean ‘given by Helios’, the Greek sun–god. The corpus of known Greek personal names from the Hellenistic Far East is very small, but we find further instances of theophoric Helios-names. There were two Graeco-Bactrian or Indo-Greek kings named ‘Heliokles’: one (reigned c. 145–130 BC) was the last Greek-named king to rule in Bactria, and the other (reigned c. 95–80 BC) was one of the myriad competing Indo-Greek kings. Is the recurrence of Helios significant? Is ‘Helios’, in fact, a translation of something else?

In the Hellenistic world it was common for the same gods to be known by different names, whether through deliberate, sometimes politically motivated syncretism of a Greek with an indigenous god, or through conventional equations of the gods of different pantheons with one

[46] A question I have discussed elsewhere, especially with regard to material from Ai Khanoum: Mairs, ‘Greek Identity and the Settler Community in Hellenistic Bactria and Arachosia’, 2008, p. 23, and Mairs, ‘The “Temple with Indented Niches” at Ai Khanoum’, 2013. See also Mairs, *The Archaeology of the Hellenistic Far East*, 2011, pp. 14–19.

another.[47] In my discussion of Heliodotos' dedication to 'Hestia' in the 'grove of Zeus', I proposed that these deities may have been known by different names, even to worshippers within the same sanctuaries, and noted that the excavated temples of Hellenistic Bactra – at Ai Khanoum and Takht-i Sangin – reveal a diversity of religious practice within the same compounds.

Figure 2. Coin of Kanishka with image of Helios and Greek legend.
© Trustees of the British Museum.

The 'Greek gods' of the Hellenistic Far East were (or became) something more complex than that, and some of the most decisive evidence relates specifically to Helios. The coins of Graeco-Bactrian and Indo-Greek kings bear many divine images with familiar Classical iconography. Even the most quintessentially Greek of these 'images from a foreign pantheon' may well have been susceptible to alternate readings by the local peoples of Central Asia and India.[48] Images of Helios, with his 'sunburst' crown, and driving a chariot, appear on the coins of the Graeco-Bactrian king Plato.[49] Helios is also depicted, in bust form, on cult objects from both Ai

---

[47] The topic is too large to be treated in full here, but see, for example, the inscriptions identifying various Greek and Iranian deities at the sanctuary of Antiochos I of Commagene at Nemrud Dag (Sanders, *Nemrud Dagi*, 1996), or the syncretised cult of Serapis in Ptolemaic Egypt (for the architectural format and artistic trappings of the Serapeum at Alexandria, see McKenzie, Gibson and Reyes, 'Reconstructing the Serapeum in Alexandria from the Archaeological Evidence', 2004).
[48] Boyce & Grenet, *A History of Zoroastrianism III*, 1991, p. 161.
[49] For examples, see Bopearachchi, *Monnaies gréco-bactriennes et indo-grecques*, 1991, pl. 24. Boyce & Grenet, *A History of Zoroastrianism III*, 1991, pp. 162–163, already see

Khanoum and Takht-i Sangin.[50] On other coins of Plato, Helios is depicted standing and holding a sceptre, again with his distinctive sun rays. This image survives onto the coinage of the Kushan emperor Kanishka in the early second century AD, where it undergoes a reinterpretation (Fig. 2). Kanishka implemented a policy of replacing Greek legends on his coins with text in the Bactrian language, and at the same time of 'translating' captions which identified gods by their Greek names into the names of local Iranian gods.[51] The god recognisable from Plato's coins, and captioned on Kanishka's early issues, as 'Helios', becomes 'Mithra' without any further change in iconography. This 'translation' of Greek into Iranian gods was only the culmination of a long process of syncretism which had begun under Graeco-Bactrian rule. Multiple such assimilations might be possible for any individual 'Greek' god: in addition to Helios, in his solar aspect, Mithra, might also be equated with Zeus.[52]

All this has certain implications for 'Greek' naming practices in the Hellenistic Far East. In contemporary Egypt, bilingual double-naming was practised by some sectors of the population, and an individual might choose to use either their Greek or Egyptian name – or both in combination – depending upon the circumstances.[53] I do not propose that this same phenomenon was at work in the Hellenistic Far East, but it is possible that specific Greek personal names were chosen, not necessarily to translate or complement an 'indigenous' name by which the individual was also known, but precisely because 'Helios' was, to a local audience, suggestive of 'Mithra'. Among the other known personal names from the Hellenistic Far East, local gods do feature, and the deified river Oxus is an especially popular choice.[54] The selection of particular, locally resonant Greek names may have offered a way of conforming to local

---

an evolution in the imagery of Helios on these coins towards that more typical of the Indian god Surya or the Iranian god Mithra.

[50] Noted by Shenkar, 'On the Temple of the Oxus in Bactria, III (Review Article)', 2012, p. 140. The objects in question are a plaque depicting Cybele from the Temple with Indented Niches at Ai Khanoum (Francfort, *Fouilles d'Aï Khanoum III*, 1984, pp. 93–104) and a silver plaque from the Temple of the Oxus (Litvinskii, *Храм Окса в Бактрии (Южный Таджикистан). Том 3: Искусство, Художественное Ремесло, Музикальные Инструменты*, 2010).

[51] Cribb, 'Money as a Marker of Cultural Continuity and Change in Central Asia', 2007, pp. 366–367.

[52] Martinez-Sève, 'Pouvoir et religion dans la Bactriane hellénistique', 2010, pp. 8–9.

[53] Quaegebeur, 'Greco-Egyptian Double Names as a Feature of a Bi-Cultural Society', 1992; see now also Coussement, *παρὰ τὸ Ἕλληνά με εἶναι: Polyonymy and the Expression of Ethnicity in Ptolemaic Egypt*, 2012.

[54] Discussed in Mairs, 'The Hellenistic Far East', 2013.

practices, and acknowledging an individual's Bactrian or Indian heritage, without discarding the outward trappings of a 'Greek' identity.

One of the most striking aspects of the inscriptions of Heliodotos and Heliodoros, in my view, is thus the extent to which they are susceptible to multiple, simultaneous readings and indeed permit and encourage them. Such variant readings do not need to stand in opposition to one another. 'Creative misunderstanding'[55] of theophoric names, superficially grounded in Greek tradition, as their local equivalents offers a mechanism for rationalising apparently aberrant 'foreign' behaviour with an accepted local framework. There is much to be said for permitting material from the Hellenistic Far East – whether inscriptions, artistic representations or material culture – to be ambiguous in this way. Polysemic readings of the evidence may in fact be much closer to the contemporary, local response.

Bibliography

Audouin, R. & P. Bernard. 'Trésor de monnaies indiennes et indo-grecques d'Aï Khanoum (Afghanistan). I. Les monnaies indiennes.' *Revue Numismatique* 5 (1973), pp. 238–289.

Bernard, P. 'Hellenistic Arachosia: A Greek Melting Pot in Action.' *East and West* 55 (2005), pp. 13–34.

Bernard, P., G.-J. Pinault & G. Rougemont. 'Deux nouvelles inscriptions grecques de l'Asie Centrale.' *Journal des Savants* (2004), pp. 227–356.

Bernard, P. & C. Rapin. 'Un parchemin gréco-bactrien d'une collection privée.' *Comptes-rendus de l'Académie des inscriptions et belles-lettres* (1994), pp. 261–294.

Bopearachchi, O. 'Les derniers souverains indo-grecs: une nouvelle hypothèse.' P. Bernard & F. Grenet (eds.), *Histoire et cultes de l'Asie centrale préislamique: Sources écrites et documents archéologiques. Actes du colloque international du CNRS (Paris, 22–28 Novembre 1988)*. Paris, 1991, pp. 235–242.

– *Monnaies gréco-bactriennes et indo-grecques: Catalogue raisonné.* Paris, 1991.

– 'Contribution of Greeks to the Art and Culture of Bactria and India: New Archaeological Evidence.' *Indian Historical Review* 32 (2005), pp. 103–125.

Bopearachchi, O. & P. Bernard. 'Deux bracelets grecs avec inscriptions grecques trouvés dans l'Asie centrale hellénisée.' *Journal des Savants* (2002), pp. 238–278.

[55] I borrow the term from White, *The Middle Ground*, 1991, esp. pp. 52–53, the relevance of which to material from the Hellenistic world is discussed at greater length in Mairs, 'The Places in Between', 2011.

Boyce, M. & F. Grenet. *A History of Zoroastrianism III: Zoroastrianism under Macedonian and Roman Rule.* (Handbuch der Orientalistik. Erste Abteilung: Der Nahe und Mittlere Osten 8.1.2.2.3.) Leiden, 1991.

Canali De Rossi, F. *Iscrizioni dello Estremo Oriente Greco: Un Repertorio.* (Inschriften Griechischer Städte aus Kleinasien 65.) Bonn, 2004.

Chakrabarti, D. K. *The Archaeology of Ancient Indian Cities.* Oxford – Delhi, 1995.

Clarysse, W. & D. J. Thompson. 'Two Greek Texts on Skin from Hellenistic Bactria.' *Zeitschrift für Papyrologie und Epigraphik* 159 (2007), pp. 273–279.

Cohen, G. M. *The Hellenistic Settlements in the East from Armenia and Mesopotamia to Bactria and India.* Berkeley, 2013.

Coussement, S. *παρὰ τὸ Ἕλληνά με εἶναι: Polyonymy and the Expression of Ethnicity in Ptolemaic Egypt.* Unpublished PhD Thesis, 2012.

Cribb, J. 'Money as a Marker of Cultural Continuity and Change in Central Asia.' J. Cribb & G. Herrmann (eds.), *After Alexander: Central Asia Before Islam.* (Proceedings of the British Academy 133.) Oxford, 2007, pp. 333–376.

Cunningham, A. *Archaeological Survey of India Vol 10: Report of Tours in Bundelkhand and Malwa in 1874–75 and 1876–77.* Calcutta, 1880.

Dar, S. R. 'A Fresh Study of Four Unique Temples at Takshasila (Taxila).' *Journal of Central Asia* 3 (1980), pp. 91–137.

Francfort, H.-P. *Fouilles d'Aï Khanoum III. Le sanctuaire du temple à niches indentées. 2. Les trouvailles.* (Mémoires de la Délegation Archéologique Française en Afghanistan 27.) Paris, 1984.

Fraser, P. M. 'The Son of Aristonax at Kandahar.' *Afghan Studies* 2 (1979), pp. 9–21.

Fussman, G. 'Southern Bactria and Northern India before Islam: A Review of Archaeological Reports.' *Journal of the American Oriental Society* 116 (1996), pp. 243–259.

Gorshenina, S. *The Private Collections of Russian Turkestan in the Second Half of the 19th and Early 20th Century.* Berlin, 2004.

Grenet, F. 'L'onomastique iranienne à Aï Khanoum.' *Bulletin de Correspondance Hellénique* 107 (1983), pp. 373–381.

Harmatta, J. 'Languages and Scripts in Graeco-Bactria and the Saka Kingdoms.' J. Harmatta, B. N. Puri and G. F. Etemadi (eds.), *History of the Civilizations of Central Asia. Vol. 2, The Development of Sedentary and Nomadic Civilizations: 700 B.C. to A.D. 250.* Paris, 1994, pp. 386–406.

Hollis, A. S. 'Greek Letters in Hellenistic Bactria.' D. Obbink & R. Rutherford (eds.), *Culture in Pieces: Essays on Ancient Texts in Honour of Peter Parsons*. Oxford, 2011, pp. 104–118.

Holt, F. L. *Alexander the Great and Bactria: The Formation of a Greek Frontier in Central Asia*. (Mnemosyne Supplements 104.) Leiden; New York, 1988.

– *Thundering Zeus: The Making of Hellenistic Bactria*. (Hellenistic Culture and Society 32.) Berkeley, 1999.

– *Into the Land of Bones: Alexander the Great in Afghanistan*. (Hellenistic Culture and Society 47.) Berkeley, 2005.

Iliakis, M. 'Greek Mercenary Revolts in Bactria: A Re-Appraisal.' *Historia: Zeitschrift für Alte Geschichte* 62 (2013), pp. 182–195.

Irwin, J. 'The Heliodorus Pillar at Besnagar.' *Purātattva* 8 (1975–76), pp. 166–176.

Karttunen, K. *India and the Hellenistic World*. (Studia Orientalia 83.) Helsinki, 1997.

Khare, M. D. 'Discovery of a Vishṇu Temple near the Heliodoros Pillar, Besnagar, Dist. Vidisha (M.P.).' *Lalit Kalā* 13 (1966), pp. 21–27.

– 'Besnagar.' A. Ghosh (eds.), *An Encyclopaedia of Indian Archaeology*. New Delhi, 1989, p. 62.

Litvinskii, B. A. *Храм Окса в Бактрии (Южный Таджикистан). Том 3: Искусство, Художественное Ремесло, Музикальные Инструменты*. Moscow, 2010.

Litvinskii, B. A., Y. G. Vinogradov and I. R. Pichikyan. 'Вотив Атросока из Храма Окса в Северной Бактрии.' *Вестник Древней Истории* (1985), pp. 85–110.

Mairs, R. 'Hellenistic India.' *New Voices in Classical Reception* 1 (2006), pp. 19–30.

– 'Greek Identity and the Settler Community in Hellenistic Bactria and Arachosia.' *Migrations and Identities* 1 (2008), pp. 19–43.

– *The Archaeology of the Hellenistic Far East: A Survey. Bactria, Central Asia and the Indo-Iranian Borderlands, c. 300 BC – AD 100*. (BAR International Series 2196.) Oxford, 2011.

– 'The Places in Between: Model and Metaphor in the Archaeology of Hellenistic Arachosia.' A. Kouremenos, S. Chandrasekaran & R. Rossi (eds.), *From Pella to Gandhara: Hybridisation and Identity in the Art and Architecture of the Hellenistic East*. (BAR International Series 2221.) Oxford, 2011, pp. 177–189.

– '*Sopha Grammata*: Greek Acrostichs in Inscriptions from Arachosia, Nubia and Libya.' J. Kwapisz, D. Petrain, and M. Szymanski (eds.), *The Muse at Play: Riddles and Wordplay in Greek and Latin Poetry*. (Beiträge zur Altertumskunde.) Berlin, 2012, pp. 277–304.

– ‘The Hellenistic Far East: From the *Oikoumene* to the Community.’ E. Stavrianopoulou (ed.), *Shifting Social Imaginaries in the Hellenistic Period: Narratives, Practices, Images*. (Mnemosyne Supplements 363.) Leiden, 2013.

– ‘The “Temple with Indented Niches” at Ai Khanoum: Ethnic and Civic Identity in Hellenistic Bactria.’ R. Alston, O. M. van Nijf and C. Williamson (eds.), *Cults, Creeds and Contests: Religion in the Post-Classical City*. (Groningen-Royal Holloway Studies on the Greek City after the Classical Age. Volume 3.) Leuven, 2013.

Marshall, J. H. ‘Notes on Archaeological Exploration in India, 1908–9.’ *Journal of the Royal Asiatic Society* (1909), pp. 1053–1056.

Martinez-Sève, L. ‘À propos du temple aux niches indentées d’Aï Khanoum: quelques observations.’ P. Carlier & C. Lerouge (eds.), *Paysage et religion en Grèce antique: mélanges offerts à Madeleine Jost*. Paris, 2010, pp. 195–207.

– ‘Pouvoir et religion dans la Bactriane hellénistique. Recherches sur la politique religieuse des rois séleucides et gréco-bactriens.’ *Chiron* 40 (2010), pp. 1–27.

McKenzie, J. S., S. Gibson, and A. T. Reyes. ‘Reconstructing the Serapeum in Alexandria from the Archaeological Evidence.’ *Journal of Roman Studies* 94 (2004), pp. 73–121.

Narain, A. K. *The Indo-Greeks*. Oxford, 1957.

Quaegebeur, J. ‘Greco-Egyptian Double Names as a Feature of a Bi-Cultural Society: The Case Ψοσνευς ὁ καὶ Τριάδελφος.’ J. H. Johnson (ed.), *Life in a Multi-Cultural Society: Egypt from Cambyses to Constantine and Beyond*. (Studies in Ancient Oriental Civilization 51.) Chicago, 1992, pp. 265–272.

Rapin, C. ‘Les inscriptions économiques de la trésorerie hellénistique d’Aï Khanoum (Afghanistan).’ *Bulletin de correspondance hellénique* 107 (1983), pp. 315–381.

– ‘Hinduism in the Indo-Greek Area: Notes on Some Indian Finds from Bactria and on Two Temples in Taxila.’ A. Invernizzi (ed.), *In the Land of the Gryphons: Papers on Central Asian Archaeology in Antiquity*. (Monografie di Mesopotamia 5.) Firenze, 1995, pp. 275–291.

– *Indian Art from Afghanistan: The legend of Śakuntalā and the Indian Treasure of Eucratides at Ai Khanum*. New Delhi, 1996.

Rawlinson, H. G. *Bactria: From the Earliest Times to the Extinction of Bactrio-Greek Rule in the Punjab (being the Hare University Prize Essay, 1908)*. Bombay, 1909.

Robert, L. ‘De Delphes à l’Oxus: Inscriptions grecques nouvelles de la Bactriane.’ *Comptes-rendus de l’Académie des inscriptions et belles-lettres* (1968), pp. 416–457.

Rowlandson, J. 'Gender and Cultural Identity in Roman Egypt.' F. McHardy & E. Marshall (eds.), *Women's Influence on Classical Civilization*. London, 2004, pp. 151–166.
Salomon, R. *Indian Epigraphy: A Guide to the Study of Inscriptions in Sanskrit, Prakrit, and the Other Indo-Aryan Languages*. (South Asia Research.) New York; Oxford, 1998.
Sanders, D. H. (ed.). *Nemrud Dagi: The Hierothesion of Antiochus I of Commagene: Results of the American Excavations Directed by Theresa B. Goell*. Winona Lake, Ind., 1996.
Sartre, M. *Histoires grecques: Snapshots from Antiquity*. (Revealing Antiquity 17.) Cambridge, 2009.
Senior, R. C. & D. MacDonald. *The Decline of the Indo-Greeks: A Re-Appraisal of the Chronology From the Time of Menander to that of Azes*. (Monographs of the Hellenic Numismatic Society 2.) Athens, 1998.
Shenkar, M. 'On the Temple of the Oxus in Bactria, III (Review Article).' *Studia Iranica* 41 (2012), pp. 135–142.
Stride, S. 'Regions and Territories in Southern Central Asia: What the Surkhan Darya Province Tells Us about Bactria.' J. Cribb & G. Herrmann (eds.), *After Alexander: Central Asia Before Islam*. (Proceedings of the British Academy 133.) Oxford, 2007, pp. 99–117.
Tarn, W. W. *The Greeks in Bactria and India*. Cambridge, 1951 [1938].
Tripathi, K. K. *Archaeology of Vidiśā (Daśārṇa) Region*. Delhi, 2002.
White, R. *The Middle Ground: Indians, Empires, and Republics in the Great Lakes Region, 1650–1815*. (Cambridge Studies in North American Indian History.) Cambridge, 1991.

CULTURAL ENCOUNTERS AND IDENTITY FORMATION AMONG THE URBAN ELITE IN EARLY NEO-BABYLONIAN SOCIETY

JOHN P. NIELSEN

Abstract. Cuneiform documents dating from the eighth and seventh centuries B.C. (the early Neo-Babylonian period) reveal an emergent use of family names among the elite inhabitants of many of southern Mesopotamia's traditional cultic centers. In *Sons and Descendants* the author applied a structuralist approach to examine this phenomenon. Less developed were the related questions of to whom the urban elite were projecting their identities and why it had become advantageous to claim such identities. The current work will address these questions by examining cultural contacts between the urban elite, the Assyrian empire, and the Aramean and Chaldean tribal groups present in southern Mesopotamia, and by considering to what degree the use of family names represented a nascent form of Babylonian national consciousness among the urban elite.

1. Introduction

A distinctive feature of Neo-Babylonian society was the dominant position enjoyed by a wealthy and educated urban gentry whose private archives reveal their close involvement in the temples as administrators and prebendaries, their control of agricultural land, or their participation in entrepreneurial enterprises that at times intersected with institutional interests.[1] The activities of this segment of society are most visible in the wealth of tablets dating from the long sixth century – the period of prolonged social stability and economic growth that stretched from the accession of Nabopolassar in 625 during the Assyrian Empire's demise to 484 BC when Xerxes suppressed a Babylonian revolt against the Persian Empire[2] – but their importance in Babylonian society can be traced further back in time due to the frequent use of distinctive family names by many members of this social class. Indeed, the antecedents of family name usage can be traced back to the Kassite period and therefore

[1] Jursa, *Aspects of the Economic History of Babylonia*, 2010, pp. 3–5.
[2] Jursa, *Aspects of the Economic History of Babylonia*, 2010, pp. 29-30.

predate Neo-Assyrian expansion and the appearance of Arameans and Chaldeans in southern Mesopotamia.[3] But it was during the first half of the first millennium, particularly during the eighth and seventh centuries, that the use of family names became more common among the urban gentry and that the textual conventions for designating such affiliations became more established and standardized.[4] It is impossible to point to a single cause for these developments, but there does seem to have been a correlation between the expanding and evolving use of family names by the urban gentry as a means for projecting their social identities and the urban gentry's contacts with both the tribal groups in southern Mesopotamia and Assyria's imperial apparatus.[5] In turn, these contacts shaped how the urban gentry understood themselves as a distinct population and conceived of Babylonia as a geographic entity.

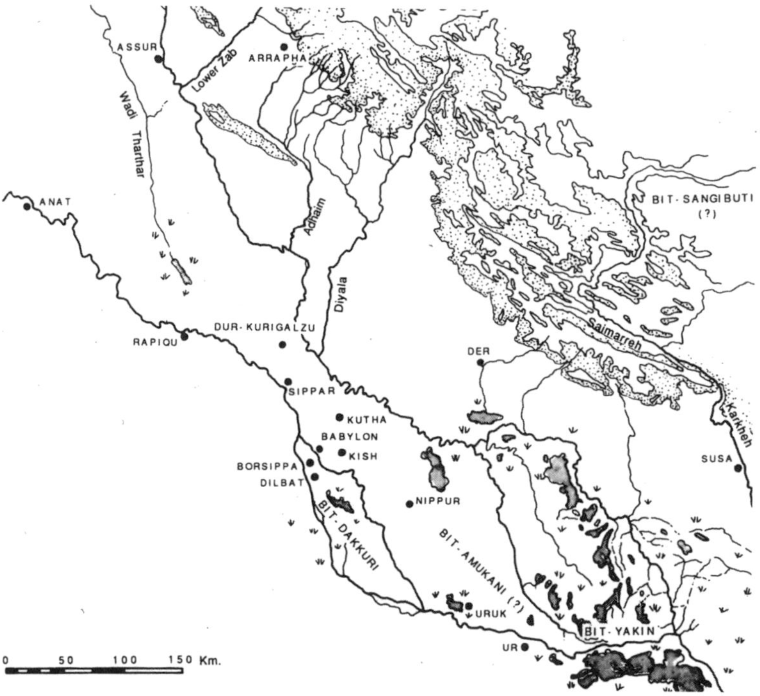

Map of Southern Mesopotamia (after Cole, *Nippur in Late Assyrian Times*, 1996, p. 109)

[3] Nielsen, *Sons and Descendants*, 2011, p. 13.
[4] Nielsen, *Sons and Descendants*, 2011, pp. 223–229.
[5] Brinkman first made this suggestion in, 'Babylonia under the Assyrian Empire', 1979, pp. 237–238.

Over the course of the first half of the first millennium the Chaldean and Aramean presence in southern Mesopotamia increased and the Assyrians extended their reach into the region.[6] The populations of the traditional cultic centers had no choice but to accommodate these new groups. Made up as they were of the descendants of the Sumerians, Amorites, and Kassites, the ethnic identity of these urban populations had blurred into a common "older Babylonian" or "Akkadian" identity based on socio-cultural traditions that were many centuries old and a strong tradition of affiliation with their respective cities and the local institutions housed within.[7]

All of these populations contributed significantly to the political history of southern Mesopotamia in the early first millennium.[8] For much of the first quarter of the millennium there had been little dynastic continuity in Babylon and it was unusual that a monarch was able to govern effectively the highly heterogeneous population of southern Mesopotamia.[9] Assyria's involvement in southern Mesopotamia until the empire's final collapse evolved into an effort to stabilize the region and diminish the power of the tribes in order to further its own imperial interests.[10] In the shifting political climate that resulted, the cities of southern Mesopotamia were not always unified. Epistolary evidence from the Assyrian imperial archives and from the *šandabakku*'s (governor's)

---

[6] Nearly a half million Arameans and Chaldeans were deported from southern Mesopotamia according to Assyrian sources. Even if this number was an exaggeration, it points to the significant size of the tribal population in southern Mesopotamia (Brinkman, 'Babylonia under the Assyrian Empire', 1979, p. 227). Likewise, the rich tribute that the Chaldean kings sent to Shalmaneser III after his Babylonian campaigns (Grayson, *Assyrian Rulers of the Early First Millennium BC, II*, 1996, A.0.102.) was a testament to the wealth these tribes were able to amass, probably through their control of trade routes at the head of the Persian Gulf (Brinkman, 'Babylonia c. 1000–748 B.C.', 1982, pp. 305–306). Tribal control of trade in southern Mesopotamia probably motivated Tiglath-pileser III's campaign against the Arameans and Chaldeans, and the seizure of the Babylonian throne by Nabû-mukīn-zēri, a Chaldean, eventually compelled Tiglath-pileser III to take the Babylonian throne himself (Brinkman, 'Babylonia under the Assyrian Empire', 1979, p. 229).

[7] The term "older Babylonian" is used by Brinkman in *Prelude to Empire*, 1984, p. 11 and by Cole in *Nippur in Late Assyrian Times*, 1996, pp. 43–44, while Frame designates the same population as "Akkadian" in *Babylonia 689-627 B.C.*, 1992, pp. 35–36.

[8] A summary of the history of this period can be found in the appendix below.

[9] For the history of Babylonia after the demise of the Second Dynasty of Isin and prior to the accession of Nabonassar see Brinkman, *A Political History*, 1968, pp. 157–226 and 'Babylonia, c. 1000–748 B.C.', 1982, pp. 282–313. Coverage of Babylonian history up to the end of Assyrian rule can be found in Brinkman, *Prelude to Empire*, 1984 and Frame, *Babylonia 689-627 B.C.*, 1992.

[10] Machinist, 'The Assyrians and Their Babylonian Problem', 1984–85, pp. 353–364 and Frame, 'Babylon', 2008, pp. 21–31.

archive from Nippur indicates that cities and tribes had competing claims to land, water, and privileges, and that these conflicting interests resulted in tensions and, on occasion, open hostilities.[11] Even though the Assyrian emperor often attempted to cultivate the allegiance of the Babylonian cities, the Assyrian presence was not universally welcome in southern Mesopotamia. Anti-Assyrian sentiments existed among the urban population, but often efforts to drive the Assyrians out of southern Mesopotamia were led by Chaldeans who had managed to secure the Babylonian throne. In the ensuing struggles it became increasingly difficult for native Babylonians from the urban gentry to secure the Babylonian crown without the backing of one group or the other and the throne was frequently occupied by either Chaldean or Assyrian claimants.

Both Assyrians and Chaldeans tried to win over the urban gentry by turning them against the other. The Chaldean monarchs who held the Babylonian throne had success in enlisting significant portions of the urban population in their efforts to resist Assyrian expansion,[12] and the Assyrians cultivated the loyalty of pro-Assyrian elements, particularly in those cities that felt threatened by the power of the Chaldeans, through preferential treatment and by appealing to a shared cultural heritage.[13] But

---

[11] Cole details the alliances and strained relations that the *šandabakku* of Nippur had with neighboring tribes in the mid-eighth century in *Nippur in Late Assyrian Times*, 1996, pp. 31–32. These years also witnessed fighting between tribes and cities in the vicinity of Babylon and Borsippa; Erība-Marduk had to expel Arameans from fields and orchards near Babylon and Borsippa (Grayson, *Assyrian and Babylonian Chronicles*, 1975, pp. 182–183 l. 9-13). Strife continued to swirl around Borsippa under Erība-Marduk's successor, Nabû-šuma-iškun. Nabû-šuma-imbi, the governor of Borsippa, claims to have fought with the people of Babylon and Dilbat as well as Arameans and Chaldeans over fields belonging to the Borsippians (Frame, *Rulers of Babylonia*, 1995, B.6.14.2001 i 15'b-21'). These tensions carried over into the reign of Nabonassar, who had to suppress a revolt at Borsippa (Brinkman, *Prelude to Empire*, 1984, p. 40). Assyrian rule did not eliminate these divisions. Brinkman (*Prelude to Empire*, 1984, p. 76 and n. 373) has suggested that Nippur and Bīt-Dakkuri did not embrace Esarhaddon's rebuilding of Babylon due to fears that the city would divert agricultural resources, a fear that was later realized in the *šandabakku*'s complaint that Babylon had cut Nippur off from access to water (Reynolds, *The Babylonian Correspondence of Esarhaddon*, 2003, No. 70 r. 5–10).

[12] Merodach-baladan was particularly adept at assembling an anti-Assyrian coalition. Part of his success may have been due to his claim of descent from the Chaldean, Erība-Marduk, whose earlier rule of Babylonia was viewed favorably (Brinkman, *Prelude to Empire*, 1984, p. 47).

[13] Assyrian emperors regularly paid homage to Babylonian gods, a practice they did not adopt with other subject peoples, in part to ingratiate themselves to the Babylonians (Brinkman, 'Babylonia under the Assyrian Empire', 1979, p. 229). The cities of northern Babylonia were less likely to favor Assyrian rule, though Esarhaddon's plan to return Marduk received support from the elite in Babylon (Nielsen, 'Marduk's Return', 2012, pp. 9-10). On the other hand, Nippur after c. 651 and the southern cities of Ur, Uruk, and Kissik, which often had tense relations with their Chaldean neighbors, tended to favor

in spite of the divisions between cities that periodically manifested themselves, common cause between segments of the urban gentry and the Assyrians or Chaldeans never resulted in the emergence of a common identity. Rather, it is apparent that the economic, cultural, and social networks that linked the various cities helped to foster an awareness among the urban population that they shared a distinct socio-cultural identity even though their respective ethnic identities had long since disappeared.[14]

One way in which this socio-cultural identity found expression was through the use of family names. By the mid-seventh century, family names had become an essential part of the urban gentry's identity in Babylon, Borsippa, Dilbat, and Sippar in the north, and can be seen to have been emerging in southern Babylonia, in Uruk and, to a lesser extent, in Ur.[15] The practice appears to have been rejected at Nippur for reasons that are not entirely evident, though political circumstances created by inter-city tensions and the Assyrian-Chaldean rivalry may have been a contributing factor.[16] Family-name usage had the dual effect of communicating social class and civic identity and was utilized much more frequently than civic gentilics (e.g., Nippurian or Borsippian) in texts. Family names were typically derived from either ancestral names, a few of which belonged to recognizable legendary or semi-legendary figures from Babylonia's past, or occupational titles, some of which were also synonymous with temple offices and prebendaries.[17] The specific and local values that many family names embodied coalesced around the city and temple, cultural symbols that were common to all the traditional cult centers of southern Mesopotamia. The urban gentry may not have used a common designator to define themselves as Babylonians, but the

Assyrian rule (Brinkman, 'Babylonia under the Assyrian Empire', p. 236), a position that would become pronounced during the Šamaš-šuma-ukīn revolt (Frame, *Babylonia 689-627 B.C.*, 1992, pp. 149-150 and 157–167).

[14] Frame, *Babylonia 689-627 B.C.*, 1992, pp. 33–34.

[15] Nielsen, *Sons and Descendants*, 2011, pp. 123–125, 154–155 and 217–220.

[16] Nielsen, *Sons and Descendants*, 2011, pp. 177–180.

[17] The antecedents of this practice may have their roots in the Kassite period (Brinkman, 'The Use of Occupation Names as Patronyms in the Kassite Period', 2006, pp. 23–43). Quite a few Neo-Babylonian family names were derived from the various offices of the *šangû* priest (e.g., Šangû-Dilbat, Šangû-Ištar-Bābili, or Šangû-Šamaš), and even though the family names communicated affiliation with a specific city or local deity, the names were not exclusive to those locales. Similarly, holders of occupational family names were not always affiliated with that profession. However, there are some examples of individuals with occupational names being engaged in prebendary activities associated with the occupation; members of the Ṣāḫit-ginê family, for example, held oil-presser (*ṣāḫitu*) prebends at Sippar (Bongenaar, *The Neo-Babylonian Ebabbar Temple at Sippar*, 1997, p. 269).

hundreds of family names that they did use can be interpreted as serving a similar purpose; those who bore family names distinguished themselves from the other, newer groups and asserted their claims to be the heirs to the much older cultural and institutional legacies upon which their own social positions were predicated. Members of these families could amass a great deal of local influence, but few individuals from this class rose to the throne; those who did could only hold power briefly or did so with external backing.[18] Lacking significant political power, the urban gentry instead exploited their cultural identities as leading local figures in the cultic and administrative function of the temples in their interactions with the Assyrians, Chaldeans, and Arameans, a response that would have ramifications for their own identities during a period that was a prelude to imperial power shifting south to Babylon.

2. Assyrian Interventions

Assyrian relations with Babylonia changed significantly over the course of the first half of the first millennium. As Assyrian involvement in southern Mesopotamia evolved, so too did their understanding of the region, with implications for the native populations. The two kingdoms were on roughly equal footing at the dawn of the millennium and little can be said about their relations until the accession of Šamaš-mudammiq late in the tenth century. A contemporary of the Assyrian king Adad-nārārī II (911–891), his reign was marked by loss of territory to the Assyrians.[19] In the century that followed, the relationship between the two kingdoms saw several shifts. Nabû-šuma-ukīn and Adad-nārārī exchanged daughters in a diplomatic marriage that led to an alliance and peace.[20] During this period Babylonian power even eclipsed that of Assyria, but as the peace broke down, Assyria regained the upper hand, to Babylonia's detriment, and began to project its power southward.[21]

Assyrian attempts to incorporate southern Mesopotamia into its empire, first by eliminating the influence of the Chaldeans and insinuating themselves into the cultic lives of the various cities and then by direct rule, were certainly novel in that they represented the first time in Mesopotamian history that Babylonia was under foreign rule for a

---

[18] Marduk-zākir-šumi of the Arad-Ea kin group, Bēl-ibni of the Rab-banê kin group, and Nergal-ušēzib of the Gahal kin group (Nielsen, *Sons and Descendants*, 2011, pp. 28–31).
[19] Brinkman, *A Political History*, 1968, pp. 177–180.
[20] Brinkman, *A Political History*, 1968, p. 169.
[21] Brinkman, *A Political History*, 1968, pp. 204–213, and 'Babylonia c. 1000–748 B.C.', 1982, pp. 307–311.

protracted period of time.[22] Initially, Assyrian emperors conducted diplomatic relations with kings at Babylon before ultimately attempting to incorporate southern Mesopotamia into their empire. However, rather than absorb Babylonia into the Assyrian provincial system or administer it as a client state, as was the Assyrian practice throughout the rest of its empire, Assyrian emperors elected to take the Babylonian crown themselves, designate a member of the Assyrian royal family as king of Babylon, or raise a non-royal Babylonian to the throne.[23] Assyrian involvement had an impact on the political organization of the region and represents an invaluable etic perspective on the political organization of the region. By adopting Babylonian royal titulary,[24] participating in the

---

[22] The only other foreign ruler to have exerted control over Babylonia previously was Tukultī-Ninurta I who claimed Babylonian royal titulary and ruled Babylonia indirectly through appointed vassals and possibly directly as king of Babylon (Yamada, 'Tukulti-Ninurta I's Rule over Babylonia and its Aftermath', 2003, pp. 153–177). His rule over Babylonia does not appear to have been particularly stable; Llop-Raduà suggests that Tukultī-Ninurta's conquest of Babylonia was a product of continuous military pressure and not the result of an outright victory against Babylonia as Tukultī-Ninurta's inscriptions would have us believe (Llop-Raduà, 'The Boundary between Assyria and Babylonia', 2011, p. 215).

[23] Brinkman, 'Babylonia under the Assyrian Empire', 1979, p. 232.

[24] Tiglath-pileser III claimed the title "king of Babylon, king of Sumer and Akkad" in his inscriptions (Tadmor & Yamada, *The Royal Inscriptions of Tiglath-pileser III and Shalmaneser V*, 2011, No. 40:2 and passim). Sargon II used the title "viceroy of Babylon, king of Sumer and Akkad" in his Babylonian inscriptions (Frame, Rulers of Babylonia, 1995, passim in B.6.22); and Sennacherib eschewed such titles. Esarhaddon called himself both "king" (Frame, Rulers of Babylonia, 1995, B.6.31.2–8 and 13–14) and "viceroy" (9-12 and 15–21) of Babylon in his Babylonian inscriptions in addition to calling himself "king of Sumer and Akkad" (9-18 and 21). Esarhaddon never used the title "king of Babylon" in his Assyrian inscriptions, preferring "viceroy of Babylon" in addition to the titles "king of Sumer and Akkad" and "king of Karduniaš" (passim in Leichty, *The Royal Inscriptions of Esarhaddon*, 2011). Ashurbanipal assiduously avoided using Babylonian royal titulary in his royal inscriptions, while his brother, Šamaš-šuma-ukīn did use such titles (Frame, Rulers of Babylonia, 1995, B.6.33). Babylonian scribes who dated tablets with the regnal years of Assyrian emperors who claimed the Babylonian throne tended to use the titles "king of Assur", "king of the lands", or "king of the world" and typically did not attach the title "king of Babylon" to the monarch's name. Tiglath-pileser III and Shalmaneser V were never given the title; Sargon II was given the title "king of Babylon, king of Sumer and Akkad" (LUGAL KÁ.[DINGIR].[RA^{ki}] [LUGAL] KUR KI.IN.GI *u* URI.KI) in IM 57900:44–45, one of the four tablets dated to his reign; Sennacherib was not given the title in the three tablets dated to his rule; Esarhaddon was called king of Babylon (LUGAL.E in San Nicolò, *Babylonische Rechtsurkunden*, 1951, No. 4 r. 11' and Waerzeggers, 'Neo-Babylonian Tablets in the Royal Museums of Art and History in Brussels', 2005, No. 18:23'; and LUGAL TIN.TIR^{ki} in Jakob-Rost, 'Urkunden des 7. Jahrhunderts v. u. Z. aus Babylon', 1970, No. 3:7) in only three of the twenty-nine tablets dated to his reign; and Ashurbanipal was never given the title. The Assyrian princes who occupied the Babylonia throne, Aššur-nādin-šumi and Šamaš-šuma-ukīn, were regularly given the title "king of Babylon".

akītu festival at Babylon,[25] and by allowing tablets to be dated by Babylonian regnal years in southern Mesopotamia rather than by Assyrian eponyms,[26] Assyrian emperors elected to acknowledge the traditional primacy of Babylon in southern Mesopotamia. Simultaneously, the Assyrians recognized and exploited to their advantage the reality that political power in the region was fragmented among several groups, each with their own internal organizations.[27] The administrative hierarchy of Babylonia was not integrated into Assyria's imperial organization so that Babylon mediated communications between the Assyrian emperor and the other cities of southern Mesopotamia. Rather the emperor circumvented Babylon and interacted directly with the various cities, all of which had long-standing traditions of self-governance through local assemblies,[28] appointing or removing officials from the leading families when necessary and possible.[29] Babylonia, for the emperor, was a network of administrative nodes in which Babylon had ideological significance.[30]

The Assyrian emperor may have encouraged a decentralized network in his governance of Babylonia, but it is clear that from the beginnings of Assyrian expansion in southern Mesopotamia, the Assyrians conceived of Babylonia as a distinct geographic entity. The Neo-Assyrian rulers who were responsible for the first phase of imperial expansion in the ninth century were all cognizant of a Babylonian territory in the accounts of their campaigns, first calling the region Karduniaš and eventually Akkad. From the initial Assyrian perspective, Babylonia possessed a king and

---

[25] Tiglath-pileser III (Brinkman, *Prelude to Empire*, 1984, p. 43) and Sargon II (p. 53) both participated in the festival, while Sennacherib probably never did (p. 55). Esarhaddon intended to return Marduk personally to Babylon (Frame, *Babylonia 689-627 B.C.*, 1992, pp. 76–78), but the task fell to his son, Šamaš-šuma-ukīn (pp. 103–105).

[26] Two tablets dated at Babylon with non-canonical eponyms indicate that there were failed attempts to introduce the Assyrian *limmu* into Babylonia during the reigns of Esarhaddon and Šamaš-šuma-ukīn (Frame, 'Another Babylonian Eponym', 1982, p. 166 and *The Archive of Mušēzib-Marduk*, 2013, pp. 180–187).

[27] Brinkman, 'Babylonia under the Assyrian Empire', 1979, p. 233.

[28] Barjamovic, 'Civic Institutions and Self-Government', 2004, pp. 47–98.

[29] In Dietrich, *The Babylonian Correspondence of Sargon and Sennacherib*, 2003, No. 39, Qišti-Marduk reminds Sargon that only Sargon is capable of installing a *šatammu* just as only Sargon can appoint a governor.

[30] In this regard, Assyrian rule over Babylonia might be seen to resemble the paradigm of the "network-empire" proposed by Liverani as a model for Assyria's expansion into the Habur region (Liverani, 'The Growth of the Assyrian Empire in the Habur / Middle Euphrates Area', 1988, pp. 81–98). Assuming the title king of Babylon or installing Assyrian princes on the throne helped to thicken the mesh of the network, but it was necessary to create a matrix of communication with local leaders of different cities to keep the region under Assyrian rule and to manage the more intractable tribal regions.

stretches of definable border: Adad-nārārī II and Ashurnasirpal II both captured border fortresses in Babylonian territory and returned them to Assyria;[31] and after suppressing a revolt in Suḫu in 878 and defeating Nabû-apla-iddina, whom he called king of Karduniaš, Ashurnasirpal II claimed that the fear of his dominion reached as far as Karduniaš.[32] The territorial organization of the regions beyond that border, however, was less clear to the Assyrians. Ashurnasirpal's inscriptions demonstrate a vague awareness of a Chaldea – his inscriptions include the first mention of their presence in southern Mesopotamia – beyond the border with Babylonia to which the awe of his weapons extended.[33] It is only after Shalmaneser III campaigned in 851 and 850 in support of Marduk-zākir-šumi and followed up those campaigns with an invasion of Chaldea that the Assyrian understanding of southern Mesopotamian geography began to distinguish between a Babylonia defined by the network of the traditional cultic cities of Babylon, Borsippa, and Cutha in the north, where Shalmaneser made offerings to the patron gods, and a Chaldea to the south, where multiple kings ruled over a non-Babylonian population.[34] The introduction in Shalmaneser's royal inscriptions of "Land of Akkad" and "Sealand" as toponyms for Babylonia and Chaldea respectively also suggests that the Assyrians had gained a more developed understanding of the political geography of southern Mesopotamia,[35] in all likelihood adopting terminology in use locally as their involvement in the region increased.

The revival of Neo-Assyrian fortunes from the mid-eighth century until the last quarter of the seventh century was marked by an intensification of Assyrian involvement in southern Mesopotamia that elicited a range of responses from the native populations. Assyrian emperors continued to differentiate between the traditional cult centers and the regions dominated by Chaldeans and Arameans in royal inscriptions, but their understanding of these groups became more sophisticated. Tiglath-pileser III, who campaigned against Chaldeans and Arameans in Babylonia and removed the Chaldean Nabû-mukīn-zēri from the Babylonian throne, was the last emperor to refer to the region as Karduniaš and the first to take the titles "King of Babylon" and "King of Sumer and Akkad" and to be

[31] Grayson, *Assyrian Rulers of the Early First Millennium BC, I*, 1991, A.0.99.2: 29 and passim in the inscriptions of Ashurnasirpal II, A.0.101.1.

[32] Grayson, *Assyrian Rulers of the Early First Millennium BC, I*, 1991, A.0.101.1 iii 23.

[33] Grayson, *Assyrian Rulers of the Early First Millennium BC, I*, 1991, A.0.101.1 iii 24.

[34] Passim in the inscriptions of Shalmaneser III, Grayson, *Assyrian Rulers of the Early First Millennium BC, II*, 1996, A.0.102.

[35] Passim in Grayson, *Assyrian Rulers of the Early First Millennium BC, II*, 1996, A.0.102.

accepted as king of Babylon in the native tradition.[36] And while Tiglath-pileser's boast of having received the remnants of the sacrificial meals from Babylon, Borsippa, and Cutha indicates that the Assyrians continued to appreciate those cities and their temple personnel,[37] the telling passage in which he claimed to have made offerings at Sippar, Nippur, Babylon, Borsippa, Cutha, Kish, Dilbat, and Uruk before asserting that he ruled over Karduniaš[38] reveals that the Assyrians had come to conceive of Babylonia as an expanded network of cities that stretched from Sippar in the north to Uruk in the south, the control of which was achieved not through conquest but rather by participating in the religious rituals and cultivating the allegiance of the priesthood at each city.

Subsequent building inscriptions produced by both Assyrians and Chaldeans on the Babylonian throne make it apparent that the desire to cultivate local loyalties by renovating temples and city walls was paired with an appreciation of Sumer and Akkad as a network of cult centers and an emphasis on Babylon's primacy of place within that network. The Chaldean Merodach-baladan's building inscription from the Eanna in Uruk typifies this approach which he employed throughout Babylonia during his reign.[39] Even though Ištar, Uruk's patron goddess, and Eanna, the chief temple in Uruk, figured prominently in the text, Merodach-baladan emphasized the importance of Marduk, Marduk's temple the Esaggil, and Babylon to his reign and stressed his activities not just at Uruk but throughout Sumer and Akkad, claiming that he defeated the Assyrians, stabilized the land, and renovated the residences of the gods of Akkad. He also stressed the otherness of the Assyrians, whom he identified with the archaic name Subarians, stressing that Marduk had turned away from the land in anger during the seven years of Assyrian rule.[40]

A comparable outlook is present in Esarhaddon's efforts to rebuild Babylon after his father had destroyed the city. His building activities at Babylon were not only celebrated in that city, but also elsewhere in southern Mesopotamia. In building inscriptions from Nippur[41] and Uruk,[42] Esarhaddon combined dedications of local projects with similar

---

[36] Brinkman, *A Political History*, 1968, pp. 240–241.
[37] Tadmor & Yamada, *The Royal Inscriptions of Tiglath-pileser III and Shalmaneser V*, 2011, No. 24:5–7.
[38] Tadmor & Yamada, *The Royal Inscriptions of Tiglath-pileser III and Shalmaneser V*, 2011, No. 47:11b-13a.
[39] Brinkman, 'Merodach-Baladan II', 1964, pp. 12–18.
[40] Frame, Rulers of Babylonia, 1995, B.6.21.1.
[41] Frame, Rulers of Babylonia, 1995, B.6.31.11–12.
[42] Frame, Rulers of Babylonia, 1995, B.6.31.15–18.

language that described how he rebuilt Babylon and how Marduk had become reconciled to Babylon and had resumed residence in Esaggil, clear indications that Esarhaddon deemed his endeavors in Babylon to be salient to the populations of those other cities as well. Ashurbanipal and Šamaš-šuma-ukīn continued to employ their father's tropes in their own building inscriptions from southern Mesopotamia with one exception, Ashurbanipal omitted descriptions of Babylon's rebuilding in his inscriptions from Nippur and eschewed the titles of king or viceroy of Babylon for Esarhaddon, having never used the title himself.[43] The Assyrians may have conceived of Babylonia as a geographic network, but this did not prevent them from attempting to manipulate that network to keep the region under control.

Though the Assyrians attempted to govern Babylonia through the Babylonian throne and local institutions, their involvement compelled the locals to adjust to the Assyrian perspective. The boasts of Assyrian emperors that they received the leftovers from the gods' meals are echoed in a letter to Sargon from Babylon informing him that Tiglath-pileser and Shalmaneser had come to Babylon to dispose of the gods' meals and encouraging him to do the same in order to establish a pact with Babylon and Borsippa.[44] Letters petitioning the emperor for the restoration of temple prebends and reminding the emperor that only he had the power to appoint temple and civic officials spoke to the very local concerns of those Babylonians who were most likely to use family names,[45] but those concerns existed within a broader framework of temples about which the locals were also cognizant. The report sent by the Babylonian Bēl-iddina to Sargon II may exemplify the effects that the added layer of imperial administration had on the temples in southern Mesopotamia. In the letter, Bēl-iddina stated that he had examined writing boards from temples spanning from the south to the north and would send his report on them to the emperor via the Assyrian official Šarru-ēmuranni, having already entrusted a previous report on temples to the *qīpu* (royal appointee) of the Esaggil, and would soon examine the temples in the vicinity of Babylon.[46]

Just as the temples all came under the imperial administrative umbrella, so too were they linked together ideologically in a network in which Babylon was central. One writer wrote to Esarhaddon to tell him that by setting foot in Babylon he would be setting foot in the center of the

---

[43] Frame, Rulers of Babylonia, 1995, B.6.32.15.
[44] Dietrich, *The Babylonian Correspondence of Sargon and Sennacherib*, 2003, No. 23.
[45] Dietrich, *The Babylonian Correspondence of Sargon and Sennacherib*, 2003, Nos. 34 and 39.
[46] Dietrich, *The Babylonian Correspondence of Sargon and Sennacherib*, 2003, No. 43.

lands.[47] Similarly a letter from Nemed-Laguda in the south informs Sargon that he would receive regular reports from the city once Sargon had entered Babylon and kissed the ground before Marduk and Zarpanitu.[48] The *akītu* festival that marked the New Year was the ultimate expression of this network. Ideally, the gods from cities both in the north and south of southern Mesopotamia were understood to convene at Babylon for the festival to reconfirm the place of Marduk at the head of the pantheon. The participation of Assyrian kings in the celebration and reports on Chaldean involvement at other times point to the ideological importance attached to the festival with regard to kingship, but it was significant also to the urban gentry. The visible participation of segments of the urban gentry aligned with the temples – men who would have made use of family names – in parades and processions was a public reification of their special identities in the eyes both of their peers and of the Chaldeans and Arameans known to be present at Babylon for the festivities.[49]

3. Contacts with Arameans and Chaldeans

The Assyrian presence in southern Mesopotamia was a product of empire. When necessary, Assyrian armies campaigned in Babylonia, but at no point were permanent Assyrian garrisons established in the region.[50] Likewise, there was not a significant corps of Assyrian administrators in southern Mesopotamia; imperial control relied primarily on manipulating local power structures. As a consequence, ethnic Assyrians never constituted a significant population in southern Mesopotamia. This absence did not prevent cultural contacts between Babylonians and Assyrians – representatives from Babylonian cities traveled to and from the imperial court and Babylonian scholars were in the employ of the emperor or corresponded with him[51] – but it did mean that the distinction

---

[47] Dietrich, *The Babylonian Correspondence of Sargon and Sennacherib*, 2003, No. 84.

[48] Dietrich, *The Babylonian Correspondence of Sargon and Sennacherib*, 2003, No. 146.

[49] The observance of the *akītu* festival involved a range of cultic personnel including the *šangû* priest, various other priests who had the right to enter the sanctuary of the god known as *ērib-bīti*s (temple enterers), and *kalû*s (lamentation priests) (Bidmead, *The* Akītu *Festival*, 2002, pp. 119-122). These priests and cultic functionaries participated in the procession of the god and king to the *akītu* house before onlookers from the general population (Bidmead, pp. 94–101). Ritual texts make no mention of the familial affiliations of these participants, but it is evident from legal and administrative texts that holders of these positions often had family names.

[50] Brinkman, 'Babylonia under the Assyrian Empire', 1979, p. 235.

[51] Barjamovic's discussion of civic assemblies quotes several letters that reference embassies sent to the emperor that were comprised of such dignitaries ('Civic Institutions and Self-Government', 2004, pp. 77–78). Furthermore, two tablets dated at Assur using

between Assyrian and Babylonian was quite clear. By contrast, the presence of Arameans and Chaldeans in southern Mesopotamia relegated the residents of southern Mesopotamia's traditional urban centers in the northwest alluvium and the south to being one constituent within a broader population. Whereas the Assyrians remained primarily an external group in southern Mesopotamia, contacts with Arameans and Chaldeans were more immediate and circumstances were potentially more conducive to a blurring of cultural identities.

The presence of significant rural populations that were not ethnically aligned with the cities was not a unique phenomenon; over the span of Mesopotamian history the urban populations had to interact with semi-sedentary and nomadic tribal groups present in the countryside. Under ideal conditions, a symbiotic relationship often existed between city and countryside, but at times of crisis this system could collapse as urban populations came under pressure from tribal groups or opted themselves to resort to pastoral lifestyles.[52] The Aramean and Chaldean presence in southern Mesopotamia was no different. Both groups were of West Semitic origins and both undermined political centralization and came to dominate significant portions of the rural hinterlands: the Chaldeans, whose apparently well-established presence in Babylonia was first attested in 878,[53] controlled parts of southern and western Babylonia;[54] and the Arameans, who entered southern Mesopotamia in the eleventh century and contributed to the political instability at the end second millennium,[55] tended to be concentrated further to the east along the Tigris River closer to the Elamite border.[56] These regions were conceptualized as territorial polities by both the Assyrians and Babylonians, but membership in these groups was determined not by residency but rather by descent, permitting both Chaldeans and Arameans

Babylonian regnal years attest to the presence of Babylonian communities in Assyria who conducted their private affairs with other Babylonians while there using native conventions (80-B-12, an unpublished sale of an orchard dated in 679 in which one of the witnesses was designated as being from Uruk and in which no participant had a personal name with a theophoric element naming the god Ashur, and San Nicolò, *Babylonische Rechtsurkunden*, 1951, No. 51). Most of the Babylonian scholars who sent letters to the imperial court are characterized by Parpola as having been part of the emperor's "outer circle" (Parpola, SAA 10, 1993, p. xxv), but one, Bēl-ušēzib, belonged to the emperor's "inner circle" and resided at Nineveh (Fabritus, 'Bēl-ušēzib', 1999, pp. 338–339).

[52] Cole, *Nippur in Late Assyrian Times*, 1996, pp. 13–16; Richardson, 'The World of Babylonian Countrysides', 2007, pp. 13–29; and Stone, 'Mesopotamian Cities and Countrysides', 2005, p. 143.

[53] Grayson, *Assyrian Rulers of the Early First Millennium BC, I*, 1991, A.101.1 iii 24.

[54] Frame, *Babylonia 689-627 B.C.*, 1992, pp. 36–43.

[55] Brinkman, *Prelude to Empire*, 1984, pp. 12–14.

[56] Frame, *Babylonia 689-627 B.C.*, 1992, pp. 43–48.

to retain their distinct identities even when members resided in one of the old cities of southern Mesopotamia.[57]

Just as Chaldeans and Arameans understood themselves to be the descendants of ancestors eponymous with the names of their respective tribes, so too the urban elite used the language of descent when designating their family names. The history of family name usage would suggest that this was not simply a matter of imitation on the part of the urban population, but rather an assertion of identity that allowed them to reclaim an idealized past that had been lost due to an historical rupture caused by the arrival of the Chaldeans and Arameans. The most conspicuous examples of this sentiment is represented by the family names derived from the ancestral names Sîn-leqe-unninnī and Arad-Ea, both of whom were believed to be scribes and scholars who served notable monarchs: Sîn-leqe-unninnī, a distinctly Urukian family name, was associated with the semi-legendary king of Uruk, Gilgamesh,[58] and members of the Arad-Ea kin group claimed, perhaps with some justification, descent from an eponymous scribe who served the dynamic Kassite king Kurigalzu.[59] Both kin groups were closely associated with temple or civic offices, the Sîn-leqe-unninnīs were often *kalû* priests at Uruk and several members of the Arad-Ea kin group held the office of *bēl pīḫati*.[60] There is also evidence that other family names were traced to ancestors who may have been less illustrious than Sîn-leqe-unninnī or Arad-Ea but were nevertheless believed to have been real figures, descent from whom brought with it claims to offices or privileges.[61]

The need to articulate claims of this kind through descent-based family names may be the result of historical memories stating that the arrival of the Chaldeans and Arameans in southern Mesopotamia had caused a break with the past and that traditional rights and privileges had been placed in jeopardy as a result. The contents of the "Sun-god Tablet" of Nabû-apla-iddina,[62] a stone tablet inscribed to commemorate the reinstallation of the cult-statue of Šamaš at Sippar, exemplify this mentality. The stone tablet records the testimony of a *šangû* priest of

---

[57] Barjamovic, 'Civic Institutions and Self-Government', 2004, p. 89 and Frame, *Babylonia 689-627 B.C.*, 1992, p. 45.

[58] Beaulieu, 'The Descendants of Sîn-lēqi-unninni', 2000, 1–16.

[59] Nielsen, *Sons and Descendants*, 2011, pp. 36–37.

[60] In the late second and early first millennia, the *bēl pīḫati* appears to have been a provincial official of uncertain function, and after the middle of the eighth century, the *bēl pīḫati* could act as a province governor (Brinkman, *A Political History*, p. 304).

[61] See for example the family names Aqar-Nabû and Abunaya in Nielsen, *Sons and Descendants*, 2011, pp. 74–78.

[62] King, *Babylonian Boundary-Stones*, 1912, No. 36.

Sippar from the second quarter of the ninth century regarding the destruction of the cult image of Šamaš by the Sutians and the subsequent attempts to maintain the cult during the tenure of his ancestor, who had also been a *šangû* priest of Sippar, in the late eleventh century. The title *šangû* of Sippar was not formally used as a family name on the tablet, but, as Bongenaar has argued, it was functionally identical to the family name Šangû-Sippar in the text.[63] "The Sun-god tablet" represents perhaps the most compelling example of an occupational or official family name functioning as a claim to traditional privileges in the face of historic rupture; ancestral association with an occupation or title that carried with it significant material benefits reached a point where the identity of the family became indistinguishable from the office or occupation its members fulfilled.

The threat posed by non-native populations to religious observances at the traditional cultic centers – and by extension those populations who participated in and benefited from their continuation – became a familiar trope in texts produced by the urban elite as well as by the Assyrians who were trying to win their allegiance. At the same time, efforts by Chaldeans and Arameans to participate in the religious institutions may also have represented a threat that shaped Babylonian identity. Arameans as a population appear to have been the more disruptive of the two groups, the example from the Babylonian Chronicle of Arameans preventing Nabû from coming out of Borsippa for the *akītu* festival for two successive years during the mid-eighth century being the most famous.[64]

In spite of the problems they could cause, Arameans and Chaldeans were not hostile to the practice of Babylonian religion. The Chaldean kings Erība-Marduk and Merodach-baladan II, as well as other Chaldeans, had Akkadian names with theophoric elements that communicated their adherence to Babylonian gods. Erība-Marduk and Merodach-baladan II also expressed this devotion by sponsoring renovations of Babylonian sanctuaries.[65] They also consecrated temple-enterers who continued to serve after the Assyrians took power according to a letter sent to Esarhaddon by a temple-enterer who had been consecrated by Sennacherib.[66] Other Chaldean monarchs were viewed

---

[63] The Sutians are often linked with the Arameans in the earliest Babylonian references to Arameans prompting the suggestion from Brinkman (*A Political History*, 1968, pp. 285–287) that the two groups were identical.

[64] Grayson, *Assyrian and Babylonian Chronicles*, 1975, pp. 137–138 iii 4'-15'.

[65] Erība-Marduk restored the Eḫiliana at Uruk according to an inscription of Esarhaddon (Frame, Rulers of Babylonia, 1995, B.6.31.18:11–13) and Merodach-baladan renovated portions of the Eanna according to his own inscriptions (B.6.21.1–3).

[66] Reynolds, *The Babylonian Correspondence of Esarhaddon*, 2003, No. 82.

more negatively. The governor of Borsippa only acknowledged that Nabû-šuma-iškun was "king" in his own building inscription, while including that he was also a Chaldean from the Bīt-Dakkuri tribe, and claimed that open hostilities broke out between the people of Borsippa and the people of Babylon and Dilbat and the Chaldeans and Arameans who were occupying their land.[67] A later literary-historical composition is even more damning, claiming that Nabû-šuma-iškun committed blasphemies against the gods, violated taboos of the temple-enterers at Borsippa, and deported the people to the Chaldeans and the Arameans.[68] Not surprisingly, Assyrian sources also leveled accusations of blasphemy against Chaldeans: Sargon sought to discredit Merodach-baladan II's accomplishments in his own inscriptions,[69] and Sennacherib vilified Mušēzib-Marduk for robbing for the treasury of Esaggil.[70] These claims resonated with the Babylonians. A Babylonian writing to Esarhaddon reported on a rebellious father and son in the country whom he identified as "fathers of the Chaldeans", claiming that the father of the elder had been with the Chaldean king Nabû-mukīn-zēri when he removed twelve talents of silver from the temple at Borsippa.[71]

The otherness of the Chaldeans and the Arameans is most pronounced in texts where they threatened the observation of religious festivals or occupied agricultural land in the vicinity of the cities, but their ability to coexist peacefully with the urban gentry may have elicited the most pronounced cultural reactions. One example may be BM 40548, a tablet from the early eighth century in which a significant amount of land was purchased from a group of men, some of whom were from Aramean tribes or had Aramaic names, who were collectively identified as "The Sons of the Farmer".[72] This sale occurred at approximately the same time that the governor of Borsippa was fighting with Chaldeans and Arameans over fields near Borsippa. Both examples represent efforts to re-appropriate tribally held land, an effort that may have prefigured the organization of agricultural land into a special category called *hanšû* a few decades later. *Hanšû* land is still imperfectly understood, but the system appears to have supported the prebendary families affiliated with the temple, and became closely associated with those families, particularly at Borsippa.[73]

---

[67] Frame, Rulers of Babylonia, 1995, B.6.14.2001 I 15'-21'.
[68] Frame, Rulers of Babylonia, 1995, B.6.14.1.
[69] Frame, Rulers of Babylonia, 1995, B.6.22.3.
[70] Luckenbill, *The Annals of Sennacherib*, 1926–27, No. 42:17–37.
[71] Reynolds, *The Babylonian Correspondence of Esarhaddon*, 2003, No. 102.
[72] Brinkman, 'A Legal Text from the Reign of Erība-Marduk (c. 775 BC)', 1989, pp. 37–47.
[73] Van Driel, *Elusive Silver*, 2002, pp. 297–300.

The ability of Arameans and Chaldeans to coexist and interact with their Babylonian neighbors likely compelled the urban elite to exclude non-Babylonians from their circles lest these new populations displace them from their privileged positions within the temples. The author of one letter to the emperor reported with great annoyance that Bēl-iqīša, a member of the Aramean Gambulu tribe, had succeeded in marrying his daughters to different Babylonian temple officials, thereby gaining possession of temple property.[74] While individuals with family names typically had Babylonian personal names, there is at least one example of such a person with an Aramaic name, Zabidā of the prominent Sîn-leqe-unninnī family.[75] This man, who was affiliated with the Eanna at Uruk, had a father, brother, sons, and a nephew, all of whom had Babylonian personal names, but his name and Uruk's status as a southern outpost of Babylonian culture in the midst of the Chaldean-controlled Sealand raise the possibility that his lineage contained Chaldean or Aramean elements.

The tendency toward exclusivity is also evident in the legal and administrative documents, nearly all of which were composed at one of the major urban centers and reflect the institutional concerns or the private dealings of the propertied class. One result of the very parochial nature of the tablets was that the participants and witnesses in most of the transactions were often from the urban gentry that tended to use family names. But even in these texts the presence of non-Babylonian populations beyond the confines of the urban centers is apparent. Individuals with West Semitic names indicating Aramean or Chaldean identity occur in promissory notes that formalized *ḫarrānu* ventures (investments in caravans for long-distance trade) and herding contracts; presumably the urban population needed to go outside their immediate social networks when pursuing economic interests outside of the city.[76] Similarly there are examples of West Semitic names in the few tablets dated at rural settlements and even geographic terms for locales that have West Semitic derivations.[77] The unavoidable impression that results is

---

[74] Reynolds, *The Babylonian Correspondence of Esarhaddon*, 2003, No. 156.

[75] Nielsen, *Sons and Descendants*, 2011, pp. 208–210.

[76] The archive of Šumā of the Nappāḫu kin group consists primarily of promissory notes that probably supported his interests in long-distance trade based on the terminology they contain (Jursa, *Neo-Babylonian Legal and Administrative Documents*, 2005, p. 72). Several personal names belonging to Aramean, Chaldean, or even Arab individuals appear in the archive. Herding contracts from the Ebabbar at Sippar demonstrate that the shepherds were drawn from the tribal populations, a good example being BM 82563 published in Da Riva, 'Sippar in the Reign of Sîn-šum-līšir (626 BC)', 2001, pp. 48–49.

[77] For example, a tablet dated at Bīt-Uqata (Jakob-Rost, 'Urkunden des 7. Jahrhunderts v. u. Z. aus Babylon', 1970, pp. 54–55 No. 5), a town that may have been in the vicinity of Babylon (Zadok, *Geographical Names*, 1985, p. 109) included a witness with the West

that the cities were enclaves of traditional cultural identity surrounded by a multi-ethnic landscape. These circumstances may have caused the urban gentry to perceive a threat to their unique identity compelling them to favor family names in order to preserve and communicate their status. The Aramean Bēl-iqīša may have been able to marry his daughters into priestly families, but the practice of cultural differentiation pursued by the urban gentry was part of a trend toward greater social exclusivity. This tendency is highlighted by endogamous marriage practices evident from the sixth century onward that were intended to guarantee that priests had the proper ancestral backgrounds.[78]

4. Was there a Babylonian National Identity?

Developments among the urban gentry in response to both external and domestic pressures contributed to the formation of Babylonian nationalism during the first half of the first millennium that would manifest itself in the Nabopolassar's successful overthrow of Assyrian rule.[79] The question of nation/nationalism is a thorny subject and one that scholars of antiquity have understandably questioned or avoided. A compelling definition of nation is provided by Benedict Anderson, who characterizes it as an imagined community whose members "will never know most of their fellow-members, meet them or even hear of them" but who are yet capable of identifying with the nation as an abstract entity limited, both in terms of membership and geographic expanse, and sovereign as a political entity or having a claim to sovereignty.[80] For Anderson, however, nationalism is only possible within the modern nation state with its technological innovations, expanding middle class, and trend toward secularism and popular sovereignty, but his concept of the imagined community is much more fluid and is not limited by the same temporal restrictions. Anthony Smith, Steven Grosby, and Aviel Roshwald, advocates of a primordialist or perennialist understanding of nationalism,[81] provide grounds for applying Anderson's "imagined community" to antiquity. All three are of the opinion that the modern character of nation states should not preclude the possibility that there

---

Semitic patronym Tagābbi-ili (Zadok, *On West Semites in Babylonia*, 1977, p. 119). Zadok also suggested that name of the town was also derived from an Arabian name Uqāta (p. 163).

[78] Waerzeggers, 'On the Initiation of Babylonian Priests', 2008, pp. 1–38.

[79] Frame, *Babylonia 689-627 B.C.*, pp. 257–261. Frame uses the phrase "nationalist sentiment", perhaps not wanting to commit fully to the term nationalism.

[80] Anderson, *Imagined Communities*, 2006 (rev. ed.), pp. 5–7.

[81] Grosby, *Biblical Ideas of Nationality,* 2002, Smith, *The Antiquity of Nations*, 2004 and Roshwald, *The Endurance of Nationalism*, 2006.

were historical expressions of nationalism in pre-modernity, preferring to understand the emergence of nations as linked "to more general processes of human activity and politics which can already be discerned in the earliest civilizations."[82] As a consequence it is possible to consider the existence in the early first millennium of a geographic entity that was recognized as Babylonia, a group that imagined their identity within the context of that entity, and one that claimed sovereignty on the basis of that identity.

Nationalism is evoked here guardedly despite the frequency with which the term Babylonia has been used by modern scholars to describe a southern Mesopotamian state that stretched southeastward from the region around Sippar and Dur-Kurigalzu in the north toward Uruk and Ur and as far east as Der. While it is true that native terms never existed for a Babylonian nation or nationality,[83] the absence of such terms should not imply that there was not a native conception of Babylonia as a geographic entity. For over a millennium, the notion that one city could exercise at least hegemonic power over southern Mesopotamia had currency,[84] and for much of that time, the city that exerted that power was Babylon. Even when political power was at its most decentralized in southern Mesopotamia, scribes in cities throughout the region retained the practice of dating tablets by the regnal year of the king of Babylon and references to the land of Sumer and Akkad, though anachronistic, remained current in royal inscriptions. Furthermore, it is clear that from the Assyrian vantage point there was a Babylonia, and that Assyrian involvement in southern Mesopotamia both shaped their own conceptions of Babylonia and likely shaped those of the native populations to their south.

It is an open question how strong Babylonian identity would have been had Assyria not attempted to incorporate southern Mesopotamia into its empire. Conceptualizations of Babylonia as a geographic entity and the capacity to imagine an identity based on that entity appear to have been greatly diminished in the mid-eighth-century building inscription of Nabû-šuma-imbi, governor of Borsippa, describing his city's conflicts

---

[82] Smith, *The Antiquity of Nations*, 2004, p. 4.

[83] Von Dassow raised these points when questioning the existence of a Babylonian state in her review of Frame in 'On Writing the History of Southern Mesopotamia', 1999, pp. 241–245.

[84] This mentality found expression in the Sumerian King List (Jacobsen, *The Sumerian King List*), a programmatic composition the earliest known examplar of which dates from the Ur III period in the early second millennium (Steinkeller, 'An Ur III Manuscript of the Sumerian King List', 2003, pp. 267–292). Michalowski, 'History as Charter', 1983, pp. 237–248, has argued that the author of the list intended to legitimate one city's rule over all of southern Mesopotamia by recounting how dominion had first come down from heaven to the city of Eridu and then passed to other cities at the will of the gods.

with Babylon, Dilbat, and Chaldeans and Arameans.[85] And they do not appear much stronger during the subsequent reign of Nabonassar when two brothers in Uruk rebuilt the *akītu* temple there – an act which was traditionally the royal prerogative – though the cylinders commemorating the event were dated to Nabonassar's fifth regnal year.[86] Babylonian identity may have been galvanized after Tiglath-pileser III claimed the Babylonian throne in 729, at times in resistance to Assyrian rule but also in conformance with Assyria's imperial apparatus which engaged with Babylonia as a geographic entity consisting of a network of cities. This is not to say that for the urban gentry Babylonian identity superseded civic identity, rather that their civic identity, which found expression in their family names, became contextualized within the network of traditional cult cities. This network had strong ideological underpinnings that may have been strengthened by economic developments that were underway in the seventh century. Efforts by both Chaldean and Assyrian monarchs to stabilize Babylonia and revitalize its agricultural base set Babylonia on a trajectory of economic expansion and integration that peaked in the sixth century.[87]

Finally, it must be asked if this identity was the basis for claims to sovereignty. Each city had a tradition of popular assemblies that oversaw local affairs and, due to the distant power of the Emperor, these cities enjoyed a degree of semi-autonomy with the urban gentry exercising their influence within the assemblies. Assyrian and Chaldean representatives could address these assemblies, but it does not appear that non-citizens could participate in deliberations. While civic governance was handled by the assembly, the status of the city was conferred by the monarch. Of great importance to the urban gentry at all the old cities was the continuation of their freedoms and privileges and the protected status of their citizens.[88] "The Advice to a Prince",[89] in which the obligations of the king to the citizens – in this case of Babylon, Sippar, and Nippur – are described, epitomizes the significance of this special status and we have several examples of letters from different cities to the emperor reminding him of their special status or asking him to restore it. One letter from Nippur even quotes "The Advice to a Prince" when addressing the emperor and, significantly, adds that Nippur is privileged in the same way that Babylon

[85] Frame, Rulers of Babylonia, 1995, B.6.14.2001.
[86] Frame, Rulers of Babylonia, 1995, B.6.15.2001.
[87] Jursa, *Aspects of the Economic History of Babylonia*, 2010, pp. 62–152 and 768.
[88] Brinkman, 'Babylonia under the Assyrian Empire', 1979, pp. 228 and 233.
[89] Cole, *The Early Neo-Babylonian Governor's Archive from Nippur*, 1996, No. 128 and Reiner, 'The Babylonian Fürstenspiegel in Practice', 1982, pp. 324–326.

is.[90] This awareness of the privileges of other cities and desire for parity among them is not unusual and sums up the identity that emerged among the urban gentry due in part to their interaction with Arameans, Chaldeans, and Assyrians: the urban population that used family names did so to distinguish themselves from tribal groups they deemed to be "others" and to project their claims to rights and privileges within the local institutions that defined their cities.

The nationalist sentiments that linked the urban gentry persisted as this class continued to flourish and continued to utilize family names to project their social identity. Following Nabopolassar's revolt, imperial power shifted from Assur to Babylon, but the more immediate presence of a Babylonian emperor did nothing to curtail the importance of the urban gentry. Rather this class thrived as land owners and power brokers within the temples, all the while perpetuating Babylonian scholarship and culture. Even when Babylon fell to Cyrus in 539 and imperial power was removed eastward to Susa, the urban gentry found ways to prosper, possessing the pragmatism to take advantage of changes in the political situation. But the embers of Babylonian nationalism did not die out. In 484 the urban gentry in the northern cities supported a revolt against Xerxes. When Xerxes suppressed the rebellion later in that same year, the urban gentry bore the brunt of his reprisals. Xerxes removed members of the elite from temple and civic offices wholesale and replaced them with new men elevated from a different social class.[91]

Appendix: A Brief Historical Sketch of the Early First Millennium B.C.

The history of southern Mesopotamia in the first millennium BC prior to the emergence of the Neo-Babylonian Empire following the accession of Nabopolassar in 625 is treated most extensively in J. A. Brinkman's two monographs *A Political History of Post-Kassite Babylonia, 1158–722 B.C.* and *Prelude to Empire*, G. Frame's *Babylonia 689–627 B.C.*, and A. K. Grayson's contributions to *The Cambridge Ancient History*. What follows here is a short chronological sketch detailing the major figures and events discussed above for the benefit of those readers who are unfamiliar with this history.

Assyria's rise to pre-eminence defined the history of the Near East during this period and the growth of its empire can be separated into two phases: an initial imperial expansion that was inaugurated by Aššur-dān

[90] Reynolds, *The Babylonian Correspondence of Esarhaddon*, 2003, No. 124.

[91] Waerzeggers, 'The Babylonian Revolts against Xerxes', 2003/2004, pp. 150–173 and Kessler, 'Urukäische Familien versus babylonische Familien', 2004, pp. 237–262.

II (934–912) and perpetuated by Adad-nārārī II (911–891), Tukultī-Ninurta II (890–884), Ashurnasirpal II (883–859), and Shalmaneser III (858–824) but which began to decline under Šamšī-Adad V (823–811) and Adad-nārārī III (810–783) and a later reassertion of empire that began during the reigns of Tiglath-pileser III (744–727) and his son, Shalmaneser V (726–722). Sargon II (721–705) usurped Shalmaneser V and under the Sargonid line of emperors – Sennacherib (704–681), Esarhaddon (680–669), and Ashurbanipal (668–c. 627) – the Assyrian Empire reached its zenith.

The trajectory of Babylonian fortunes during this time was one of decline. Prior to and throughout the first phase of Assyrian growth (934–824), native kings occupied the Babylonian throne, but their grasp on power appears to have been tenuous at times. Nabû-mukīn-apli's long reign (978–943) was marred by the actions of hostile Arameans, but he was succeeded on the throne by his two sons, Ninurta-kudurrī-uṣur II (943) and then Mār-bīti-aḫḫē-iddina (942–?). Šamaš-mudammiq[92] and Nabû-šuma-ukīn I[93] both had to contend with Assyrian aggressions. Nabû-šuma-ukīn I and Adad-nārārī II eventually exchanged daughters in marriage, issuing in a period of relatively peaceful relations between Babylonia and Assyria, and Nabû-šuma-ukīn's dynasty was able to hold the Babylonian throne for most of the ninth century. When the accession of Nabû-šuma-ukīn's grandson, Marduk-zākir-šumi I, in or before 851 was threatened by a rebellion, Shalmaneser III intervened on the new king's behalf. Marduk-zākir-šumi would later return the favor when Shalmaneser's son, Šamšī-Adad V, faced an insurrection at the outset of his own reign. However, the humiliating treaty Marduk-zākir-šumi imposed on Šamšī-Adad effectively ended the peace between Babylonia and Assyria; Šamšī-Adad would campaign against Babylonia, taking Marduk-zākir-šumi's son, Marduk-balāssu-iqbi, captive in about 813 and returning in 812 to depose his successor Babu-aḫa-iddina.

Šamšī-Adad V's Babylonian campaigns created a power vacuum over the next century that several Chaldean rulers from the Bīt-Dakkuri, Bīt-Amukāni, and Bīt-Yakīn tribes exploited by seizing the Babylonian throne, thus creating a new challenge for the Sargonid line in their dealings with Babylonia. Chief among these Chaldean kings were Erība-Marduk (reign ended c. 760) and Merodach-baladan II (721–710 and 703), whose initial reign may be regarded as a turning point in the relationships between Assyria, Babylonia, and the Chaldean tribes.

[92] Šamaš-mudammiq's reign was contemporary with those of Aššur-dān II (934–912) and Adad-nārārī II (911–891).

[93] Nabû-šuma-ukīn I's reign was contemporary with that of Adad-nārārī II (911–891).

Whereas previous Assyrian emperors had sought to stabilize southern Mesopotamia by campaigning against the Chaldean tribes in the south on behalf of often weaker Babylonian monarchs, Merodach-baladan succeeded in uniting many of Babylonia's urban centers with Chaldean tribes in opposition to Assyria, a dynamic that would persist during subsequent Babylonian rebellions to the detriment of Assyria. The revolt that marked the beginning of the end of the Assyrian Empire was initiated by Šamaš-šuma-ukīn (667–648), the son of Esarhaddon and brother of Ashurbanipal whom Esarhaddon had designated as the heir to the Babylonian throne. The chief supporters of Šamaš-šuma-ukīn's uprising, which lasted from 652 to 648, were the urban centers in Babylonia's north and the Chaldean tribes. While Ashurbanipal succeeded in suppressing the rebellion, he was compelled to follow up his victory with campaigns against Elam and the Arabs, both of whom had given aid to Šamaš-šuma-ukīn. The cumulative effect of the rebellion and follow-up campaigns proved detrimental to Assyria; little is known about Ashurbanipal's final years and the Assyrian Empire did not long survive his death in or around 627. With the accession of Nabopolassar to the Babylonian throne in 626, Babylonia would soon find itself in the ascendancy.

Bibliography

Anderson, B. *Imagined Communities. Reflections on the Origin and Spread of Nationalism*. Revised edition. London, 2006.

Barjamovic, G. 'Civic Institutions and Self-Government in Southern Mesopotamia in the Mid-First Millennium BC.' J. G. Dercksen (ed.), *Assyria and Beyond. Studies Presented to Mogens Trolle Larsen.* (PIHANS 100.) Leiden, 2004, pp. 47–98.

Beaulieu, P.-A. 'The Descendants of Sîn-lēqi-unninni.' Marzahn, J., H. Neumann and A. Fuchs (eds.), *Assyriologica et Semitica: Festschrift für Joachim Oelsner anläßlich seines 65. Geburtstages am 18. Februar 1997.* (Alter Orient und Altes Testament 252.) Münster, 2000, pp. 1–16.

Bidmead, J. *The* Akītu *Festival: Religious Continuity and Royal Legitimation in Mesopotamia.* (Gorgias Dissertations: Near Eastern Studies 2.) Piscataway, 2002.

Bongenaar, A. C. V. M. *The Neo-Babylonian Ebabbar Temple at Sippar: Its Administration and its Prosopography.* (PIHANS 80.) Leiden, 1997.

Brinkman, J. A. 'Merodach-Baladan II.' R. D. Biggs & J. A. Brinkman (eds.), *Studies Presented to A. Leo Oppenheim*. Chicago, 1964, pp. 6–53.

– *A Political History of Post-Kassite Babylonia. 1158–722 B.C.* (Analecta Orientalia 43.) Rome, 1968.
– 'Babylonia under the Assyrian Empire, 745–627 B.C.' M. T. Larsen (ed.), *Power and Propaganda: A Symposium on Ancient Empires.* (Mesopotamia 7.) Copenhagen, 1979, pp. 223–250.
– 'Babylonia c. 1000–748 B.C.' J. Boardman, I. E. S. Edwards, N. G. L. Hammond and E. Sollberger (eds.), *Cambridge Ancient History*, vol. 3 part 1, 2nd ed. Cambridge, 1982, pp. 282–313.
– *Prelude to Empire: Babylonian Society and Politics, 721–626 B.C.* Philadelphia, 1984.
– 'A Legal Text from the Reign of Erība-Marduk (c. 775 BC).' H. Behrens, D. Loding and M. T. Roth (eds.), DUMU-E2-DUB-BA-A. *Studies in Honor of Å. Sjöberg.* (Occasional Publications of the Samuel Noah Kramer Fund 11.) Philadelphia, 1989, pp. 37–47.
– 'The Use of Occupation Names as Patronyms in the Kassite Period: A Forerunner of Neo-Babylonian Ancestral Names?' A. K Guinan, M. d.-J. Ellis, A. J. Ferrara, S. M. Freedman, M. T. Rutz, L. Sassmannshausen, S. Tinney and M. W. Waters (eds.), *If a Man Builds a Joyful House: Assyriological Studies in Honor of Erle Verdun Leichty.* (Cuneiform Monographs 31.) Leiden, 2006, pp. 23–43.
Cole, S. *The Early Neo-Babylonian Governor's Archive from Nippur.* (Oriental Institute Publications 114.) Chicago, 1996.
– *Nippur in Late Assyrian Times c. 755–612 BC.* (State Archives of Assyria Studies 4.) Helsinki, 1996.
Da Riva, R. 'Sippar in the Reign of Sîn-šum-līšir (626 BC).' *Altorientalische Forschungen* 28 (2001), pp. 40–64.
von Dassow, E. 'On Writing the History of Southern Mesopotamia.' *Zeitschrift für Assyriologie und Vorderasiatische Archäologie* 89 (1999), pp. 227–246.
Dietrich, M. *The Babylonian Correspondence of Sargon and Sennacherib.* (State Archives of Assyria 17.) Helsinki, 2003.
van Driel, G. *Elusive Silver. In Search of a Role for a Market in an Agrarian Environment. Aspects of Mesopotamia's Society.* (PIHANS 95.) Leiden, 2002.
Fabritus, K. 'Bēl-ušēzib.' K. Radner (ed.) *The Prosopography of the Neo-Assyrian Empire*, Vol. 1/II, B-G. Helsinki, 1999, pp. 338–339.
Frame, G. 'Another Babylonian Eponym.' *Revue d'assyriologie et d'archeologie orientale* 76 (1982), pp. 157–166.
– *Babylonia 689–627 B.C. A Political History.* (PIHANS 69.) Leiden, 1992.

– *Rulers of Babylonia from the Second Dynasty of Isin to the End of the Assyrian Domination (1157–612 BC).* (Royal Inscriptions of Mesopotamia, Babylonian Periods 2.) Toronto, 1995.
– 'Babylon: Assyria's Problem and Assyria's Prize.' *Journal of the Canadian Society for Mesopotamian Studies* 3 (2008), pp. 21–31.
– *The Archive of Mušēzib-Marduk son of Kiribtu and Descendant of Sîn-nāṣir: A Landowner and Property Developer at Uruk in the Seventh Century BC.* (Babylonische Archive 5.) Dresden, 2013.
Grayson, A. K. *Assyrian and Babylonian Chronicles.* (Texts from Cuneiform Sources 5.) Glückstadt, 1975.
– *Assyrian Rulers of the Early First Millennium BC, I (1114–859 BC).* (The Royal Inscriptions of Mesopotamia, Assyrian Periods 2.) Toronto, 1991.
– 'Assyria: Tiglath-Pileser III to Sargon II (744–705 B.C.).' J. Boardman, I. E. S. Edwards, E. Sollberger and N. G. L. Hammond (eds.), *Cambridge Ancient History*, vol. 3 part 2, 2nd ed. Cambridge, 1992, pp. 71–102.
– 'Assyria: Sennacherib and Esarhaddon (704–669 B.C.).' J. Boardman, I. E. S. Edwards, E. Sollberger and N. G. L. Hammond (eds.), *Cambridge Ancient History*, vol. 3 part 2, 2nd ed. Cambridge, 1992, pp. 103–141.
– 'Assyria 668–635 B.C.: The Reign of Ashurbanipal.' J. Boardman, I. E. S. Edwards, E. Sollberger and N. G. L. Hammond (eds.), *Cambridge Ancient History*, vol. 3 part 2, 2nd ed. Cambridge, 1992, pp. 142–161.
– *Assyrian Rulers of the Early First Millennium BC, II (858–745 BC).* (The Royal Inscriptions of Mesopotamia, Assyrian Periods 3.) Toronto, 1996.
Grosby, S. *Biblical Ideas of Nationality: Ancient and Modern.* Winona Lake, 2002.
Jursa, M. *Neo-Babylonian Legal and Administrative Documents.* (Guides to the Mesopotamian Textual Record 1.) Münster, 2005.
– (ed., with contributions by J. Hackl, B. Janković, K. Kleber, E. E. Payne, C. Waerzeggers and M. Weszeli) *Aspects of the Economic History of Babylonia in the First Millennium BC.* (Alter Orient und Altes Testament 377.) Münster, 2010.
Jacobsen, T. *The Sumerian King List.* (Assyriological Studies 11.) Chicago, 1939.
Jakob-Rost, L. 'Urkunden des 7. Jahrhunderts v. u. Z. aus Babylon.' *Forschungen und Berichte* 12 (1970), pp. 49–60.
Kessler, K. 'Urukäische Familien versus babylonische Familien. Die Namengebung in Uruk, die Degradierung der Kulte von Eanna und der

Aufstieg des Gottes Anu.' *Altorientalische Forschungen* 31 (2004), pp. 237–262.

King, L. W. *Babylonian Boundary-Stones and Memorial Tablets in the British Museum*. London, 1912.

Leichty, E. *The Royal Inscriptions of Esarhaddon, King of Assyria (680–669 BC)*. (The Royal Inscriptions of the Neo-Assyrian Period 4.) Winona Lake, Ind., 2011.

Liverani, M. 'The Growth of the Assyrian Empire in the Habur / Middle Euphrates Area: A New Paradigm.' *State Archives of Assyria Bulletin* 2 (1988), pp. 81–98.

Llop-Raduà, J. 'The Boundary between Assyria and Babylonia in the East Tigris Region during the Reign of Tukultī-Ninurta I (1233–1197 BC).' P. Miglus & S. Mühl (eds.) *Between the Cultures: The Central Tigris Region from the 3rd to the 1st Millennium BC. Conference at Heidelberg, January 22nd – 24th, 2009*. (Heidelberger Studien zum Alten Orient 14.) Heidelberg, 2011, pp. 209–215.

Luckenbill, D. D. *The Annals of Sennacherib*. (Oriental Institute Publications 2.) Chicago, 1926–27.

Machinist, P. 'The Assyrians and Their Babylonian Problem: Some Reflections.' *Wissenschaftskolleg zu Berlin. Jahrbuch 1984–85*, 1984–85, pp. 353–364.

Michalowski, P. 'History as Charter: Some Observations on the Sumerian King List.' *Journal of the American Oriental Society* 103 (1983), pp. 237–248.

Nielsen, J. P. *Sons and Descendants: A Social History of Kin Groups and Family Names in the Early Neo-Babylonian Period, 747–626 BC*. (Culture and History of the Ancient Near East 43.) Leiden, 2011.

– 'Marduk's Return: Assyrian Imperial Propaganda, Babylonian Cultural Memory, and the *akītu* Festival of 667 BC.' M. Bommas, J. Harrisson and P. Roy (eds.), *Memory and Urban Religion in the Ancient World*. (Cultural Memory and History in Antiquity.) London, 2012, pp. 3–32.

Parpola, S. *Letters from Assyrian and Babylonian Scholars*. (State Archives of Assyria 10.) Helsinki, 1993.

Reiner, E. 'The Babylonian Fürstenspiegel in Practice.' M. A. Dandamayev, N. J. Postgate and M. T. Larsen (eds.) *Societies and Languages of the Ancient Near East: Studies in Honour of I. M. Diakanoff*. Warminster, 1982, pp. 324–326.

Reynolds, F. *The Babylonian Correspondence of Esarhaddon*. (State Archives of Assyria 18.) Helsinki, 2003.

Richardson, S. 'The World of Babylonian Countrysides.' G. Leick (ed.), *The Babylonian World*. New York – London, 2007, pp. 13–38.

Roshwald, A. *The Endurance of Nationalism. Ancient Roots and Modern Dilemmas*. Cambridge, 2006.
San Nicolò, M. *Babylonische Rechtsurkunden des Ausgehenden 8. und des 7. Jahrhunderts v. Chr.* Munich, 1951.
Smith, A. *The Antiquity of Nations*. Cambridge, 2004.
Steinkeller, P. 'An Ur III Manuscript of the Sumerian King List.' W. Sallaberger (ed.), *Literatur, Politik, und Recht in Mesopotamien: Festschrift für Claus Wilcke.* Wiesbaden, 2003, pp. 267–292.
Stone, E. 'Mesopotamian Cities and Countryside.' D. Snell (ed.), *A Companion to the Ancient Near East*. Oxford, 2005, pp. 141–154.
Tadmor, H.& S. Yamada, *The Royal Inscriptions of Tiglath-pileser III (744–727 BC) and Shalmaneser V (726–722 BC), Kings of Assyria.* (The Royal Inscriptions of the Neo-Assyrian Period 1.) Winona Lake, Ind., 2011.
Waerzeggers, C. 'The Babylonian Revolts against Xerxes and the "End of Archives".' *Archiv für Orientforschung* 50 (2003/2004), pp. 150–173.
– 'Neo-Babylonian Tablets in the Royal Museums of Art and History in Brussels.' *Akkadica* 126 (2005), pp. 133–158.
– (with a contribution by M. Jursa) 'On the Initiation of Babylonian Priests.' *Zeitschrift für Altorientalische und Biblische Rechtsgeschichte* 14 (2008), pp. 1–38.
Yamada, S. 'Tukulti-Ninurta I's Rule over Babylonia and its Aftermath - A Historical Reconstruction.' *Orient* 38 (2003), pp. 153–177.
Zadok, R. *On West Semites in Babylonia.* Jerusalem, 1977.
– *Geographical Names According to New- and Late-Babylonian Texts.* (Répertoire géographique des textes cunéiformes 8.) Wiesbaden, 1985.

QUR'ĀNIC REVELATIONS AND ECONOMIC ADMINISTRATIVE ADJUSTMENTS

JØRGEN B. SIMONSEN

Abstract. Among historians a discussion has prevailed for ages as to how we present our interpretation(s) of the past. We agree on the importance of sources, but when it comes to how to use the sources differences among trained historians surface. In this article I will conduct an analysis of sources pertaining to three different encounters in early Islamic history and show how these encounters can be analytically used to document a social dynamic present in the early caliphate that is not mentioned directly in the sources themselves. The social dynamic only becomes visible when the modern historian creates history by carefully using the available sources – usually left for posterity by sheer coincidence.

INTRODUCTION

People, ideas, languages, religions, empires and armies have been involved and engaged in encounters all through history. In this article I will look at and analyze three encounters, beginning with an encounter between different religious traditions as it surfaced in Mecca and Medina on the Arabian Peninsula in the early 7th century when Muhammad received what he and his supporters considered to be revelations from the one and only God. I will then turn to a different kind of encounter taking place in Egypt from 639 and a few years onwards, when a caliphal army engaged in a struggle with the Byzantine Empire about political control of the prosperous province of Egypt, an event that ended with a complete victory for the caliphate.[1] Finally, a third encounter will be analyzed: a clash between the Arab Muslims on the one hand and part of the local population in Egypt and other conquered provinces who had converted to Islam. The conversion was not at all supported by the Arab Muslim elite, but once set in motion it challenged the ideology on which the early

[1] The caliphal army constituted Arabs who had converted to Islam, but many Arabs from the peninsula participated in the early conquest as it became clear that booty was at hand. As the conquest went on segments of the previous Byzantine army entered the caliphal army as did segments of the previous Sassanid army; see Baladhuri (dead 892), *Futuh al-Buldan,* 1866 pp. 471ff. See also Kennedy, *The Armies of the Caliphs,* 2001.

caliphate was established. The process resulted in a new and quite different interpretation of the caliphate and Islam.

I am aware that these encounters are rooted in different contexts, but in line with Hayden White[2] I rely on the obligation of the modern historian to *create* history by using sources of different kinds that have been passed on to posterity by agents participating in decision making and in ordinary life in the past. Accordingly, it is my aim to present an explanatory interpretation of how the three analyzed encounters became intertwined as new social dynamics forced the caliphate to have a critical look at how the empire was organized. The outcome was a new interpretation of Islam that politically and legally held sway in the Middle East until the late 19th century.[3]

ENCOUNTER I: ISLAM, ARAB POLYTHEISM, ARAB JEWS AND ARAB CHRISTIANS

The birth of Islam in Mecca and Medina from 610 until the prophet Muhammad passed away in 632 offers an example of a religious encounter that began peacefully but ended violently as the differences became insurmountable.[4] Muhammad's revelations introduced to his co-citizens a belief in one omnipotent and omnipresent God. The people of Mecca in the early 7th century were followers of a local religious belief based on the acceptance of a number of different gods venerated in the Kaʿba, a local temple in Mecca and celebrated in a number of localities in and around Mecca and in other places, where local trade was conducted at the same time.[5] Muhammad's revelations as expressed in the Qurʾān constituted a complete break with local religious traditions.[6] During the preceding century the ruling elite in Mecca under the leadership of Quraish had established an elaborate system of alliances with tribes and

[2] Cf. H. White, *The Content of the Form,* 1990.
[3] The views in this paper were originally presented in Simonsen, *Studies in the Genesis and Early Development of the Caliphal Taxation System,* 1988, and have since been elaborated further. See also Morimoto, *The Fiscal Administration of Egypt*, 1981; Hussein, *Das Steuersystem in Ägypten*, 1982; and Morony, 'Economic Boundaries?', 2004, pp. 166–194.
[4] Watt, *Muhammad at Mecca,* 1972, and *Muhammad at Medina,* 1974.
[5] Cf. Bonner, '"Time has come Full Circle"', 2011; Simon, *Meccan Trade and Islam*, 1989; and Kister, 'Mecca and Tamin', 1965. Patricia Crone (*Meccan Trade and the Rise of Islam,* 1987) launched a strong critique of the traditional scholarly interpretation of the size and the extension of the trade conducted by the traders rooted in Mecca. Her critique, however, does not infringe on the importance of trade to be extrapolated from the Qurʾān. For Arabs in a longer historical perspective see Hoyland, *Arabia and the Arabs*, 2001.
[6] For a long time modern research has documented that many traditions were Islamized, cf. Izutsu, *God and Man in the Koran,* 1980, and *Ethico-religious Concepts in the Qurʾān,* 2002.

localities in the western part of the Arab peninsula that was based on mutually recognized religious ideas and values. In this environment Muhammad's revelations were from day one perceived as a threat to this carefully developed system.[7] Most of his co-citizens remained skeptical about his call to embrace Islam; they declined conversion and for years remained loyal to local religious beliefs and traditions.

Long before Muhammad entered history, the Arabs in the peninsula had been introduced to religious monotheism. During the previous centuries both Judaism and Christianity had gained followers among the Arabs in the western part of the peninsula, and this entailed a religious conflict between Muhammad and Arab Jews and Christians, who soon began to question the content of his revelations originally directed to the polytheists in Mecca.[8]

From the beginning, Muhammad claimed that the revelations he received and introduced to his fellow citizens originated from God, and the early parts of the Qur'ān repeatedly reverted to the idea that throughout history his God had sent a number of prophets and messengers to different peoples with divinely endorsed rules and regulations, which made it possible for people to welcome a prophet or a messenger who would organize their society in line with the wishes of God. According to the Qur'ān all of these prophets had been sent by the same God, a central idea underlined in Sura 3 verse 84: "Say: 'We believe in God, and in what has been revealed to us and what was revealed to Abraham, Isma'il, Isaac, Jacob, and the Tribes, and in the books given to Moses, Jesus and the prophets from their Lord: we make no distinction between one and another among them, and to God do we bow our will.'"

The Qur'ān accordingly defined Muhammad as the seal of the prophets, the *khatim al-nabiyin,* as mentioned in Sura 33 verse 40: "Muhammad is not the father of any of your men, but he is the apostle of God and the seal of the prophets: and God has full knowledge of all things." In this way Islam is presented not as a new religion, but as the final and complete revelation of the true monotheistic belief. With Muhammad, the revelation came to an end and mankind needed no further revelation.

Early on in the Qur'ānic revelations Abraham is designated as a true monotheist and a Muslim as explained in Sura 3 verse 67: "Abraham was

---

[7] Hamidullah, 'Al-Ilaf ou les rapports économico-diplomatiques', 1957.

[8] Lecker, *Jews and Arabs in pre- and early Islamic Arabia*, 1998; Trimingham, *Christianity among the Arabs in pre-Islamic Times*, 1979. Gerald R. Hawting (*The Idea of Idolatry and the Emergence of Islam*, 2000) has offered an alternative interpretation of the Qur'ānic concept of idolatry; according to him, the word was actually referring to monotheists who had misunderstood monotheism.

not a Jew, nor yet a Christian; but he was true in faith (hanifan in Arabic, designating a true and upright believer in monotheism) and bowed his will to God's (musliman in Arabic)."[9]

Muhammad elaborated this idea further and accused the (Arab) Jews and the (Arab) Christians of deliberate manipulation of the revelation their prophets had once received in order to delete promises about the future coming of Muhammad, promises that were originally part of the revelation their prophets were expected to pass on to their people.

It can hardly surprise that the (Arab) Jews and the (Arab) Christians in Mecca and Medina were annoyed by such accusations, and the two monotheistic groups joined forces with the Arab polytheists in their criticism and rejection of the revelation presented by Muhammad. His revelations thus collided with both local polytheists and monotheists, a collision that can be found in a number of revelations constituting the so-called punishment stories.[10] These revelations offer examples of how the one and only God throughout history sent prophets and messengers with revelations to mankind. And like Muhammad in Mecca in the early 7th century, prophets in the past had also been ridiculed by their contemporaries and mocked for being crazy and obsessed by demons.[11]

Moses is portrayed in the Qur'ān as an earlier prophet, who was rejected by his fellow men, but most often we are told how he was rejected and persecuted by the Egyptian king, the Pharao, who is mentioned no less than 74 times in the Qur'ān.[12] For instance in Sura 10 verse 88–92, where Moses utter a prayer to God in order for God to help him and Banu Isra'il (the Qur'ānic reference to the Jews): "(88) Moses prayed: "Our Lord! Thou hast indeed bestowed on Pharao and his Chiefs splendour and wealth in the life of the present, and so, our Lord, they mislead men from thy path. Deface, our Lord, the features of their wealth and send hardness to their hearts, so they will not believe until they see the grievous penalty". (89) God said: "Accepted is your prayer, so stand ye straight, and follow not the path of those who know not." (90) We took the children of Israel across the sea: Pharao and his hosts followed them in insolence and spite. At length, when overwhelmed with the flood, he said: "I believe that there is no god except Him whom the children of Israel believe in. I am of those who submit" (in Arabic: *wa ana min al-muslimin*)."

---

[9] For the concept of *hanif*, see McAuliffe (ed.), *Encyclopaedia of the Qur'ān,* Vol. II p. 402 (U. Rubin).

[10] *Encyclopaedia of the Qur'ān,* Vol. 4, pp. 318ff. (D. Marshall) and Brinner, *Lives of the Prophets*, 2002.

[11] Cf. Qur'ān 81:22.

[12] Cf. *Encyclopaedia of the Qur'ān,* Vol. 4 pp. 66f. (R. Firestone).

According to this text, Pharao seems to have converted to Islam shortly before he was drowned by God along with his army. The medieval Muslim tradition nevertheless generally depicts Pharao as the one who on Doomsday will lead his people into the hellfire for eternal punishment as a result of his efforts to fight Moses and the Jews.[13] Other punishment stories in the Qur'ān are using other prophets familiar in both the Jewish and the Christian traditions, such as Lot, Noah and Aaron. But prophets from outside the Jewish and Christian traditions are also mentioned in the Qur'ān, for instance the prophet Hud who was sent to a tribe called ʿAd, and the prophet Salih sent to a tribe called Thamud.[14]

Islam as a religion was not yet elaborated nor formulated in theological and legal dogmas when Muhammad's death in 632 brought the revelation to an end. The Qur'ān as we know it nevertheless offers an example of how the idea of monotheism – already alive among both Jews and Christians – was appropriated by Muhammad and given new meaning.[15] The central idea was maintained in the sense that the common link between the three monotheistic religions symbolized in Abraham was underlined. But the core content of monotheism was reinvented and reformulated in order to serve Muhammad's interpretation of himself.[16]

Through the ensuing centuries Muslim theologians and Muslim legal scholars discussed among themselves how the Qur'ān was to be interpreted.[17] The early discussion was rooted in an environment, where Islam only was a matter for the Arabs and where the appropriation of the monotheistic idea formulated in the Qur'ān resulted in a severe critique

---

[13] Cf. Wheeler, *Moses in the Quran and Islamic Exegesis*, 2002, and Joost Kramer's article in this volume.

[14] For the prophet Hud, see Qur'ān 7:65 and 26:124; for Salih, see Qur'ān 7:73, 75 and 77; 11:61–62.

[15] I use the concept of appropriation as defined in H. Read (ed.), *Thames and Hudson Dictionary of Art and Artists*, 1994, p. 19: "The direct duplication, copying or incorporation of an image (painting, photographs, etc.) by another artist who represents it in a different context, thus completely altering its meaning and questioning notions of originality and authenticity." I am not considering Muhammad as an artist, but certainly as a religious person appropriating ideas from others and reformulating them in line with his own understanding; cf. Schneider, 'On "Appropriation"', 2003 p. 215–229; and Ziff & Rao (eds.), *Borrowed Power*, 1997.

[16] Orientalist research in the late 19th and early 20th century focused a lot on the textual and conceptual inter-relationship between Judaism, Christianity and Islam; cf. Geiger, *Was hat Muhammed aus dem Judenthume aufgenommen,* 1902; Rudolph, *Die Abhängigkeit des Qurans von Judentum und Christentum*, 1922; Andrea, *Der Ursprung des Islams und das Christentum*, 1926; and R. Bell, *The Origin of Islam in its Christian Environment*, 1926.

[17] Cf. Wensinck, *The Muslim Creed*, 1965; Cook, *Early Muslim Dogma*, 1981; Nagel, *The History of Islamic Theology*, 2000; Melchert, *The Formation of the Sunni Schools of Law*, 1997; and Hallaq, *The Origins and Evolution of Islamic Law*, 2005.

by the Arab Jews and Christians. They rejected his claim to be the final monotheistic prophet, and they dismissed his idea of being the one who had received the revelations from the God they worshipped.

The interpretation of Islam that was formulated in the decades following the death of Muhammad was intimately linked to the Arab peninsula and not to the many different Jews and Christians living in the territories that were conquered by the caliphate after his death. The early Muslim scholars interpreted the victory of Islam over the Arab polytheists and the Arab Jews and Christians as a result of God's support for his last prophet who had been sent to introduce the final monotheistic revelation to the Arabs, be they polytheists, Jews or Christians. In line with this view, Muslim scholars later claimed that Muhammad had already invited the rulers of the various parts of the Middle East to convert to Islam prior to the military conquests. Muslim historians of the 8th and 9th century presented a number of letters sent by Muhammad to the rulers in the region, for instance the Byzantine Emperor, the Sassanid king, and the Muqawqis in Egypt being the head of the Christians in Egypt, inviting them to convert to Islam or to be subjugated by the new polity established by Muhammad and his followers in Medina – a polity that after the exodus from Mecca to Medina in 622 gradually changed the political structure of the Arabian Peninsula and later of the region at large.[18]

The religious conflict Muhammad and his followers had with the local polytheists on the one hand and the Arab Jews and Christians on the other had turned full circle. The Muslims won and succeeded in establishing a new dynamic and powerful polity that was transformed into a caliphate when Muhammad died in 632, where the first caliph Abu Bakr (ruled 632–634) was elected as his successor.[19] He and his successors were to organize the conquests that eventually left the Christian empire of Byzantium greatly diminished in size and the Sassanid Empire completely routed.

ENCOUNTER II: THE CALIPHAL CONQUEST OF EGYPT

An encounter of quite a different sort surfaced in 640, when a small detachment of the caliphal army conquering Palestine went south towards Egypt, passed Gaza, and initiated a conquest of the former Byzantine province. The Byzantine army was routed in al-Fustat, a locality later to be absorbed by Cairo; and shortly after Alexandria was conquered as well.

---

[18] The embedded and long-term changes became visible when Muhammad around 615 sent off a number of newly converted Muslims to the Negus in Abyssinia, cf. Watt, *Muhammad at Mecca*, 1972.

[19] Cf. Crone & Hinds, *God's Caliph*, 1990.

A Byzantine re-conquest was organized but to no avail, and from 642 onwards Egypt became part of the caliphate.

The caliphal conquest has often been interpreted as an expansion of Islam,[20] but as will be argued here such an interpretation does not comply with sources dating back to the years following the conquest of the former Byzantine province of Egypt.[21] There was nothing Islamic about the conquest itself, but certainly about the explanation Muslim scholars later formulated in order to explain the success of the caliphal expansion as already mentioned. This view will be elaborated further below.

We have no contemporary Arab sources to help us understand how the impressive caliphal expansion was made possible, but we do have a small amount of very interesting papyri from 642–643 today preserved in the Rainer Collection in Vienna. The papyri were found in Ahnas in 1877/78 and were first presented briefly by J. Karabacek, *Papyrus Erzherzog Rainer, Führer durch die Ausstellung* (Wien 1894),[22] and have since then been published in a variety of contexts. In all there are 12 papyri. The papyri in question here stem from the local Egyptian administration, and they show how the conquering caliphal army demanded forage for their animals and food for their soldiers while doing their best to finish the conquest of the rich province that for ages had served as the grain chamber of the Byzantine Empire.[23]

The papyri in the Rainer Collection give no examples of payments in cash paid by the local administration to the conquering army, but one of them (PERF 554) documents how the local Byzantine administration was still busy collecting taxes in cash from the local population. In several cases the papyri mention the name of the pagarch,[24] the person in charge of the local administration, indicating that although a military encounter between a recently established polity centered in Medina and the Byzantine Empire was going on, the local administration was maintaining its work as the final outcome of the struggle was not yet decided. In other words, the local Byzantine administration was working as usual.

The Rainer Collection papyri also show how the administration took all needed precautions to be able to account for the expenses caused by the supply of forage and food demanded by the caliphal army,

---

20 Cf. Kaarsh, *Islamic Imperialism*, 2007.

21 Cf. Donner, *The Early Islamic Conquests*, 1981.

22 For a recent contribution to the insight to be harvested by using papyri, see Sijpestein & Sundelin (eds.), *Papyrology and the History of Early Islamic Egypt*, 2004.

23 Simonsen, *Studies in the Genesis and Early Development of the Caliphal Taxation System*, 1988, pp. 81ff.

24 Liebeschuetz, 'The Origins of the Office of the Pagarch', 1973; and Atiya (ed.), *The Coptic Encyclopedia,* Vol. 6, pp. 1871f.

documenting a local administrative practice where accountability apparently was an important principle.

The caliphal army succeeded in its efforts and conquered Egypt, and the caliphate therefore had to establish a system for the administration of the province once the conquest was completed. The larger part of the conquering army was placed in al-Fustat and in Alexandria, and minor groups were placed in a number of medium-sized cities in the province for shorter intervals.[25] They were placed in separate quarters of the cities and it seems that the army in Egypt purposely was settled in areas segregated from the local population, apparently in order to reduce the interaction between the conquering army on the one hand and the local conquered population on the other. Al-Fustat became a *misr,* a city or an area where the caliphal army settled just like in Kufa and Basra in Iraq.[26]

A similar principle of segregation between conquerors and conquered is documented in a large number of papyri that demonstrate how the administration was organized after the inclusion of Egypt into the caliphate.[27] The administrative system established after the successful conquest was headed by the governor of the province, who was always an Arab Muslim stationed in al-Fustat. He was appointed by the caliph, and his power was secured and supported by the caliphal army stationed in Egypt. The governor was assisted in his work by a local administration, which throughout Egypt was headed by local pagarchs, i.e. large landowners who represented the local elite. The pagarchs had been central to the Byzantine administration as well, and to judge by the many papyri from different places in Egypt, these men were recognized as indispensable by the conquerors once the conquest was successfully finished. The local elites had something to offer the Arab conquerors, and this mutual dependence was recognized by both groups and paved the way for "a middle ground".[28]

We do not know the number of Arab Muslims who settled in Egypt after the conquest, but they were certainly too few to uphold the administration themselves.[29] The conquerors were therefore in dire need of an agreement with the local elite if they wanted to extract taxes and other services from the population. This situation explains why the conquerors allowed the continuation of a local administration rooted in a Byzantine tradition.

---

[25] Simonsen, *Studies in the Genesis and Early Development of the Caliphal Taxation System*, 1988, pp. 81f.
[26] Kubiak, *Al-Fustat*, 1987.
[27] See note 34.
[28] Cf. R. White, *The Middle Ground*, 1991.
[29] Donner, *The Early Islamic Conquests*, 1981.

The pagarchs were probably appointed by the governor; at least we have a number of papyri documenting how the provincial governor threatened pagarchs to be removed from office if they did not comply with the governor's orders.[30] But neither the Arab governor nor any other Arab Muslim were directly involved in the administration at the local level. The governor and his staff in al-Fustat only supervised the administration, ensuring that all demands of taxes in kind and cash were paid and that all other demands were complied with. The local pagarch had a number of assistants at hand who assisted him in the daily administration of the pagarchy, and the papyri make clear how these men stayed in office for a longer or shorter period of time. Some papyri also document how a person in charge of one part of the local administration later came to be in charge of other areas.[31]

When the Byzantines surrendered Egypt the administration was left to the caliphate who kept the existing administration intact as far as the lower level was concerned and only introduced changes in the upper levels of the administration. The papyri allow us to say that taxes in cash and kind were levied on the local population as had been the case during Byzantine times. In the Greek and Coptic papyri we find the same technical words as those used during the Byzantine period, whereas the authors of the Arab papyri had to come up with terms that could be used in the new administrative context where taxes now were levied on a conquered population.[32] In the first decades after the conquest, the taxes remained mainly the same, the only difference being that taxes in kind and cash were now used to pay the caliphal army as well as the upper layers of the Arab administration in Egypt and to pay pensions to the Arab Muslim elite in Mecca and Medina at a regular basis.[33] The papyri offer no clues to anything Islamic as far as the taxes in kind and cash are concerned.

Another very large amount of papyri from Aphrodito – a locality in the central part of Egypt south of modern Asyut – allow us a closer look at the organization of the administration.[34] The administration in Aphrodito was in the hands of a certain Baselios, one of the many pagarchs in charge

---

[30] Cf. Bell, *Greek Papyri in the British Museum IV*, 1910 (P. Lond IV 1338 and 1339).

[31] Simonsen, *Studies in the Genesis and Early Development of the Caliphal Taxation System*, 1988, pp. 113ff.

[32] The earliest Arabic papyri use the word *djizya* for taxes in cash levied on the population. The word was later defined as a poll-tax to be paid by all Jews and Christians, but this was clearly not the meaning of the word in the early papyri, cf. Encounter III discussed below.

[33] Baladhuri, *Futuh al-Buldan*, 1866, pp. 448ff.

[34] Bell, *Greek Papyri in the British Museum IV*, 1910; and Grohmann, *Arabic Papyri in the Egyptian Library I–VI*, 1934–1962. A very large number of papyri from Vienna have been edited in *Corpus Papyrorum Raineri*.

of the local administration throughout Egypt. The Arab governor Qurra ibn Sharik served as provincial governor for all of Egypt from 709 to 714, and the Aphrodito-papyri contain a large number of letters that show in detail what the caliphal administration in al-Fustat required to be paid by the pagarchy of Aphrodito.

These papyri also contain a number of accounts run both by the provincial administration in al-Fustat as well as the pagarch in Aphrodito, and these offer an interesting and fascinating view into both the provincial and the local administration of Egypt in the late 7th and early 8th century. When the provincial administration in al-Fustat needed payments in cash or kind, the governor sent requisition notes to the local administration via a messenger who presented the request to the local pagarch. The local administration then had to divide the requested amount among the local tax-paying population, organize its collection, and finally bring the contributions to the central administration in al-Fustat. In the Aphrodito papyri we can follow how the requests change character and become increasingly differentiated as time passes. When the caliph Abd al-Malik (reigned 685–705) decided to build a new large mosque in Jerusalem, one papyrus shows that Aphrodito had to contribute its part of the total costs.[35] The governor in Egypt apparently received a request from Damascus to supply a number of craftsmen to the construction of the new mosque, and the provincial governor worked out a plan and decided which pagarchy was to contribute how much. When this had been done, requisition notes were dispatched to the pagarchs, who then had to decide how the request could be met. Other papyri in the Aphrodito collection show how the same pagarchs in Egypt occasionally had to supply other craftsmen for work elsewhere, for instance when roads in Palestine needed maintenance or when the governor in al-Fustat decided to have a new palace built. All expenses incurred by the caliphal administration were covered in a similar manner, be it salaries for army personnel or cash needed to pay the pensions to the Arab Muslim elite.

The conquerors were well aware that this practice had its limits. In several cases, the Arab governor Qurra ibn Sharik took pains to encourage Basilios to be fair and just in the way he divided the caliphal requests among the local population, and he was asked to be careful not to demand too much from the same group of people.[36] And in one particular case, where payments in kind had been requested and the pagarch had divided the requested amount among the single villages in the pagarchy, the governor demanded Basilios to conduct a test of the weights used to make

---

[35] Cf. Bell, *Greek Papyri in the British Museum IV*, 1910 (P. Lond IV 1366).
[36] Cf. Bell, *Greek Papyri in the British Museum IV*, 1910 (P. Lond IV 1345 and 1349).

sure that they were correctly adjusted in order to prevent fraud; any case of discrepancy would be met with strict punishment by the provincial administration.

The interaction between conquerors and conquered in the early caliphate was limited, and the general administrative practice followed by the Arab Muslim governors in al-Fustat was simple: The caliph had the right to demand whatever was needed from the conquered local population. It was his plain right. The conquered population simply had to comply, and the papyri clearly document that they did. After the conquest, the local elite realized that they had something the conquerors needed: administrative knowledge and experience – and this knowledge could be traded. If the Arab Muslim conquerors granted the local elite autonomy and left them to do what they had done for ages, the local elite would secure that payments requested in cash and kind would be honored. Both the Arab Muslim elite and the local elite benefited from this arrangement, a situation that very much resembles what Richard White has labeled the "middle ground" of cultural encounters.[37]

Eventually this delicate balance came to an end, and a new encounter of ideological nature surfaced in the caliphate from the beginning of the 8th century. The middle ground that was established with the conquest of Egypt lasted for decades, but the balance that characterized this situation was eroded by dynamics not originally taken into consideration when the system was first established in 640.

Encounter III: A different definition of Islam

Even if the many Egyptian papyri from the 7th and early 8th century differ in content, they all pertain to the actual daily administration of the caliphate and do not focus on the conquerors, the Arab Muslims who settled in the former Byzantine province. The conquerors were clearly those who benefited from the many requisition notes, but the papyri actually do not say much about them. The explicit segregation between conquerors and conquered documented in the papyri can be taken as a strong indication of a surprisingly low level of interaction between the two groups. The social segregation left the conquered population to themselves, and as long as taxes in kind and cash were paid and required services were honored and complied with, the Arab Muslims kept to themselves and did not interfere in the local administration. As a result of this, the local population could carry on with their lives more or less unchanged in spite of the fact that they were now subjects to the caliph in

[37] R. White, *The Middle Ground*, 1991.

Damascus instead of the emperor in Constantinople. In one respect they were better off than before. The Coptic Church and its bureaucracy had been submitted to various forms of suppression as a result of serious dogmatic disagreements between the Byzantine church on the one hand and the local Copts on the other; these disagreements were related to differences in their respective view of Jesus during the last centuries of Byzantine power. With the advent of the caliphate this suppression came to an end, and the local Christian population was left to handle its own affairs without interference from the caliphate.

Anything to do with Islam was a matter for the conquerors, and during the first century after the conquest the Arab Muslims struggled among themselves several times on a number of issues. There were intense fights for political power between different groups, and there were intellectual debates as well as discussions about the correct interpretation of the Qur'ān and the formulation of Islamic dogma. But during the 7th century Islam was perceived by the Muslim Arab conquerors as something for them alone, and no serious initiatives were taken to try to convert the conquered population. The established idea was that the conquerors had the right to rule and were entitled to take what they needed from the conquered people. This fundamental principle was in effect for several decades and it constituted the *raison d'être* for the established middle ground, which had its obvious advantages for the Arab Muslim elite as well as for the local Christian elite.

We have barely any Arabic sources from the 7th century that allow us to get a deeper understanding of how the Arab Muslim elite organized themselves in the conquered province of Egypt. But important information can be found in Arabic works from the 8th century onwards, and many of these later works contain detailed and valuable historical information through their extensive quotes from earlier works. This makes it possible for us to trace the changes in the perception of the conquests as formulated by later Muslim historians.

As mentioned above, Islam in the Qur'ān was defined as the original and authentic monotheistic belief. The Qur'ān contained the final revelation and it was left to the Muslims to interpret the text and to make sure that society was ruled in compliance with the Qur'ānic revelation. The early discussions between Muslim scholars had no immediate repercussions for the population living in the conquered provinces as they had been granted extensive local autonomy when they were incorporated into the caliphate. The Arab-Muslim sources of the 8th and 9th century explain and interpret the conquest of territories outside the Arab peninsula as a continuation of the support the Muslims were granted by God when they overcame the polytheists in Mecca.[38] In the Muslim historical tradition the expansion is described as an obvious and inevitable consequence of the support the Muslims had from God when they struggled with the Arab polytheists. God had supported his prophet, and after his death, supported the ruling caliph.

As time went on, the original small groups of Muslims settled in the conquered provinces grew in size, and Arab Muslims enrolled in the army and placed in the conquered territories married local women and had children. Entering the 8th century, the Arab Muslim sources mention the presence of a new social group, the *mawali*, a technical term used for non-Arabs who converted to Islam and became Muslims. They were all attached to the Arab Muslims as clients; they were rooted in the conquered provinces and originally took no part in the discussions among Arab Muslims about such matters as political legitimacy. But they soon focused on the apparent discrimination between Muslims belonging to the conquerors and their descendants vis-à-vis converted Muslims from the different provinces.[39] The converts and their children were declined the right to pensions paid by the caliphate to successors of the early Arab Muslims, and they were for long denied the right to be enlisted as salaried members of the standing caliphal army funded exclusively by the taxes paid by the locals.[40] They felt discriminated against and lacked recognition by the Arab Muslims as equals in spite of the egalitarian principle formulated several places in the Qur'ān.[41]

Muslim theologians and legal scholars from the early 8th century gradually formulated a new interpretation of Islam that emphasized the universality of the Qur'ānic revelation. According to this view, it was not a revelation only for the Arabs alone but one for all mankind and thus also a religion for the population in the conquered provinces as well. This is clear, for instance, in Sura 34,28: "We have not sent thee but as a universal[42] (Messenger) to men, giving them glad tidings and warning them (against sin), but most men understand not." A consequence of this

---

[38] The Arab Muslim historian Ahmad ibn Yahya al-Baladhuri (died 892), author of *Futuh al-Buldan (The Conquest of the Countries)* about the caliphal expansion, introduced his book with an account on the Muslims' exodus from Mecca to Medina in 622.

[39] *Encyclopaedia of Islam,* Vol. 6 pp. 874ff, 1986 (P. Crone) rightly focus on the inevitable need of the assistance of the *mawali* for the caliphal administration.

[40] Kennedy, *The Armies of the Caliphs*, 2001.

[41] During the 9th and 10th century non-Arab Muslims responded to this attitude on behalf of the Arab Muslim as better Muslims in the so called *shu'ubiyya*-movement, cf. *Encyclopaedia of Islam* (2nd edition) Vol. IX pp. 533ff. (S. Enderwitz).

[42] The Arabic word used here is *kâffatan*, meaning "one and all, altogether", cf. Ambros, *A Concise Dictionary of Koranic Arabic*, 2004, p. 240. All quotations from the Qur'ān in this article is from Ali, *The Holy Qur'an. Translation and Commentary*, 1946.

made it increasingly difficult – if not impossible – to uphold the unfair treatment and discrimination of the converts compared to how Arab Muslims were treated. We do not know the number of converts, but the *mawali* can be traced as actively involved in the intra-Muslim political struggles going on in the first half of the 8th century.[43] A strong critique of the political legitimacy of the ruling Umayyad family also surfaced among some Arab Muslims, and when members of the Abbasid family began to organize and prepare a revolt against the Umayyads the concerns of the *mawalis* were taken seriously.[44] The converts were now so many that a change was needed, and this was recognized by the Muslim legal scholars who set out to formulate a new interpretation of Islam in line with the growing demand formulated by the *mawali* for equality for all Muslims, Arabs or not.

The Qur᾽ān has a number of references to *ahl al-kitab*, the People of the Book,[45] and as mentioned above, the Qur᾽ān recognizes that some of the previous prophets revealed their revelations in book(s). Among the People of the Book were the Jews and the Christians, and the many Christians as well as the Jews in the conquered provinces like the Arab Jews and the Arab Christians living in the peninsula rejected the idea that Islam constituted the true monotheism. The Arab polytheists had constituted the prime goal for the revelation Muhammad had brought to his city of birth, but their fate was doomed after Muhammad and his followers conquered Mecca in 630.

In Sura 9, revealed shortly after the Muslims conquered Mecca in 630, it is stated that the Muslims were to accept and meet all treaties signed with the polytheists for the time agreed upon in the single treaty, but after the deadline they had to convert to Islam or be killed. Sura 9:5 has the following text: "But when the forbidden months are past, then fight and slay the Pagans where ye find them".

The Qur᾽ān uses the word *dhimma* for the security polytheists could obtain from Muhammad and his followers if they supported his struggle against Quraish in Mecca. Also the Arab Jews and the Arab Christians are addressed in Sura 9, where they are demanded to choose between conversion to Islam or to accept the payment of a tax called *jizya* to prove they had been subjected as stated in Sura 9: 29: "Fight those who believe not in God nor the Last Day, nor hold that forbidden which hath been forbidden by God and His Apostle, nor acknowledge the Religion of

---

43 Cf. C. F. Robinson, *Empire and Elites after the Muslim Conquest*, 2000.
44 Sharon, *Black Banners from the East*, 2004.
45 Qur᾽ān 2:144–146; 3:64–65, 69-72, 98–100, and 7:169-170.

Truth, (even if they are) of the People of the Book until they pay the jizya with willing submission".

The Muslim legal scholars who discussed Islam in the early 8th century were well aware of the struggle Muhammad had with the Arab polytheists in the early 7th century, but as the category polytheists no longer existed it became possible to establish a link between *dhimma, ahl al-kitab* and *jizya*.[46] The *ahl al-kitab* constituted the majority of the population in the caliphate at large and the autonomy that was granted to the conquered population and their elites after the conquest could now be legitimized as the protection (*dhimma*) mentioned in the Qur'ān. In legal terms, the People of the Book were allowed the right to maintain their religious and legal autonomy, but they had to pay *jizya* to the caliph for this autonomy, which was now recognized as *dhimma*. During Muhammad's lifetime the concept was used for all groups willing to cooperate with the Muslims in their struggle with Quraish. In the new interpretation *dhimma* was redefined and *jizya* was defined as the tax demanded from the individual subject, whether it was a Jew or a Christian.

The conquered population had paid taxes to the caliphate ever since they were incorporated into it, and in this respect nothing was changed. The Arab Muslim conquerors did not originally pay taxes, but as they and their descendants engaged in economic activities as traders, craftsmen and peasants the original administrative system met increasing difficulties as the local converts to Islam had to pay taxes as all other subjects did. The new caliphal ideology underlined that all subjects had to pay tax, but the kind of tax paid was dependent on the religious affiliation of the individual subject. In this new system everybody had to pay taxes: Muslims and non-Muslims, but the kind of taxes the single tax-payer had to pay was based on his or her religious belief.

CONCLUSION

Sources are indispensable for historians trying to interpret the dynamics of human history. But sources can only answer the questions raised, they never speak by themselves, and not all sources can answer all questions. These principles are important to keep in mind when trying to understand the political encounter between the armies of the Byzantine Empire and the caliphate in Egypt beginning in 640 and ending in 642, when it became clear that the Byzantine re-conquest was of no avail. The papyri analyzed above demonstrate how the local Byzantine administration

---

[46] Simonsen, *Studies in the Genesis and Early Development of the Caliphal Taxation System*, 1988, pp. 135 ff.; and McAuliffe (ed.), *Encyclopaedia of the Qur'ān*, Vol. 5, p. 192 (P. L. Heck on 'taxation').

continued to work as usual, and when the power struggle was settled in favor of the caliphate, the local Egyptian elite and the conquerors made a deal to the advantage of both parties.

The ideological framework for the caliphate was the revelations collected after the death of the prophet Muhammad in the Qur'ān. The Arab Muslim conquerors did nothing to try to convert the conquered populations, but conversion was inevitable in the longer run. The caliphal army was settled in the conquered provinces, and the enlisted soldiers married local women. As the expansion lost momentum, the Arabs Muslim settlers began to engage in the local economy, and during this process the seeds were planted for the later conflict between the *mawali* and the Arab Muslims. The converts became Muslims, but the descendants of the original Arab Muslim conquerors refused to extend the same rights and privileges they themselves enjoyed. The conflict was used politically when the Abbasids organized their revolt against the Umayyads, and where the Abbasid propaganda promised to implement a more egalitarian interpretation of Islam. The early distinction between conquerors and conquered was thus reduced to history and a new ideology was formulated according to which all subjects had to pay tax. The kind of taxes to be paid differed and depended on the religious affiliation of the single subject. Christians were to pay a poll tax and were legally and religiously granted autonomy and could thus maintain their religious and legal traditions without interference from the caliphate.

The new interpretation of Islam was legitimized by reference to the Qur'ān, and thus the religious encounter between Islam, the Arab polytheists and the Arab Jews and Christians was invoked when the original agreement between the Arab Muslim conquerors and the local elite was given up. The structure of the political encounter between the caliphate and the Byzantine Empire had been eroded by mass conversion, and a new one was established which came to be formulated in terms and principles that were to endure in the region until late in the 19th century.

BIBLIOGRAPHY

Ali, A. Y. *The Holy Qur'an. Translation and Commentary*. London, 1946.

Ambros, A. A. *A Concise Dictionary of Koranic Arabic*. Wiesbaden: Reichert Verlag, 2004.

Andrea, T. *Der Ursprung des Islams und das Christentum*. Uppsala, 1926.

Atiya, A. S. (ed.). *The Coptic Encyclopedia*. 8 vols. New York, 1991.

Baladhuri, A. ibn Yahya al-. *Futuh al-Buldan* (ed. M. J. de Goeje). Lugdoni Batavorum, 1866.
Bell, H. I. *Greek Papyri in the British Museum, Vol. IV. The Aphrodito Papyri.* London, 1910.
Bell, R. *The Origin of Islam in its Christian Environment.* London, 1926.
Bonner, M. '"Time has come Full Circle": Markets, Fairs and the Calendar in Arabia before Islam.' A. Q. Ahmad, B. Sadeghi and M. Bonner (eds.), *The Islamic Scholarly Tradition. Studies in History, Law, and Thought in Honor of Professor Michael Allan Cook.* Leiden, 2011, pp. 13–48.
Brinner, W. M. *Lives of the Prophets.* Leiden, 2002.
Cook, M. *Early Islamic Dogma. A Source-Critical Study.* Cambridge, 1981.
Crone, P. *Meccan Trade and the Rise of Islam.* Princeton, 1987.
Crone, P. & M. Hinds. *God's Caliph: Religious Authority in the first Centuries of Islam.* Cambridge, 1990.
Donner, F. M. *The Early Islamic Conquests.* Princeton, 1981.
Encyclopaedia of Islam. Second edition, 11 vols. (eds. P. J. Bearman, Th. Bianquis, C. E. Bosworth, E. van Donzel and W. P. Heinrichs). Leiden, 1960–2002.
Encyclopedia of the Qur'ān. 6 Vols. (ed. J. D. McAuliffe). Leiden, 2001–2004.
Geiger, A. *Was hat Muhammed aus dem Judentume aufgenommen?* Leipzig, 1902.
Grohmann, A. (ed.). *Arabic Papyri in the Egyptian Library I–VI.* Cairo, 1934–1962.
Hamidullah, M. 'Al-Ilaf ou les rapports économico-diplomatiques de la Mecque pré-islamique.' *Mélanges Louis Massignon,* Vol. II. Damas, 1957, pp. 293–312.
Hallaq, W. *The Origins and Evolution of Islamic Law.* Cambridge, 2005.
Hawting, G. R. *The Idea of Idolatry and the Emergence of Islam: From Polemic to History.* Cambridge, 2000.
Hoyland, R. G. *Arabia and the Arabs: from the Bronze Age to the Coming of Islam.* London, 2001.
Hussein, F. *Das Steuersystem in Ägypten von der arabischen Eroberung bis zur Machergreifung der Tuluniden 19-254/639-868 mit besonderer Berücksichtigung der Papyruskunden* (Heidelberger Orientalistische Studien 3.) Frankfurt am Main, 1982.
Izutsu, T. *God and Man in the Koran.* Tokyo, 1980.
– *Ethico-religious Concepts in the Qur'ān.* Montreal, 2002.
Kaarsh, E. *Islamic Imperialism. A History.* New Haven – London, 2007.

Kennedy, H. *The Armies of the Caliphs: Military and Society in the Early Islamic State*. London, 2001.
Kister, M. 'Mecca and Tamim (Aspects of their Relations).' *Journal of the Economic and Social History of the Orient* 8 (1965), pp. 117–163.
Kubiak, W. B. *Al-Fustat. Its Foundation and Early Urban Development*. Cairo, 1987.
Lecker, M. *Jews and Arabs in pre- and early Islamic Arabia*. Aldershot, 1998.
Liebeschuetz, W. 'The Origins of the Office of the Pagarch.' *Byzantinische Zeitschrift* 66 (1973), pp. 38–46.
McAuliffe, J. D. (ed.) *Encyclopaedia of the Qur'ān*. 6 Vols. Leiden, 2001–2006.
Melchert, C. *The Formation of the Sunni Schools of Law*. Leiden, 1997.
Morimoto, K. *The Fiscal Administration of Egypt in the Early Islamic Period.* (Asian Historical Monographs 1.) Dohosa, 1981.
Morony, M. G. 'Economic Boundaries? Late Antiquity and Early Islam.' *Journal of the Economic and Social History of the Orient* 47 (2004), pp. 166–194.
Nagel, T. *The History of Islamic Theology*. Princeton: Marcus Rienner Publishers, 2000.
Qur'an, the Holy. Translation and commentary by A. Y. Ali. (The Islamic Propagation Centre International.) London. 1946.
Read, H. (ed.) *Thames and Hudsons Dictionary of Art and Artists*. London, 1994.
Rudolph, W. *Die Abhängigkeit des Qurans von Judentum und Christientum*. Stuttgart, 1922.
Robinson, C. F. *Empire and Elites after the Muslim Conquest. The Transformation of Northern Mesopotamia*. Cambridge, 2000.
Robinson, N. *Discovering the Qur'an. A Contemporary Approach to a Veiled Text*. Washington, 2004.
Schneider, A. 'On "Appropriation". A Critical Reappraisal of the Concept and its Application in Global Art Practices.' *Social Anthropology* 11 (2003), pp. 215–229.
Sharon, M. *Black Banners from the East. The Establishment of the Abbasid State*. Jerusalem, 2004.
Sijpestein, P. & L. Sundelin (eds.). *Papyrology and the History of Early Islamic Egypt*. Leiden – Boston, 2004.
Simon, R. *Meccan Trade and Islam: Problems of Origin and Structure*. Budapest, 1989.
Simonsen, J. B. *Studies in the Genesis and Early Development of the Caliphal Taxation System*. Copenhagen, 1988.

Trimingham, J. S. *Christianity among the Arabs in Pre-Islamic Times*. London, 1979.

Watt, W. M. *Muhammad at Mecca*. Oxford, 1972.

Watt, W. M. *Muhammad at Medina*. Oxford, 1974.

Wensinck, A. J. *The Muslim Creed. Its Genesis and Historical Development*. London, 1965.

Wheeler, B. *Moses in the Quran and Islamic Exegesis*. London – New York, 2002.

White, H. *The Content of the Form: Narrative Discourse and Historical Representation*. Baltimore, 1990.

White, R. *The Middle Ground: Indians, Empires, and Republics in the Great Lakes Region, 1650–1815*. Cambridge, 1991.

Ziff, B. & P. V. Rao. *Borrowed Power. Essays on Cultural Appropriation*. New Brunswick, 1997.

IDENTITY AND SOCIAL PRACTICE

Aegean-Type Pottery in the Southern Levant

PHILIPP W. STOCKHAMMER

Abstract. Identities are mostly created in the context of social practices through a process where individuals or groups define themselves. Transculturality as an important feature of human existence is in conflict with the process of self-identification, and at the same time it offers a means for self-identification. In this article, I focus on the dialectic relationship between transcultural entanglements and processes of self-identification. I draw on four case studies from the Late Bronze Age and Early Iron Age Southern Levant of the 13th and 12th centuries BCE. My focus lies on the (non-) appropriation of Aegean-type pottery by different actors and the relevance of this pottery for the actors' identities.

INTRODUCTION[1]

In the archaeology of the Eastern Mediterranean Late Bronze and Iron Age studies on identity have focused on ethnic identity for a long time.[2] Bryan Feuer has recently reviewed the extensive discussions on this topic and ethnic identity still remains his major focus.[3] Without literary sources, however, the reconstruction of ethnic identity seems to be an impossible task. Therefore, discussions on past ethnicities should not play such a major role in archaeological discourse. When using terms like "Mycenaeans" or "Minoans", we have to be aware of the fact that these terms do not reflect past ethnic entities but are nothing else than inventions by archaeologists.[4] They should be regarded as useful only as analytical concepts.

---

1 This contribution is part of my postdoctoral research within the Cluster of Excellence "Asia and Europe in a Global Context" at Heidelberg University. I would like to thank the organizers of the conference for kindly inviting me to Copenhagen and to contribute to the publication.

2 Mac Sweeney, 'Beyond Ethnicity', 2009.

3 Feuer, 'Being Mycenaean', 2011.

4 Middleton, 'Mycenaeans, Greeks, Archaeology and Myth', 2002.

In contrast to ethnicity, other kinds of identity and processes of identity formation have not been extensively studied so far in the period and area under study. When using the term "identity," I am aware of the fact that this term can refer to both individual and collective self-identifications. However, for the discussion that follows I will concentrate on collective identities. My understanding of "collective identity" follows Alberto Melucci's inasmuch as collective identities are "an interactive and shared definition produced by several individuals (or groups at a more complex level) and concerned with the orientations of action and the field of opportunities and constraints in which the action takes place."[5] This understanding emphasizes the dynamics of identity formation, which is also the focus of the four case studies in this paper. They all shed light on groups of individuals who generate a joint non-ethnic identity by particular social practices with Aegean-type pottery.

Transculturality as an important feature of human existence is in conflict with the process of self-identification while, at the same time, transculturality offers the basis for self-identification.[6] Following Wolfgang Welsch, I define "transculturality" as the on-going process of transformation which results from intercultural contacts.[7] However, my conceptualization of "transculturality" also goes beyond Welsch's notion. In common with the Heidelberg Cluster of Excellence "Asia and Europe in a Global Context: The Dynamics of Transculturality", I believe that the term can refer to both a particular object and also to a methodological approach that understands cultures as processes and intercultural encounter as a basis of past and present human existence. Cultures – and also collective identities as well as otherness – are permanently produced and altered.

Identity cannot exist without otherness. From a psychological point of view, the definition of identity is necessary for individuals and groups and a prerequisite for social cohesion and orientation. Self-identification is inseparably connected with the differentiation between the self and the other, with inclusion and exclusion. This distinction and the self-identification connected therewith have to be conceptualized as on-going processes and not as single events. The borderline between the self and the other is continuously re-defined. This is due to the fact that individuals continuously encounter something new and have to decide whether they want to appropriate the new and thereby also transform their own identity or if they want to re-define their identity by the rejection of the other.

[5] Melucci, 'The Process of Collective Identity', 1995, p. 44.
[6] Enwezor, 'Introduction. Travel Notes', 1997.
[7] Welsch, 'Transculturality – the Puzzling Form of Cultures Today', 1999.

There is no doubt that the encounter with foreign objects plays a crucial role in the definition and transformation of identities. I am aware of the fact that foreignness is not a permanent attribute of an object or a social practice. The perception of foreignness and otherness need not endure long before the object or practice is integrated into the own objects and practices. Hans P. Hahn describes this process aptly: "Perception in this very moment is not a mere recognition of object features, but a mutual exchange of human and object. During the very first moment, things are not thought, but felt."[8] Therefore, otherness is not a state, but most often only a moment of individual, emotional perception. Consequently, its analysis perhaps requires an over-individual and uniform perception.[9]

In many cases, identities are only created in the context of social practices with the objects. Jürgen Straub notes that the processual, constructed and unstable character of identity is in clear opposition to the individual's/group's claim to demonstrate continuing, stable and exclusive essentials with their identity.[10]

In the discussion that follows, I shall focus my analysis on the appropriation of pottery of Aegean type in the Late Bronze Age and Early Iron Age Levant of the 13th and 12th centuries BCE.[11] I choose this case study in order to shed light on the very different reactions of the different actors to their encounter with the foreign pottery and to analyse the role of social identities for the (non-)appropriation of Aegean-type pottery. In my contribution, I shall focus on four different phenomena:

1. Identity by non-appropriation
2. Identity by transculturality
3. Identity by migration
4. Identity by opposition.

1. Identity by Non-Appropriation: Elite Contexts

During the 14th and 13th centuries BCE large quantities of fine ware pottery, produced in workshops in the north-eastern Peloponnese on the Greek mainland, were brought to the Southern Levant. So far, current research is dominated by the idea that this attractive pottery of foreign origin was primarily acquired by local Levantine elites, who then could

---

[8] Hahn, *Materielle Kultur*, 2005, p. 30.

[9] Cf. Stockhammer, *Kontinuität und Wandel*, 2008, p. 273.

[10] Straub, 'Identität', 2004.

[11] As questions of origin and places of production will not be discussed further here, I will use the term "pottery of Aegean-type" instead of "Mycenaean pottery." In my definition, Aegean-type pottery comprises all vessels produced in a Mycenaean or Minoan (Cretan) tradition of forming – irrespective of where such vessels were actually produced.

enforce their status position and social identity by the conspicuous consumption of these vessels.[12] This hypothesis is based on the argument that a particularly large number of Aegean-type sherds were found during the excavations of Late Bronze Age palaces in the Southern Levant, especially in Hazor and Megiddo (Fig. 1).[13]

During the recent excavations of the Late Bronze Age "Royal Precinct/Ceremonial Palace" on the Upper Tell of Hazor, 781 completely preserved vessels were found together with a considerable number of exceptional small finds. This singular *in situ* context results from the violent destruction of the structure in the 13th century BCE.[14] There is no doubt that this complex provides a unique insight into the role of material culture within elite rituals and is representative of elite ritual performances in Late Bronze Age Hazor. Despite this exceptionally well-preserved context, not one Aegean type vessel has been found complete or at least as multiple sherds.[15] A very similar situation is documented in Megiddo, where single sherds of Aegean type vessels were found in the Late Bronze Age palace, but complete vessels are missing.[16] During the excavation of the Megiddo palace in 1948, the excavator, Gordon Loud, described how one of the Aegean type sherds was found inside a mud brick used in the construction of the palace.[17] This should have long been taken as a cautionary tale when drawing conclusions from the Aegean-type sherd material from the building. However, complete vessels are documented from non-palatial residential contexts at both sites. There is no doubt that the Aegean-type sherds from the palaces in Hazor and Megiddo were relocated by being within mud bricks. Therefore, those sherds cannot be taken as evidence for the appropriation of Aegean-type

[12] Steel, 'Consuming Passions', 2002; van Wijngaarden, *Use and Appreciation of Mycenaean Pottery*, 2002, pp. 95–96; Yasur-Landau, 'Old Wine in New Vessels', 2005, p. 176; Zuckerman, 'Dating the Destruction of Canaanite Hazor without Mycenaean Pottery?', 2007, p. 626; Josephson Hesse, *Contacts and Trade at Late Bronze Age Hazor*, 2008, pp. 135, 144, 202, 211.

[13] Leonard & Cline, 'The Aegean Pottery at Megiddo', 1998.

[14] Zuckerman, 'Slaying Oxen and Killing Sheep, Eating Flesh and Drinking Wine', 2007; Zuckerman, 'Fit for a (not-quite-so-great) King', 2008; Zuckermann, pers. comm.

[15] Altogether, 90 single Aegean type sherds were discovered. Most of the sherds were very fragmented and badly worn and they were all clearly found in a secondary context, often in Iron Age layers (Zuckerman, 'Dating the Destruction of Canaanite Hazor without Mycenaean Pottery?', 2007, pp. 623, 624 fig. 2, 626; Josephson Hesse, *Contacts and Trade at Late Bronze Age Hazor*, 2008, pp. 135, 144, 202, 211).

[16] Leonard & Cline, 'The Aegean Pottery at Megiddo', 1998, p. 9 fig. 4, 16. However, only a few complete Canaanite and Cypriot vessels were discovered in the palace so that the evidence is less significant than that from Hazor.

[17] Loud, *Megiddo*, II, 1948, pl. 137, 5. See also Leonard & Cline, 'The Aegean Pottery at Megiddo', 1998, pp. 5–6, 21 No. 5.

vessels by the local elites. With my contextual analysis I was able to demonstrate that the local elites defined their social identity by the almost exclusive use of locally made, Canaanite-type pottery shapes and not with the help of imported vessels.[18]

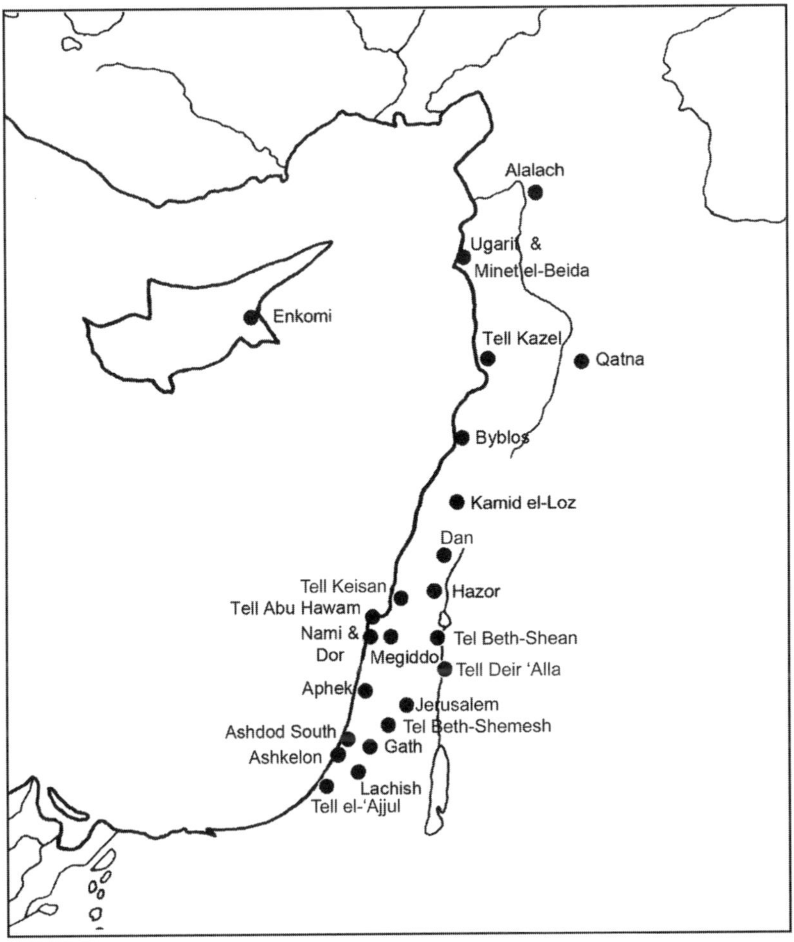

Figure 1. The Levant in the late 2nd millennium BCE (after Fischer, *Ägyptische und ägyptisierende Elfenbeine aus Megiddo und Lachish. Inschriftenfunde, Flaschen, Löffel*, 2007, pl. 1).

[18] Stockhammer, 'Entangled Potter', 2012; Stockhammer, *Materielle Verflechtungen*, 2013.

However, if it was not the elite, then which element of society was acquiring Aegean type pottery and which identity groups decided to appropriate those vessels in Hazor and Megiddo? I would like to shed further light on the relevant actors by concentrating only on a certain vessel shape, i.e. the amphoroid krater. Amphoroid kraters are large, open vessels and – in contrast to other Aegean-type krater shapes – were almost exclusively produced for the export to Cyprus and to the Levant.

There are only a very small number of meaningful *in situ* contexts with amphoroid kraters in the Levant. One of them is room 1817 in Area CC in Megiddo, where one largely preserved amphoroid krater was found together with other complete vessels on the floor. Room 1817 is part of an inconspicuous house within the settlement of Stratum VIIA.[19] In addition to the aforementioned amphoroid krater, fragments of a second krater were found in the room – unfortunately not enough to postulate a second krater *in situ* – together with a large number of other finds but with no other feasting dishes other than the krater. The findings from the room excavated by Gordon Loud include, for instance, a storage amphora, a so-called cup-and-saucer vessel, a bowl made of basalt, a clay wall bracket of Cypriot type and many small finds like spindle whorls, pendants of different material, rings, a human figurine etc.[20] As Loud only documented those ceramic vessels that were completely or largely preserved or of foreign origin, it is improbable that other feasting dishes were kept in the same room together with the kraters. This evidence corresponds with the result of my quantitative analysis of Aegean-type kraters and drinking vessels in southern Levantine settlements:[21] only ten amphoroid kraters and only five Aegean-type drinking vessels were found in the settlement at Megiddo. In Tell es-Sâfī/Gath, I identified six amphoroid kraters and not a single Aegean-type drinking vessel from the excavations in 1996–2005 and 2010. From Aphek, nine kraters and seven other Aegean-type feasting vessels are known; from Hazor ten kraters and ten other feasting vessels of Aegean type; and from Lachish thirteen kraters, sixteen cups and a kylix.[22] I do not want to exclude the possibility

[19] Room 1817 comprises Locus 1817 and Locus W=1817, which is the area west of Locus 1817. Locus 1817 is the southeastern edge of a room from which only part of the eastern and southern wall was preserved (Loud, *Megiddo*, II, 1948, fig. 409). To judge from Loud's architectural plan, it seems very reasonable to consider W=1817 as the western part of the room 1817 therefore consisting of Loci 1817 and W=1817.

[20] Loud, *Megiddo*, II, 1948, 155, pl. 70, 15; pl. 140, 7–17; pl. 152, 198; pl. 158, 198; pl. 172, 31; pl. 200, 1; pl. 214, 96–97; pl. 224, 12; pl. 242, 14; pl. 249, 2. Unfortunately, Loud illustrates only a small percentage of the registered finds in his publication.

[21] Stockhammer, *Materielle Verflechtungen*, 2013.

[22] Hankey, French, Sherratt, and Magrill, 'The Aegean Pottery', 2004; Guzowska & Yasur-Landau, 'Mycenaean Pottery', 2009; Zuckerman, pers. comm.

that the drinking vessels of Aegean type at these sites were never used with the respective kraters. However, the quantitative relationship between the kraters and the drinking vessels differs so markedly from the one observed in for the Aegean – i.e. the combination of about ten drinking vessels with one krater[23] – suggests that Levantine practices of feasting with Aegean-type pottery differed from those in the Aegean. This ratio might also have been valid for the Northern Levant, as five kraters but not a single drinking vessel of Aegean-type were found under the thirty-three examples of Aegean type found in the Temple of Rhytons in Ugarit.[24] In the Aegean, we have clear indications that Mycenaean drinkers sat in pairs opposite each other drinking from pairs of nearly identical drinking vessels, specifically kylikes.[25] The few depictions of drinking practices of the Canaanite elite of the 13th and 12th centuries BCE, especially the images of drinking male rulers on ivories found in the palace of Megiddo, clearly indicate the consumption of wine from metal bowls as is also attested in the iconography of contemporaneous Egyptian rulers.[26] The use of shallow metal drinking bowls by the local elites is further evidenced by their frequent occurrence as grave goods in elite burials.[27]

As I have argued above, actors with high status stopped using Aegean-type pottery from the late fourteenth century BCE onwards. Thus, the aforementioned images cannot be used for illustrating the practices with Aegean-type pottery. They only show us that high status individuals also used krater-like vessels and that those vessels were placed in stands. Moreover, following the written sources, the consumption of wine was restricted to certain groups of high status individuals within society. However, as wine consumption was limited to the elite and these actors did not use Aegean-type pottery, which actors were willing to integrate the amphoroid kraters into their social practices? More illuminating for the practices with Aegean-type kraters are the depiction of a Canaanite

---

23 Podzuweit, *Studien zur spätmykenischen Keramik*, 2007, p. 193; Stockhammer, *Kontinuität und Wandel*, 2008, pp. 135, 169, 306, 314, 320, 325.

24 Mallet, 'Le Temple aux Rhytons', 1987; van Wijngaarden, *Use and Appreciation of Mycenaean Pottery*, 2002, pp. 60–62.

25 Wright, 'A Survey of Evidence for Feasting in Mycenaean Society', 2004; Stockhammer, *Kontinuität und Wandel*, 2008, pp. 135, 169, 306, 314, 320, 325. The unique preservation of a Mycenaean feast in the archaeological evidence of Room 8/00 of the Northeastern Lower Town of Tiryns documents the use of two pairs of kylikes and one pair of cups together with one krater (Stockhammer, *Kontinuität und Wandel*, 2008, pp. 163, 306, fig. 90, pls. 49:1194–1195, 51:1201C-F) at one feasting event.

26 Loud, *The Megiddo Ivories*, 1939, pl. 4, 2; 32, 160.

27 Yasur-Landau, 'Old Wine in New Vessels', 2005.

mercenary on a stela from Tell el-Amarna from the 14th century BCE[28] and the great number of finds of strainer tips and also, sometimes, tube elbows for drinking straws, e.g. from Tell el-Amarna and the shipwreck from Ulu Burun (Fig. 2).[29] The average people – be they possible traders or migrants in Megiddo or the fishermen in Ashdod South (in whose houses the Aegean-type kraters were found) – obviously drank beer with straws from huge vessels that were placed in the centre of a round of drinkers.[30] In most cases, kraters of Canaanite shape were most probably used for this kind of Canaanite feasting practice, as those vessels are so frequently encountered in Late Bronze Age contexts.[31] Because of the affordances of their shape, Aegean-type kraters could easily be integrated into this Levantine practice of drinking as well. Thus, there is considerable evidence that indicates a very particular use of Aegean-type kraters in the Southern Levant that differs markedly from what the Greek producers had originally envisaged to be their function.[32] Whereas the Canaanite-type kraters were often decorated with pictorial motifs,[33] but

[28] Spiegelberg & Erman, 'Grabstein eines syrischen Söldners', 1898.

[29] Griffith, 'A Drinking Siphon from Tell el-ʿAmarnah', 1926; Maeir & Garfinkel, 'Bone and Metal Straw-Tip Beer-Strainers', 1992; Simon, 'Râpes, siphons ou filtres pour pailles', 1992; Weisgerber, 'Biertrinker an Bord?', 2005; Maeir, 'The Bone Beverage Strainers', 2007. There are a great number of images depicting drinking with straws in the Near Eastern and Egyptian art of the third and second millennium BCE, especially in the glyptic of the third millennium BCE (Selz, *Die Bankettszene. Entwicklung eines 'überzeitlichen' Bildmotivs*, 1983; Homan & Ebeling, 'Baking and Brewing Beer in the Israelite Household', 2008; McGovern, *Uncorking the Past*, 2009, pp. 97–100).

[30] The Greek author Xenophon (Anabasis, IV, 5, 26) gives us an ethnohistorical description of the custom of drinking beer with straws by farmers in the Armenian mountains (Spiegelberg & Erman, 'Grabstein eines syrischen Söldners', 1898, p. 128). Even today, drinking beer with straws from huge crater-like vessels is a common habit in East Africa and Vietnam (Karp, 'Beer Drinking and Social Experience in an African Society', 1980; Homan, 'Beer and Its Drinkers', 2004, p. 86; Dietler & Herbich, 'Liquid Material Culture', 2006; Haaland, 'Porridge and Pot, Bread and Oven', 2007).

[31] Amiran, *Ancient Pottery of the Holy Land*, 1970, pp. 132–135 with pl. 41.

[32] Unfortunately, it is not possible to verify this hypothesis with scientific analysis so far. The detection of beer with residue analysis is much more difficult than that of wine. Moreover, such analyses are completely missing for amphoroid kraters found at the Southern Levant and no strainers or elbow tubes have been found inside Aegean-type kraters at the Levant so far. Ethnographic data from modern day Eastern Africa indicates that most drinking straws for beer are used without a strainer or elbow tube (Dietler & Herbich, 'Liquid Material Culture', 2006). However, nothing is preserved from such straws in an archaeological context. Another possibility for straining beer before drinking is the use of a strainer jug. Such vessels are frequently known from Levant and Egypt in the Late Bronze and Early Iron Age (Homan, 'Beer and Its Drinkers', 2004, p. 92; Homan & Ebeling, 'Baking and Brewing Beer', 2008, pp. 55–56).

[33] Choi, *Decoding Canaanite Pottery Paintings*, 2008.

Figure 2. Above: siphon and tube elbow from a drinking straw from Tell el-Amarna (with kind permission of the British Museum, London). Below: Depiction of a Canaanite mercenary on a limestone stele from Tell el-Amarna (with kind permission of the Staatliche Museen Preußischer Kulturbesitz; © Sandra Steiß, Ägyptisches Museum und Papyrussammlung, Berlin).

Figure 3. Amphoroid krater of Aegean-type (with kind permission of the British Museum, London).

hardly any scenic depictions, Aegean-type amphoroid kraters were beautifully painted with chariot scenes, bulls, or fantastic beings (Fig. 3).[34] The decorative scenes on these vessels were definitely perceived by the participants of the feast; they might have been topics of discussions and could have exerted some influence on narration during feasting.

2. Identity by Transculturality: The Nami Cemetery

In this section, I shall focus on a small group of actors out of the multitude of social groups who were willing to appropriate Aegean-type pottery. These actors lived at the small harbour site of Nami on the Carmel Coast in the north of the modern state of Israel. Nami is one of a number of

[34] Vermeule & Karageorghis, *Mycenaean Pictorial Vase Painting*, 1982.

harbour places that were founded at the southern Levantine coast in the late 13th century BCE and which all ceased to exist only 50 to 70 years later. Sites with a similar character were established at Sarepta in modern Lebanon, Nami and Dor at the Carmel Coast and Ashdod South to the very south of the Levant. I have subsumed these harbour places and the social phenomena of cultural interaction connected with these sites as the "Nami" Horizon.[35]

The settlement and cemetery of Nami are situated ca. 15 km south of modern Haifa at the Carmel Coast. The Tell Settlement is situated on a peninsula, and the contemporaneous necropolis Nami East on the adjacent coast. In the years 1986 to 1989, a team of the Centre for Maritime Studies and the Archaeological Institute of Haifa University under the direction of Michal Artzy excavated in three areas on the tell (areas G, D, D1) and in one area (area O) in Nami East.[36] So far, none of the areas have been published in a final version. Michal Artzy has published a great number of preliminary reports, which concentrate mostly on the historic contextualization.[37] Rich finds from the settlement of the late 13th and early 12th centuries BCE were encountered in the areas G and D1 on the Tell and in the cemetery of Nami East.

The material culture of Nami as well as other harbour sites of this horizon can be identified as transcultural from an etic perspective.[38] Only a small proportion of the Aegean-type pottery from the site was still produced in the Aegean – as it has been the usual case until the middle of the 13th century BCE. The majority of vessels was produced on Cyprus or in the Southern Levant. However, the transcultural character of the site becomes most obvious, when taking social practices into consideration, especially in the context of the sanctuary in area G and the cemetery in Nami East.

Most interesting is the local imitation of a conical cup of Cretan type that was found together with pumice within the sanctuary. Both the shape of the cup as well as the cultic practice of depositing pumice within such

---

35 Stockhammer, 'The "Aegean-type" pottery', in press.

36 Artzy, 'Nami Land and Sea Project 1985–1988', 1990.

37 Artzy, 'Pomegranate Sceptres and Incense Stand', 1990; Artzy, 'Nami Land and Sea Project 1985–1988', 1990; Artzy, 'Nami Land and Sea Project, 1989', 1991; Artzy, 'Conical Cups and Pumice', 1991; Artzy, 'Tel Nami, un grand port à l'âge du Bronze', 1992; Artzy, 'Tel Nami', 1993; Artzy, 'Incense, Camels and Collared Rim Jars', 1994; Artzy, 'Nami', 1995; Artzy, 'Nomads of the Sea', 1997; Artzy, 'Routes, Trade, Boats and "Nomads of the Sea"', 1998; Artzy, 'The Carmel Coast during the Second Part of the Late Bronze Age', 2006; Artzy & Zagorski, 'Cypriote "Mycenaean" IIIB Imported to the Levant', 2012. I want to thank Michal Artzy for kindly showing me all relevant findings from the site and for supporting me with a lot of so-far unpublished information.

38 Stockhammer, *Materielle Verflechtungen*, 2013.

cups clearly relate to Crete, where deposits of pumice within conical cups have been found within several sanctuaries; outside Crete, this practice is only known from Nami.[39]

At the site of the cemetery was found an Aegean-type krater with horizontal handles of Cypriot production (Fig. 4).[40] Artzy describes that the sherds were found around one of the richest burials and within several later burial pits indicating that the krater was used in the context of social practices during or after the funeral. Within the krater near the base, Artzy was able to identify traces of bronze, which she interprets as an indication for the placement of a bronze bowl within the krater.[41] In Artzy's view, the krater was very probably used for burning incense during funerary or post-funerary ceremonies. This particular use of Aegean-type vessels – mostly kylikes or stemmed bowls – for the burning of hallucinogenic substances can also be shown for other Late Bronze Age harbour sites as well as cemeteries in the Southern Levant.[42]

The ceramic finds from the graves mostly comprise stirrup-jars (Fig. 5) and alabastra of Aegean-type each of which look surprisingly uniform in their shape, fabric and decoration. Whereas the stirrup-jars seem to have been mostly produced on Cyprus, the alabastra were most probably produced in the Southern Levant itself.[43]

In addition to the pottery, rich finds of bronze and precious metal were found in the sanctuary and the necropolis. For many of these objects – e.g. a gold pendant of Southern Levantine type with the depiction of a goddess in a northern Syrian style[44] – a place of production cannot be identified on the basis of stylistic analysis and they can be attributed to what Marian Feldman calls the "International Style" of the Late Bronze Age.[45]

If one may derive past social identities of the people buried in the Nami cemetery from the combination of the grave goods, it is the evidence of the deceased person's multifaceted networks of interaction that come through rather than references to local material culture of the hinterland of the site. As I have argued above, the southern Levantine elite of the 13th century BCE clearly preferred Canaanite-type material culture.

---

[39] Artzy, 'Conical Cups and Pumice', 1991.

[40] Artzy, 'The Carmel Coast during the Second Part of the Late Bronze Age', 2006, pp. 52, 53 fig. 6, 13.

[41] Artzy, 'Nami', 1995, pp. 28–29.

[42] Stockhammer, 'Performing the Practice Turn in Archaeology', 2012, pp. 26–31.

[43] Artzy & Zagorski, 'Cypriote "Mycenaean" IIIB Imported to the Levant', 2012.

[44] Artzy, 'Incense, Camels and Collared Rim Jars', 1994, p. 125 fig. 4.

[45] Feldman, *Diplomacy by Design. Luxury Arts and an 'International Style'*, 2006.

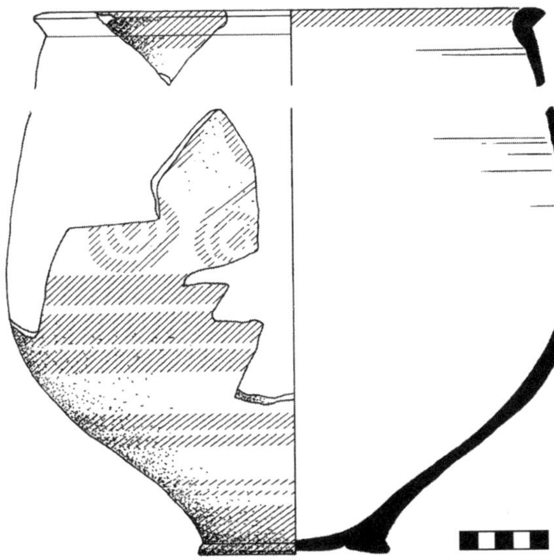

Figure 4. Nami East, Krater with horizontal handles of Aegean-type (with kind permission of Michal Artzy; drawing by Ragna Stidsing).

Figure 5. Nami East, Stirrup-jars of Aegean-type (with kind permission of Michal Artzy; drawing by Ragna Stidsing).

They considered transculturality to be in conflict with their identity. The inhabitants of Nami, however, were most probably mariners and traders and thus highly mobile actors who permanently encountered otherness. These actors obviously wished to demonstrate their intercultural networks and competences also after their death. For them, transculturality offered a basis for self-identification.

3. IDENTITY BY MIGRATION: PHILISTINE POTTERY

As a third example, I would like to discuss the pottery of the so-called Philistine settlements that emerged in the early 12th century BCE in the Southern Levant. The appearance of the Philistines has long been taken as a marker for the end of the Late Bronze Age and the beginning of the Early Iron Age in this area. For a long time, the emergence of these settlements has been considered to be one of the clearest archaeological indications for mass migration.[46] These hypotheses are based on the "deep change" of the material culture within the settlements Tel Miqne/Ekron, Ashdod, Ashkelon, Tell es-Safi/Gath and Gaza in the early 12th century after the supposed arrival of the new population. This change of material culture and social practices cannot sufficiently be explained with the integration of foreign influences and without any population movement. Most prominent novelties in the Philistine settlements are hearths with substructures made out of sherds or pebbles and cooking pots with a flat base that were set at the side of the hearth's fire. In contrast, the Late Bronze Age Canaanite-type round-bottomed cooking pots were set directly over differently constructed fireplaces. New shapes of loom-weights indicate a change of textile production technologies and ceramic idols of Aegean derivation and the sudden start of a large-scale consumption of pork are further indications. Pork had already been consumed in the Late Bronze Age Levant, however only in very small quantity. The most prominent feature of the Philistine settlements, however, has always been the large amount of fine ware pottery of Aegean-type which was locally produced and where their spectrum of shapes clearly differs from what had been imported from the Aegean during the 13th century BCE. These new ceramic vessel types were also considered to indicate new ways of food consumption and feasting practices.[47]

In my view, there is no doubt that migration took place at the beginning of the 12th century and that actors who were rooted in Aegean-type social practices and lifeworlds moved to the Southern Levant. In the following, however, I would like to demonstrate that Philistine material culture cannot be taken as a mirror of the Late Bronze Age Aegean, but has instead to be acknowledged as a complex entanglement of Aegean and Canaanite traditions. This process of intercultural entanglement is the

---

[46] For a recent overview of the long-term discussions about the Philistines, their origin and their material culture: Yasur-Landau, *The Philistines and Aegean Migration*, 2010.

[47] See Yasur-Landau, *The Philistines and Aegean Migration*, 2010 with further references.

result of the transformative potential of a migrant community, as it can still be observed nowadays.[48]

Assaf Yasur-Landau has recently pointed out that actors rooted in Canaanite-type material culture made an important contribution to what we perceive as Philistine.[49] He demonstrated that Aegean-type and Canaanite-type material objects and practices coexisted not only within one and the same Philistine settlement, but also within the same household. Cooking pots of different shapes and from different traditions were used side by side, and round-bottomed Canaanite-type cooking pots that replaced Aegean-type tripod cooking pots could be placed over the centre of the fireplace in the same manner as their counterparts.

Moreover, Philistine fine ware pottery has always been perceived as a local imitation of a foreign, Aegean-type set of dishes in order to enable the migrants to continue their traditional practices of eating and drinking. Therefore, this pottery has been intensely studied with regard to the existing range of shapes and motifs[50] as well as their possible non-Levantine region(s) of origin.[51] However, although of major importance for the whole argument, the social practices connected with the use of these vessels have not found equal interest among archaeologists. Only recently have scholars demonstrated the integration of Canaanite stylistic elements in the shaping and painting of the Philistine fine ware pottery already since its beginning, or they have enforced the overall transcultural character of the Philistine culture thereby questioning the dominating narrative.[52]

In my view, it is time to modify our perspective on the Philistine fine ware pottery. I regard this pottery and the social practices connected with it, as the result of cultural encounters and, therefore, as a creative and highly dynamic phenomenon.

On the basis of the vast amount of excavated, documented and published Philistine, Mycenaean and Canaanite pottery, I make the assumption that the quantity of a certain shape of feasting vessel in the archaeological record is 1) very roughly representative for the quantitative relationship between the different shapes in the prehistoric

---

48 Bailey, 'Turning Transnational', 2001; Bhabha, *The Location of Culture,* 2007.

49 Yasur-Landau, 'The Role of the Canaanite Population', 2012.

50 For an overview: Dothan & Zukerman, 'A Preliminary Study of the Mycenaean III C:1 Pottery Assemblages', 2004.

51 For an overview: Killebrew, *Biblical Peoples and Ethnicity*, 2005.

52 Mountjoy, 'A Note on the Mixed Origins of Some Philistine Pottery', 2010. Hitchcock, '"Transculturalism" as a Model for Examining Migration to Cyprus and Philistia', 2011.

households and 2) that a high number of vessels of a certain shape indicates its more frequent use in daily practices.[53]

As already mentioned, the most common feasting dish in Mycenaean style comprised one krater for mixing water and wine and several pairs of nearly identical kylikes used for drinking. Although other types of drinking vessels were used beside the kylikes, the latter remained the most prominent drinking vessel shape until the middle of the 12th century BCE.[54] Shallow bowls and deep bowls were also used in great numbers – most probably for eating, although I do not want to exclude that they were also sometimes used for drinking some more liquid (soup-like?) food.

Within the Canaanite ceramic repertoire, obvious drinking vessels are surprisingly rare in the archaeological evidence. The very small number of chalices and stemmed bowls that have long been used to fill this gap were in fact used as incense burners and not drinking vessels.[55] There is no doubt that the inhabitants of the Southern Levant drank beverages, but they did not use a specific shape as drinking vessel. Instead, they used straws to drink from various vessels and bowls that could be used for both eating and drinking. This is an interesting difference when compared to the apparently more specified functions of the feasting vessels in the Mycenaean pottery.

As is the case in Mycenaean Greece, the Philistine fine ware repertoire comprises a large number of shallow carinated bowls and deep bowls as well as a certain number of kraters.[56] Kylikes, however, are almost completely missing in the Philistine settlements – as are the cups and the mugs.[57] This is in clear contrast to the range of Aegean-type pottery shapes outside Philistia. As the migrants did not stop drinking after arriving at the Southern Levant, they obviously changed their drinking practices. I would like to explain this marked difference between Aegean-type and Philistine ceramic feasting assemblages by suggesting that the Philistines used their bowls for eating and drinking in a similar way as the local Canaanite population in the Southern Levant, who had done so long before the arrival of the migrants.

---

[53] I am aware of the fact that the number of sherds of a certain vessel shape in the archaeological record is the result of a highly complex process of pre- and post-vessel breakage practices with the object, ranging from the size of the vessel and the frequency of its prehistoric use to its identifiability by the archaeologist (cf. Stockhammer, *Kontinuität und Wandel*, 2008, pp. 73–76, 312–313).

[54] Stockhammer, 'From Hybridity to Entanglement' 2013, pp. 19-21 with n. 8.

[55] Stockhammer, 'Performing the Practice Turn in Archaeology', 2012, pp. 26–31.

[56] Dothan & Zukerman, 'A Preliminary Study of the Mycenaean III C:1 Pottery Assemblages', 2004, pp. 7–16.

[57] Dothan & Zukerman, 'A Preliminary Study of the Mycenaean III C:1 Pottery Assemblages', 2004, p. 22.

The Philistine deep bowls also exhibit an interesting difference in vessel size in relation to their Aegean counterparts. Deep bowls with less than 12 cm rim diameter are an exceptional rarity in the Aegean and the rim diameter almost always ranges between 12 and 18 cm with 14 to 16 cm as the most common size.[58] In Mycenaean Greece, rim fragments with deep bowl-type lips and a diameter of less than 12 cm can quite consistently be attributed to deep cups. In the Philistine settlements, however, a surprisingly high number of very small deep bowls has been found, especially at Ashdod, with only 7 to 9 cm as rim diameter.[59] The average rim diameter for deep bowls in the Philistine inventories reaches only 12 to 14 cm.[60] This might be interpreted that especially the small deep bowls were used as drinking vessels as their rim diameters fit very well to those measured for cups and carinated kylikes in the Aegean.[61]

The abandonment of the differentiation between certain vessel shapes for eating and drinking in Philistine fine ware pottery can best be explained as the result of the encounter with local Canaanite practices of consumption that triggered a process of appropriation of these practices, but which was most interestingly not accompanied by the appropriation of Canaanite vessel shapes. In my view, the Philistine ceramic feasting assemblage may be interpreted as the translation of Canaanite practices into the stylistic vocabulary of the Aegean-type pottery.

The Philistines obviously saw no need to completely reject the foreign practices they encountered in their new homeland. The integration of foreign objects and practices into their daily practices, lifeworlds and, therefore, also identities was not in contrast to their identity as migrants from a distant place or their ethnic identity, if something like a Philistine ethnic identity ever existed.

4. Identity by Opposition: Tel Beth-Shemesh

As a last example, I would like to discuss the possibility to shape one's identity by deliberately opposing the material culture and social practices of other identity groups. This can easily been done by confronting the aforementioned Philistine settlements with their Canaanite surroundings. There, the material culture and connected social practices show highly interesting phenomena of the Canaanite population's intentional

[58] E.g. Stockhammer, *Kontinuität und Wandel*, 2008, fig. 80:e, 80:f (for early 12th century Tiryns).
[59] Dothan & Zukerman, 'A Preliminary Study of the Mycenaean III C:1 Pottery Assemblages', 2004, pp. 8, 10 fig. 6, 11 tab. 4.
[60] Dothan & Zukerman, 'A Preliminary Study of the Mycenaean III C:1 Pottery Assemblages', 2004, p. 8.
[61] Stockhammer, *Kontinuität und Wandel*, 2008, fig. 82.

opposition towards the migrants. This becomes most evident in Tel Beth-Shemesh, one of the most important Canaanite settlements in the Shepelah, the hill country between the coastal plain and the Judean Mountains (Fig. 6).

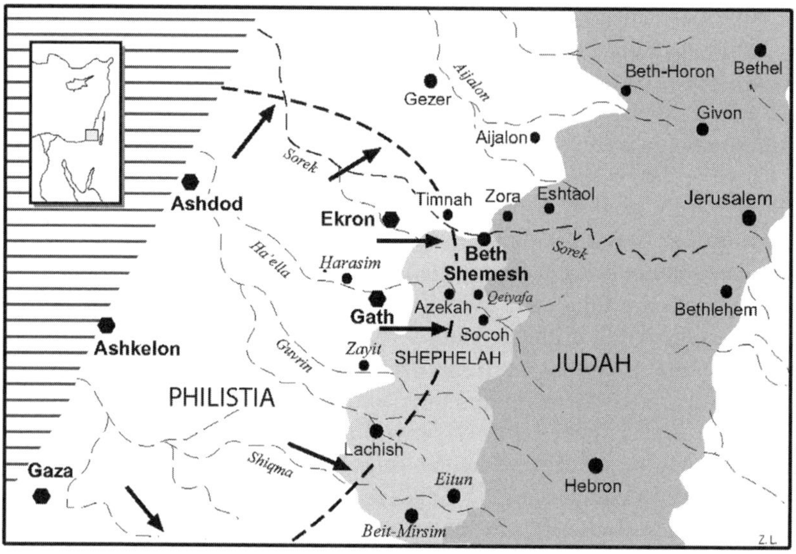

Figure 6. Philistia and surrounding areas in the 12th century BCE (after Bunimovitz & Lederman, 'Canaanite Resistance: The Philistines and Beth-Shemesh – A Case Study from Iron Age I', 2011, p. 38 fig. 1; with kind permission of Shlomo Bunimovitz and Zvi Lederman).

The first excavations at Tel Beth-Shemesh took place under Duncan Mackenzie for the British Palestine Exploration Fund in the years 1911 and 1912. Further, large-scale excavations were committed by an expedition of the Haverford College under the direction of Elihu Grant in the years 1928 to 1933.[62] Since 1990, the tell has been continuously excavated by a team from Tel Aviv University under the direction of Shlomo Bunimovitz and Zvi Lederman.[63]

Although there is only a distance of ca. 12 km between the large Canaanite-type settlement of Tel Beth-Shemesh and the Philistine-type

[62] Grant, *Beth Shemesh (Palestine)*, 1929; Grant & Wright, *Ain Shems Excavations (Palestine) V*, 1939.

[63] For the history of research cf. Bunimovitz & Lederman, 'Beth Shemesh', 1997, pp. 42–43; Bunimovitz & Lederman, 'The Archaeology of Border Communities', 2009, pp. 115–120; Bunimovitz & Lederman, 'Canaanite Resistance', 2011, pp. 37–41.

settlement of Tel Miqne/Ekron, not a single sherd of the early Philistine fine ware pottery was found at Tel Beth-Shemesh. This pottery – called Philistine I or Philistine Monochrome – characterizes the early Philistine cultural layers at Tel Miqne/Ekron. Thus, the lack of this ware at the contemporaneous and nearby Tel Beth-Shemesh came as a surprise in the beginning. Aegean-type pottery – so-called Philistine II (or Philistine Bichrome) pottery – dominates the ceramic inventories from the Philistine settlements in the late 12th and 11th century BCE: 41 % of the pottery from Tel Miqne/Ekron, 47 % in Ashdod, and 31 % in Ashkelon can be attributed to this ware. The Philistine settlement at Timnah – with a share of 34 % of Philistine pottery – is only 7 km away from Tel Beth-Shemesh, where only 5.3 % of the ceramic inventory could be identified as Philistine II pottery.[64]

Even more impressive are the changes in the consumption of pork from the Late Bronze Age to the Early Iron Age and within and outside the Philistia. One of the most characteristic features of the Philistine settlements is the large quantity of pig bones in the animal bone inventory, which indicates the extensive consumption of pork. Pork was also consumed during the Late Bronze Age in the Shepelah and the Judean Mountains – although only in small scale. At the moment of the foundation of the Philistine settlements, the consumption of pork meat suddenly stopped in the Canaanite settlements in the surrounding area.[65]

There is no doubt that the sudden refusal of pork meat has to be interpreted as an intentional action of opposition to the migrant communities nearby.[66] These actors did not only define their identity by the non-appropriation of Philistine-type pottery, but also by the conscious change of their consumption practices. The encounter with the Philistines forced the neighbouring communities to assert their own Canaanite traditions and to oppose this Canaanite-type way of living to the social world of the migrants.[67]

---

[64] Bunimovitz & Lederman, 'A Border Case', 2008, p. 24; Bunimovitz & Lederman, 'Canaanite Resistance', 2011, pp. 42–44, 44 fig. 7.

[65] Bunimovitz & Lederman, 'A Border Case', 2008, p. 25; Bunimovitz & Lederman, 'Canaanite Resistance', 2011, pp. 44–45, 45 fig. 8.

[66] The relevance of pork consumption as possible marker of group identities was particularly emphasized by Hesse 'Pig Lovers and Pig Haters', 1990 and Hesse & Wapnish, 'Can Pig Remains Be Used for Ethnic Diagnosis', 1997.

[67] Bunimovitz & Lederman, 'A Border Case', 2008; Bunimovitz & Lederman, 'Canaanite Resistance', 2011.

SUMMARY

The four case studies just presented served to demonstrate the necessity of concentrating on the process of formation of collective (and non-ethnic) identities and the active role played by objects within these processes. This formative power of objects in processes of self-identification is especially obvious when it comes to the (non-) appropriation of foreign objects.

The first case study showed that high status individuals in the Late Bronze Age Southern Levant defined their identity also by rejecting pottery of foreign type in their daily practices. At the same time, this pottery found the interest of the average population living in the same settlements. They appropriated the Aegean-type vessels by attributing them with meanings and functions that differed from those in the Aegean and thus translated the foreign objects into their own social worlds. Secondly, I discussed the harbour site of Nami, where the local actors defined their identities through the intercultural networks in which they were involved as sailors and merchants. For them, transculturality was not in opposition to their identity formation, but the basis thereof. In the case of the Philistia, new social practices and identities were created within the migrant community after the encounter with foreign people. The contemporaneous Canaanite communities, however, enforced their identity by rejecting the material culture of the Philistines and by changing their own consumption practices. The conclusions just presented largely rely on ceramic findings and the connected processes of (non-)appropriation, which enable us to gain insights into past creations of identities and ultimately also perceptions of social worlds.

All four case studies demonstrate the importance of (non-) appropriation of Aegean-type pottery for certain groups of individuals in their processes of constructing and enforcing collective identities. As these identities were produced and continuously re-affirmed by social practices with objects, these objects have the power to shape collective identities.

BIBLIOGRAPHY

Amiran, R. *Ancient Pottery of the Holy Land: From Its Beginnings in the Neolithic Period to the End of the Iron Age*. Jerusalem, 1970.

Artzy, M. 'Pomegranate Sceptres and Incense Stand with Pomegranates Found in Priest's Grave.' *Biblical Archaeology Review* 16, 1 (1990), pp. 48–51.

– 'Nami Land and Sea Project 1985–1988.' *Israel Exploration Journal* 40 (1990), pp. 73–76.

– 'Nami Land and Sea Project, 1989.' *Israel Exploration Journal* 41 (1991), pp. 194–197.
– 'Conical Cups and Pumice: Aegean Cult at Tel Nami, Israel.' R. Laffineur & L. Basch (eds.), *Thalassa: L'Égée préhistorique et la mer. Actes de la troisième Rencontre égéenne internationale de l'Université de Liège, Station de recherces sous-marines et océanographiques (StaReSO), Calvi, Korsika, 23.-25. April 1990.* (Aegaeum 7.) Liège, 1991, pp. 203–206.
– 'Tel Nami, un grand port à l'âge du Bronze.' *Le Monde de la Bible* 76 (1992), pp. 42–46.
– 'Tel Nami.' E. Stern (ed.), *The New Encyclopedia of Archaeological Excavations in the Holy Land* 3. Jerusalem, 1993, pp. 1095–1098.
– 'Incense, Camels and Collared Rim Jars: Desert Trade Routes and Maritime Outlets in the Second Millennium.' *Oxford Journal of Archaeology* 13 (1994), pp. 121–141.
– 'Nami: A Second Millennium International Maritime Trading Center in the Mediterranean.' S. Gitin (ed.), *Recent Excavations in Israel: A View to the West. Reports on Kabri, Nami, Miqne-Ekron, Dor, and Ashkelon.* (Archaeological Institute of America: Colloquia and Conference Papers 1.) Dubuque, 1995, pp. 17–40.
– 'Nomads of the Sea.' S. Swiny, R. L. Hohlfelder and H. Wylde Swiny (eds.), *Res Maritimae. Cyprus and the Eastern Mediterranean from Prehistory to Late Antiquity. Proceedings of the Second International Symposium 'Cities on the Sea', Nikosia, 18–22 October 1994.* Atlanta, 1997, pp. 1–16.
– 'Routes, Trade, Boats and "Nomads of the Sea".' S. Gitin, A. Mazar and E. Stern (eds.), *Mediterranean Peoples in Transition. Thirteenth to Early Tenth Centuries B.C.E. In Honor of Professor Trude Dothan.* Jerusalem, 1998, pp. 439–448.
– 'The Carmel Coast during the Second Part of the Late Bronze Age: A Center for Eastern Mediterranean Transshipping.' *Bulletin of the American Schools of Oriental Research* 343 (2006), pp. 45–64.
Artzy, M. & S. Zagorski. 'Cypriote "Mycenaean" IIIB Imported to the Levant.' M. Gruber, S. Aḥituv, G. Lehmann and Z. Talhir (eds.), *All the Wisdom of the East. Studies in Near Eastern Archaeology and History in Honor of Eliezer D. Oren.* (Orbis Biblicus et Orientalis 255.) Freiburg and Göttingen, 2012, pp. 1–12.
Bailey, A. J. 2001. 'Turning Transnational: Notes on the Theorisation of International Migration.' *International Journal of Population Geography* 7 (2001), pp. 413–428.
Bhabha, H. K. *The Location of Culture*. London and New York, 2007.

Blum, S. W. E. *Işıklar. Ethnoarchäologische Untersuchungen zu Formation und Transformation archäologischer Siedlungskontexte.* (Studies in Ethnoarchaeology 1.) Remshalden, 2003.

Bunimovitz, S. & Z. Lederman 'Beth Shemesh: Culture Conflict on Judah's Frontier.' *Biblical Archaeology Review* 23 (1997), pp. 42–49.

– 'A Border Case: Beth-Shemesh and the Rise of Ancient Israel.' L. L. Grabbe (ed.), *Israel in Transition: From Late Bronze II to Iron IIa (c. 1250–850 B.C.E.). Vol. 1. The Archaeology* (European Seminar in Historical Methodology 7.) New York and London, 2008, pp. 21–31.

– 'The Archaeology of Border Communities: Renewed Excavations at Tel Beth-Shemesh, Part 1: The Iron Age.' *Near Eastern Archaeology* 72 (2009), pp. 114–142.

– 'Canaanite Resistance: The Philistines and Beth-Shemesh – A Case Study from Iron Age I.' *Bulletin of the American Schools of Oriental Research* 364 (2011), pp. 37–51.

Choi, G. D. *Decoding Canaanite Pottery Paintings from the Late Bronze Age and Iron Age I: The Classification and Analysis of Decorative Motifs and Design Structures – Statistics, Distribution Patterns, and Cultural and Socio-Political Implications.* Unpublished PhD Dissertation. Jerusalem, 2008.

Dietler, M. & I. Herbich, 'Liquid Material Culture: Following the Flow of Beer among the Luo of Kenya.' H.-P. Wotzka (ed.), *Grundlegungen. Beiträge zur europäischen und afrikanischen Archäologie für Manfred K. H. Eggert.* Tübingen, 2006, pp. 395–407.

Dothan, T. & A. Zukerman 'A Preliminary Study of the Mycenaean III C:1 Pottery Assemblages from Tel Miqne-Ekron and Ashdod.' *Bulletin of the American Schools of Oriental Research* 333 (2004), pp. 1–54.

Enwezor, O. 'Introduction. Travel Notes: Living, Working, and Travelling in a Restless World.' O. Enwezor (ed.), *Trade Routes: History and Geography. 2nd Johannesburg Biennale 1997.* Singapur, 1997, pp. 7–12.

Feldman, M. H. *Diplomacy by Design. Luxury Arts and an 'International Style' in the Ancient Near East, 1400–1200 B.C.E.* Chicago, 2006.

Feuer, B. 'Being Mycenaean: A View from the Periphery.' *American Journal of Archaeology* 115, 4 (2011), pp. 507–536.

Fischer, E. *Ägyptische und ägyptisierende Elfenbeine aus Megiddo und Lachish. Inschriftenfunde, Flaschen, Löffel.* (Alter Orient und Altes Testament 47.) Münster, 2007.

Grant, E. *Beth Shemesh (Palestine). Progress of the Haverford Archaeological Expedition.* Haverford, 1929.

Grant, E. & G. E. Wright, *Ain Shems Excavations (Palestine). Part V.* Haverford, 1939.

Griffith, F. L. 'A Drinking Siphon from Tell el-ʿAmarnah.' *JEA* 12 (1926), pp. 22–23.

Guzowska, M. & A. Yasur-Landau, 'Mycenaean Pottery.' Y. Gadot & E. Yadin (eds.), *Aphek-Antipatris II. The Remains on the Acropolis. The Moshe Kochavi and Pirhyia Beck Excavations.* (Monograph Series of the Institute of Archaeology of Tel Aviv University 27.) Tel Aviv, 2009, pp. 342–361.

Haaland, R. 'Porridge and Pot, Bread and Oven: Food Ways and Symbolism in Africa and the Near East from the Neolithic to the Present.' *Cambridge Archaeological Journal* 17 (2007), pp. 165–182.

Hahn, H. P. *Materielle Kultur. Eine Einführung.* Berlin, 2005.

Hankey, V., E. B. French, E. S. Sherratt and P. Magrill 'The Aegean Pottery.' D. Ussishkin (ed.), *The Renewed Archaeological Excavations at Lachish (1973–1994).* (Monograph Series of the Institute of Archaeology of Tel Aviv University 22.) Tel Aviv, 2004, pp. 1373–1449.

Hesse, B. 'Pig Lovers and Pig Haters: Patterns of Palestinian Pork Production.' *Journal of Ethnobiology* 10 (1990), pp. 195–225.

Hesse, B. & P. Wapnish 'Can Pig Remains Be Used for Ethnic Diagnosis in the Ancient Near East?' N. A. Silberman & D. Small (eds.), *The Archaeology of Israel: Constructing the Past, Interpreting the Present.* (JSOT Supplement 237.) Sheffield, 1997, pp. 238–270.

Hitchcock, L. A. '"Transculturalism" as a Model for Examining Migration to Cyprus and Philistia at the End of the Bronze Age.' *Ancient West and East* 10 (2011), pp. 267–280.

Homan, M. M. & J. R. Ebeling 'Baking and Brewing Beer in the Israelite Household: A Study of Women's Cooking Technology.' B. A. Nakhai (ed.), *The World of Women in the Ancient and Classical Near East.* Newcastle, 2008, pp. 45–62.

Homan, M. M. 'Beer and Its Drinkers: An Ancient Near Eastern Love Story.' *Near Eastern Archaeology* 67, 2 (2004), pp. 84–95.

Josephson Hesse, K. *Contacts and Trade at Late Bronze Age Hazor: Aspects of Intercultural Relationships and Identity in the Eastern Mediterranean.* PhD Dissertation, Umeå, 2008.

Karp, I. 'Beer Drinking and Social Experience in an African Society: An Essay in Formal Sociology.' I. Karp & C. S. Bird (eds.), *Explorations in African Systems of Thought.* Bloomington, 1980, pp. 83–119.

Killebrew, A. E. *Biblical Peoples and Ethnicity. An Archaeological Study of Egyptians, Canaanites, Philistines, and Early Israel, 1300–1100 B.C.E.* Leiden and Boston, 2005.

Leonard, A. & E. H. Cline 'The Aegean Pottery at Megiddo: An Appraisal and Reanalysis.' *Bulletin of the American Schools of Oriental Research* 309 (1998), pp. 3–39.

Loud, G. *The Megiddo Ivories.* (University of Chicago Oriental Institute Publications 52.) Chicago, 1939.

– *Megiddo II: Seasons of 1935–39.* (University of Chicago Oriental Institute Publications 62.) Chicago, 1948.

Mac Sweeney, N. 'Beyond Ethnicity: The Overlooked Diversity of Group Identities.' *Journal of Mediterranean Archaeology* 22 (2009), pp. 101–126.

Maeir, A. M. & Y. Garfinkel 'Bone and Metal Straw-Tip Beer-Strainers from the Ancient Near East.' *Levant* 24 (1992), pp. 218–223.

Maeir, A. M. 'The Bone Beverage Strainers.' Y. Garfinkel & S. Cohen (eds.), *The Middle Bronze Age IIA Cemetery at Gesher: Final Report.* (AASOR 62.) Boston, 2007, pp. 119–123.

Mallet, J. 'Le Temple aux Rhytons.' M. Yon (ed.), *Le Centre de la Ville. 38e–44e Campagnes (1978–1984).* (Ras Shamra-Ougarit 3.) Paris, 1987, pp. 213–248.

McGovern, P. E. *Uncorking the Past: The Quest for Wine, Beer, and Other Alcoholic Beverages*. Berkeley – Los Angeles – London, 2009.

Melucci, A. 'The Process of Collective Identity.' H. Johnston & B. Klandermans (eds.), *Social Movements and Culture.* Minneapolis and London, 1995, pp. 41–63.

Middleton, G. 'Mycenaeans, Greeks, Archaeology and Myth: Identity and the Uses of Evidence in the Archaeology of Late Bronze Age Greece.' *Eras Journal* 3 (2002), pp. 1–11.

Mountjoy, P. A. 'A Note on the Mixed Origins of Some Philistine Pottery.' *Bulletin of the American Schools of Oriental Research* 359 (2010), pp. 1–12.

Podzuweit, C. *Studien zur spätmykenischen Keramik.* (Tiryns 14.) Wiesbaden, 2007.

Selz, G. *Die Bankettszene. Entwicklung eines 'überzeitlichen' Bildmotivs in Mesopotamien von der Frühdynastischen bis zur Akkad-Zeit.* (Freiburger Altorientalische Studien 11.) Wiesbaden, 1983.

Simon, C. 'Râpes, siphons ou filtres pour pailles: développement égyptien d'un art de boire.' *Atti, Sesto Congresso Internazionale di Egittologia, Turin, 1.-8. September 1991.* Turin, 1992, pp. 555–563.

Spiegelberg, W. & A. Erman 'Grabstein eines syrischen Söldners aus Tell Amarna.' *ZÄS* 36 (1898), pp. 126–129.

Steel, L. 'Consuming Passions: A Contextual Study of the Local Consumption of Mycenaean Pottery at Tell el-cAjjul.' *Journal of Mediterranean Archaeology* 15 (2002), pp. 25–51.

Stockhammer, P. W. *Kontinuität und Wandel – Die Keramik der Nachpalastzeit aus der Unterstadt von Tiryns*. Heidelberg, 2008. <http://www.ub.uni-heidelberg.de/archiv/8612/> (accessed 18 July 2012).

– 'Performing the Practice Turn in Archaeology.' *Transcultural Studies* 1 (2012), pp. 6–39.

– 'Entangled Pottery: Phenomena of Appropriation in the Late Bronze Age Eastern Mediterranean.' J. Maran & P. W. Stockhammer (eds.), *Materiality and Social Practice. Transformative Capacities of Intercultural Encounters. Papers of the Conference, Heidelberg, 25.–27. März 2010*. Oxford, 2012, pp. 89–103.

– *Materielle Verflechtungen – Zur lokalen Einbindung fremder Keramik in der ostmediterranen Spätbronzezeit*. Unpublished Habilitation Thesis. Basel, 2013.

– 'From Hybridity to Entanglement, from Essentialism to Practise.' P. van Pelt (ed.), *Archaeology and Cultural Mixture*. (Archaeological Review from Cambridge 28, 1.) Cambridge, 2013, pp. 11–28.

– 'The "Aegean type" pottery.' E. Stern, A. Gilboa and I. Sharon (eds.), *Tel Dor: Excavations of Area G, The Bronze and Iron Ages*. (Qedem Reports.) Jerusalem, in press.

Straub, J. 'Identität.' F. Jaeger & B. Liebsch (eds.), *Handbuch der Kulturwissenschaften. Grundlagen und Schlüsselbegriffe*. Stuttgart, 2004, pp. 277–304.

van Wijngaarden, G. J. *Use and Appreciation of Mycenaean Pottery in the Levant, Cyprus and Italy (1600–1200 BC)*. (Amsterdam Archaeological Studies 8.) Amsterdam, 2002.

Vermeule, E. & V. Karageorghis *Mycenaean Pictorial Vase Painting*. Cambridge/Mass. – London, 1982.

Weisgerber, G. 'Biertrinker an Bord? Ein seltener Fund aus Blei!' Ü. Yalçin, C. Pulak and R. Slotta (eds.), *Das Schiff von Uluburun. Welthandel vor 3000 Jahren. Katalog der Ausstellung des Deutschen Bergbau-Museums Bochum*. Bochum, 2005, pp. 157–165.

Welsch, W. 'Transculturality – the Puzzling Form of Cultures Today.' M. Featherstone & S. Lash (eds.), *Spaces of Culture: City, Nation, World*. London, 1999, pp. 194–213.

Wright, J. C. 'A Survey of Evidence for Feasting in Mycenaean Society.' *Hesperia* 73 (2004), pp. 133–178.

Yasur-Landau, A. 'Old Wine in New Vessels: Intercultural Contact, Innovation and Aegean, Canaanite and Philistine Foodways.' *Tel Aviv* 32 (2005), pp. 168–191.

– *The Philistines and Aegean Migration at the End of the Late Bronze Age*. Cambridge, 2010.

– 'The Role of the Canaanite Population in the Aegean Migration to the Southern Levant in the Late 2nd Millennium BC.' J. Maran & P. W. Stockhammer (eds.), *Materiality and Social Practice. Transformative Capacities of Intercultural Encounters. Papers of the Conference, Heidelberg, 25.–27. März 2010*. Oxford, 2012, pp. 191–197.

Zuckerman, S. 'Dating the Destruction of Canaanite Hazor without Mycenaean Pottery?' M. Bietak & E. Czerny (eds.), *The Synchronisation of Civilisations in the Eastern Mediterranean in the Second Millennium B.C. III. Proceedings of the Second EuroConference of SCIEM 2000 Held at the Austrian Academy, Wien, 28. Mai – 1. Juni 2003*. Wien, 2007, pp. 621–629.

– '"Slaying Oxen and Killing Sheep, Eating Flesh and Drinking Wine": Feasting in Late Bronze Age Hazor.' *PEQ* 139 (2007), pp. 186–204.

– 'Fit for a (not-quite-so-great) King: A Faience Lion-Headed Cup from Hazor.' *Levant* 40 (2008), pp. 115–125.

NON-VERBAL EVIDENCE FOR CULTURAL ENCOUNTERS AS SEEN IN WORKS OF THE NEO-ASSYRIAN PERIOD

IRENE J. WINTER

Abstract. Under the rubric of 'cultural encounters' in the Neo-Assyrian Period (9th – 7th centuries BCE), a variety of sub-categories emerge. Among these, it is possible to discern historical differences and perspectives in the particular instance, allowing one to then move more easily to general principles and cross-regional/inter-regional comparison. Such an approach, it is hoped, may not only clarify Assyrian engagements, facilitating thereby a more nuanced understanding of the impact of encounter(s) between particular groups, but also permit generalization related to the range of encounter(s) experienced under specific historical conditions and by different types of socio-political entities.

1. INTRODUCTION AND DEFINITIONS

For purposes of the present article, a "cultural encounter" may be loosely defined as *an interaction between identifiable entities [polities or peoples], the results of which include an impact upon one or more of the participants*. As an historical phenomenon, its examination is timely. With an increasing body of data available plus recent conceptual frameworks seeking to record social, not merely artifactual, interactions as part of the mandate of ancient studies, new perspectives are needed – both in the context of territorial and political expansion of the early Mesopotamian state in general and of the Neo-Assyrian polity in particular.

In the course of encounters between heretofore independent traditions, or as relationships of previously connected polities shift and develop, a number of questions arise, including how apparently similar concepts, materials, and representational patterns may change meaning as the result of either new encounters or changing relationships, how evidence from material culture replicates, complements or problematizes other forms of evidence, textual and archaeological, and how power factors into such encounters?

To pursue such questions, I shall argue in the present article for the desirability of a nuanced, if provisional, typology of cross-cultural encounters. Subject to evidence, some interactions may be coded positive, others negative, and all of the permutations in-between, across the broad spectrum of trade, warfare, diplomatic exchange, population movements, inter-marriage, and political absorption. Pictorial records of interactions, however inflected (it should be noted that the nature of such representations depends entirely upon the vantage point of the recording entity), would then serve no less than textual records as markers of cultural encounters between Assyria and its neighbors during the early first millennium BCE. Underlying the present exercise is the premise that the visual domain constitutes a significant medium of expression that is not merely reflective but *affective* in both marking and operationalizing the socio-political surround as it responds to "cultural encounters" and adapts to change.[1]

This inquiry seems well-suited to the mission of the Center for Canon and *Identity Formation* (italics mine) of the University of Copenhagen. With "identity" as well as "encounter" in the current scholarly frame, identities (plural) must be understood as interactive, fluid, often hybrid, and in a permanent state of re-definition.[2] Both theoretical and methodological issues underlie this proposition. For, to make progress beyond the impressionistic and the anecdotal, explicit necessary and sufficient criteria need to be developed by which to measure and then assess those markers selected as indicators of "encounter." Although the issues raised are larger than can be addressed in a single article, I shall look at selected instances manifest in the visual record when Assyria may be said to have intersected with designated "others," toward establishing both a tentative typology and a consistent terminology with respect to cultural encounters.

In those instances where encounters have been recognized to date, a variety of signs have been identified; but to my knowledge, no attempt

---

[1] This notion of the 'affective' not merely 'reflective' is one I have been working on since the mid-1980s (see, for example, Winter, 'The Body of the Able Ruler', 1989). Of interest is the ability of works we call 'art' to generate responses in audiences of the time and by so doing actually shape socialization and values.

[2] Here, I take seriously the critique of current anthropological 'identity' studies by Lauren Leve, 'Identity', 2011, in which she acknowledges that 'Identity is a powerful organizing presence', while at the same time making clear that the paradoxes encoded in modern identity politics requires that as one uses the term, one be sensitive to 'the processes that produce and extend particular ways of seeing and organizing the world, rather than inadvertently naturalizing them' (p. 513). See also Gruen, *Cultural Identity,* 2010. The caution for us as historians, then, is to be careful not to impose a modern notion of identity upon other cultures, past and present, but to attempt to reconstruct a given culture's attitudes toward identity on its own terms (on this, see van Damme, 'Cultural Encounters', 2011).

has been made to establish a systematic typology of possible interactions, long-term or transitory, cultural and/or spatial, near or distant. If one begins with a notion of identity as requiring the articulation of a set of self-representations,[3] then by adding "encounter" to the mix, one may interrogate a given identity, *any* given identity, in dialogue with a set of representations of some "other": the 'not us' as distinct from the 'us', the 'changed other' as distinct from a 'former other;' the 'changed us' as distinct from a 'former us.[4] In short, as will be discussed further below, the diachronic becomes important, as well as the nuanced variants within the categories of both 'us' and 'not-us.'

Given that the monumental in Assyria is not separate from the official, a third term/concept presently in vogue enters the picture: that of projected "memory." What is selected in order to perpetuate events or stories with an end toward formation or maintenance of group identity – i.e., cultural memory – can be added to the broader frame of inquiry, since what, after all, are monuments, but signs on a large scale that record and/or stimulate those memories that serve as a fundamental component of the cohesion of a given collective?[5]

Both positive and negative encounters may be demonstrated visually. I would argue that, within that binary, 'positive' is constituted by valued interactions with people, goods, and ideas, whereas 'negative' is coded for status-dissonance, antithetical value judgments, and tropes in opposition to the self, all viewed from the perspective of a given center. Among these, one may distinguish at least four types of cultural encounter: between equals; with dependents of high status, such as tributary or vassal states, their people and their rulers; with subordinates; and with those marked as enemy.

Each of these categories of interaction can be subject to analysis by the scholar as coded for positive and/or negative values. Within the category

---

[3] The notion of self-representation is all too rarely examined, except for royal titles and images. See, however, the important exceptions: Machinist, 'Assyrians on Assyria', 1993, and Brown, 'The Kilamua Relief', 2008.

[4] In the discussion that follows, visual differences in content and rendering are pursued, but with an emphasis on iconography more than style. For further distinctions related to style, see references below to Cifarelli, 'Gesture and Alterity', 1998, and Feldman, 'Assyrian Representation', 2011, where both style and iconography are pursued as a way of distinguishing a given 'us' from a given 'other.

[5] Halbwachs, *Cultural Memory*, 1992 (originally published in French, 1952), where the term 'collective memory' was introduced. Several permutations on cultural and collective memory have been pursued in the Anglophone literature since the early 90s. As applied in antiquity, see the papers in Scheidel (ed.), *Rome and China,* 2009; also Assmann, *Cultural Memory*, 2011 (originally published in German, 1992), who joins 'collective memory' with 'cultural identity.'

of positive interactions, one sees well-documented on sculptural reliefs the offering and receiving of gifts (however coercively or hierarchically determined); the social engagement between acceptable equals and non-equals; and the emulation, appropriation and absorption of non-indigenous elements, styles, or themes as the result of encounter. In the negative class, one observes adverse military actions, demonstrations of political dominance (hence also subservience from the perspective of the other), tropes of inappropriate behavior, or even iconoclasm – all of which require the counter-point of the "not us"!

In both positive and negative instances, an essential component of the representation is that the "other" with whom an encounter is depicted must be identifiable: whether by class, ethnicity, status, gender or race. This is often done through details of physiognomy, hairstyle, dress, emblems, or the occasional epigraphic label. Milestones in this endeavor for the study of the 1st millennium BCE have been the work of Marcus Wäffler on non-Assyrians in Assyrian relief imagery, and the many attempts to identify the delegations on the Persepolis reliefs of the Apadana with particular peoples within the extended Achaemenid polity.[6]

Toward the establishment of a set of representational categories deployed to convey the specific relationship intended in the depiction of an "other," as differentiated above, let me begin with the negative trope of encounter with an enemy.

2. The Enemy

Any political entity representing an enemy would obviously code them as negative. Textual evidence for representing the enemy in the Neo-Assyrian Period has been examined by Mario Fales and Carlo Zaccagnini.[7] Clearest in the visual domain is the occasion when Mesopotamians meet with some "other" in battle. This has been well

---

[6] Wäffler, *Nicht-Assyrer*, 1975; and for the Achaemenids, see most recently, Klinkott, 'Steuern, Zöllen, Tribut', 2007. Allen, 'Reading Identity from the Robe', 2012, has recently identified variations in the garments of royal figures at Achaemenid sites as well. For the present article, it will be noted that the distinctions recorded between self and other are largely viewed as ideologically motivated. Nevertheless, it should be stressed that the curious and the exotic are also referenced in royal texts and suggested in visual representation, as are curiousities and challenges of particular topographies. And, as Mehmet-Ali Ataç has argued (*The Mythology of Kingship*, 2010), there is likely to have been an additional layer of esoteric knowledge bedded into both subject matter and composition. The polyvalence of the representation – whether verbal or visual – should not be obscured, therefore; nor the function of imagery in context to create collective identity as well as to represent otherness.

[7] Fales, 'The Enemy in Assyrian Royal Inscriptions', 1982; Zaccagnini, 'The Enemy in the Neo-Assyrian Royal Inscriptions', 1982.

studied by Megan Cifarelli for Neo-Assyrian battle scenes on palace reliefs, where she noted not only difference in hair and clothing styles, but also in stature, posture, gesture, and often size (see, for example, fig. 1).[8]

Such a distinction was not new to the 1st millennium. It will be remembered that the Victory Stela of Naram-Sin of Agade, of the second half of the 3rd millennium BCE, clearly differentiates the upright Akkadian ruler and his soldiers from the cowering, bent enemy, identified in what remains of the original inscription as the Lullubi – arms raised in entreaty; hair in a braid; clothing including animal skins not worn by any self-respecting Mesopotamian; weapons broken in defeat (Fig. 2). The later, Neo-Assyrian depictions of a similarly-clad enemy can be seen as an instance of both topographical and garment continuity over a millennium later. For the particular image illustrated here, texts of Sargon II (721–705 BCE) refer to enemy who were said to "wear their hair like women," were clad in animal skins, and were said to come from the same geographical region as Naram-Sin's Lullubi in what is now the mountains of western Iran, just as shown in the reliefs.[9]

The visual record can simply echo what is also known from text, as pictorial statements parallel to those found in royal annals and annalistic texts, for example; and text-based historians in our field have not been slow in finding illustrations for them – as in the meetings of the American Oriental Society held in Boston in March, 2012, in which one of the plenary lectures, given by Gary Beckman, was on "Foreigners in the Ancient Near East," or the recently published discussion of the status of the foreigner in the Hebrew Bible by Jan Dušek.[10] The only good reason for having an art historian examine this topic, therefore, is to test whether for any given cultural moment the visual and verbal records are identical, overlap partially (and if so, where), or differ. Differences between image

---

[8] Cifarelli, 'Gesture and Alterity', 1998. This has been pursued by Feldman, 'Assyrian Representations', 2011, especially pp. 139-40, where it is stressed that the representation of powerlessness on monuments/works intended for the center provides a memory of conquest for the victors.

[9] Cf. Grayson, *Royal Inscriptions of Mesopotamia: Assyria* 2, 1991, pp. 207, 249: Assurnasirpal text; and for imagery, Wäffler, *Nicht-Assyrer,* 1975 plus especially Albenda, *The Palace of Sargon,* 1986, pls. 112, 117, 121, 128 (Room 2, slabs 6, 12, 18, 28–29), pls. 29, 31, 32 (Room 10, slabs 5–6, 9-1, 11–12), pl. 77 (Room 8, slab 18), for similarly represented figures in battle, as prisoners and in tribute-procession. The citadel on the relief illustrated here (Room 14, slab 2) provides an identifying caption noting the campaign in the Zagros, between Mannea and Zikirtu (Albenda, pp. 150 and 275–276).

[10] Dušek, *Aramaic and Hebrew Inscriptions*, 2012.

Figure 1. Drawing of relief of Sargon II: fortified city of Mannea under siege, Room 14, slab 2. Royal Palace, Khorsabad (original lost). (Source: Albenda, *The Palace of Sargon*, 1982, pl. 136.)

and text can take many forms, determined by selection or omission, nuance, or representational detail in the imagery, and by loci of visual accessibility in the context of a largely non-literate populace. How one then accounts for such difference between textual accounts and imagery impacts directly upon our understanding of the ancient situation.

Figure 2. Detail, Stela of Naram-Sin of Agade: enemy. Found Susa. Louvre, Paris, AO Sb 4. Drawing by Denise L. Hoffman.

That imagery reflects state rhetoric no less than the verbal record no longer needs any argument, particularly when occurring in official venues. It is clear, if only by virtue of placement of such images on palace walls and on official markers such as court seals and public stelae. Most obvious for the Assyrian case is that, by careful selection evident in these images, it is the enemy who perish, not the Assyrians (e.g., fig. 3).[11]

Military engagements, then, offer a prime opportunity to examine the obviously marked enemy other. As on the Naram-Sin stela, in Assyrian renderings of the enemy too, degrees of verisimilitude in terrain are frequently complemented by identifying details of dress, hairstyle, weapons, and behavior, in order to denote the particular spatio-temporal event as distinct from a generic or mythological locus on the one hand, and in order to contrast the enemy with Assyrian standards of decorum on the other.[12]

Figure 3. Relief of Assurnasirpal II: siege, Throneroom B, slab B.3a. Northwest Palace, Nimrud. British Museum, London, ME 124555. (Photograph courtesy of the Trustees, The British Museum.)

---

[11] See on this, Cifarelli, 'Gesture and Alterity', 1998. Cf. also Kertai, 'Kalhu's palaces of war and peace', 2011, as well as Eph'al, 'Stages and Aims in the Royal Historiography of Esarhaddon', 2014, where the extreme rarity of mentioning Assyrian defeat in textual sources is discussed.

[12] Another sort of 'encounter' with an enemy population that could be considered here is instances of purposeful abduction or destruction of divine images as recorded visually, and also textually. See on this most recently the various articles in May, *Iconoclasm and Text Destruction,* 2012, particularly those by Schaudig and Berlejung.

3. THE 'OTHER', WITH THE DESIGNATED 'US'

A converse to the negative trope of the 'enemy' other would be the representation of foreign soldiers fighting *with* the Neo-Assyrian army – included with the 'us', but still not entirely 'of us', since they are visually differentiated. Although, through specific characteristics such as hairstyle and dress, such conscripts were clearly designated 'not us' they were demonstrably with the 'us' at a given point in time. In such cases, the shift from negative other (enemy) to conscripted/allied other (still not us by identification, but now positive-by-behavior) is that the center may well value the inclusion of a recognizably non-Assyrian portion of the population. Indeed, having annexed territory and possibly required conscription, or having made allies who support and help to protect the political center in exchange for reciprocal protection and preferential treatment, the Assyrians may well *need* to identify them as 'other.' However, to the extent that they remain designated as other, they differ in value from those considered in the inner core. From the perspective of the contributing population, of course, their resultant conscription may not be as willing as the service rendered is valued. Thus, identification of the representing 'center' is a primary stage in evaluating degrees of positive and negative interaction.

Where historical annals and annalistic texts are preserved, the visual may often be seen to mirror, or to be complementary to verbal descriptions. This is particularly true of the composite army of Tiglath Pileser III (744–727 BCE) in the second half of the 8th century BCE – soldiers differentiated from co-protagonists clad in Assyrian garb and shown with typically Assyrian hairstyles. The apparently non-Assyrians are shown in distinctive short kilts and with ringlet haircurls. These signs of identity would have been readily recognizable to contemporaries, whether ally or enemy, just as the texts are explicit in providing a geographical or political name, and occasionally a brief description (Fig. 4).[13] Visual and verbal representation, then, can reinforce each other when

[13] Wäffler, *Nicht-Assyrer*, 1975, p. 186 and Figs. 104, 106, 107, and Barnett & Falkner, *Sculptures of Assurnasirpal II,* 1962, pl. XXXVI. Note also that we are fortunate in having preserved texts related to the subsidiary (vassal?) status of the western state of Sam'al, both from the reign of Tiglath Pileser III (Tadmor, *The Inscriptions of Tiglath-Pileser* III, 1994, p. 69, Ann. 14*, l. 12; p. 89, Ann. 27, l. 4; p. 109, Stele III A, l. 17, etc.) referring to tribute from Panammu of Sam'al, and from the son and successor of Panammu, Bar-Rakib (Donner & Röllig, *Kanaanäische und Aramäische Inschriften* I, 1962, pp. 223–224, No. 216; and see fig. 19, below), who notes that his father had been killed "running at the side of" the Assyrian king's chariot while fighting with the Assyrian army. Indeed, Wäffler, cited above, has shown that the particular hairdo is associated with men of Sam'al.

overlapping, and provide complementary information that is additive when they differ.

What such foreigners in the Assyrian army signify is more difficult to ascertain. In order to mark them as not fully Assyrian, their attributes of otherness must be shown; but does it code conscription, hence power and dominance, or recognition of a cosmopolitan, multi-ethnic state? And can correlations be made, especially for the time of Tiglath Pileser III, between representation and historically-grounded provincial status, marking new tropes of hybridity in Assyria?

Figure 4. Relief of Tiglath Pileser III: foreign soldiers, Central Palace, Nimrud. Archäologisches Institute, Zurich, No. 1916.

A second instance of verbal and visual doubling of those represented as others, in this case *to* the 'us', occurs in processions of foreign delegations bearing gifts to the Assyrian king/state. When indicated visually, such scenes are often depicted in prominent places in Neo-Assyrian palaces – as on the bronze door bands of Assurnasirpal II (883–859 BCE) and Shalmaneser III (859–824 BCE) from Balawat (e.g., fig.

5a) and on the Northern Façade of Court D, entry to the Throne Room in the Northwest Palace of Assurnasirpal at Nimrud/Kalah (Fig. 5b).

Figure 5a. Bronze Gate Band Relief of Assurnasirpal II: tribute. Balawat, Temple Door, right side, upper band. Mosul Museum, MM ASH II R1.

Figure 5b. Detail, Relief of Assurnasirpal II: tribute bearer carrying platter with bracelets. Court D (North Façade of Throneroom B), Northwest Palace, Nimrud. British Museum. London. (Photograph courtesy of the Trustees, The British Museum.)

In text, they are recounted on the Banquet Stela of Assurnasirpal, found within the Northwest Palace.[14] Yet one sees some differences between image and text. On the Banquet Stela, the text specifically recounts the event of the inauguration of the palace and the new capital of Kalah. On the reliefs of Court D, by contrast, individuals in regional dress bring materials in procession to the king, presumably artifacts, produce, and

[14] For the reliefs, see Meuszynski, *Rekonstruktion*, 1981, pls. 5 and 6; Curtis & Tallis (eds.), *The Balawat Gates*, 2008, Temple bands (ATB) R1, 3, 4, 5, 6, 8 and L1, 3, 4, 6, 8, pp. 47–71, Palace bands (APB) R1, 6, 7, 11, pp. 23–46, and discussions of tribute pp. 52, 73. For the Banquet Stela, see Wiseman, 'A New Stela', 1952; Kinnier Wilson, 'Lines 40–52 of the Banquet Stele', 1988; Grayson, *Royal Inscriptions of Mesopotamia: Assyria* 2, 1991, pp. 288–293. In general, see Bär, *Der assyrische Tribut,* 1996. For the bronze bands from Shalmaneser III's palace at Balawat, see the most recent discussion in Curtis & Tallis, op. cit., pp. 11–14 and Table 2.1, with prior bibliography.

resources from their native land. But the imagery cannot represent the scale of the historical event, nor is it a journalistic image since the decorative program of the palace would have to have been completed prior to the inauguration.

Such ceremonial imagery could represent anticipation of gifts to be brought to the inauguration, or the sequence could reference gifts expected on a regular basis as part of courtly ceremony/annual tribute in the future. On the bronze door bands, particularly in the sequence illustrated here (Band R1 from the Temple of Mamu), a procession of individuals in distinctive dress bearing ivory tusks and presumably bronze cauldrons, among other things, approaches the ruler standing outside an architectural structure conveniently labeled IMGUR.ENLIL, the Assyrian name of Balawat. Above the processional figures is an epigraphic text in which the approaching delegation is labeled as bearing tribute (Akk. *madattu*) from the land of Suhu.[15] In both the Court D reliefs and on the several narrative bands of the Balawat gates where tribute is depicted from a number of different polities, parts must stand for a greater whole, and so delegations must have been carefully selected and materials equally carefully edited to represent recognizable cohorts and commodities, in keeping with the historical and rhetorical purposes of the imagery. The fuller text of the Banquet Stela recounts in detail the number and places of origin of delegations, along with the extent of food and hospitality offered to visitors, and the events included in the festivities, with particular emphasis on the lavish inaugural banquet.[16] This makes the visual record partial in interesting ways, allowing us to differentiate rhetorical agendas in palace and temple decoration from the politico-historical narrative of the stela. It also permits us to distinguish cultural encounters that bring foreign delegations into the center from those where Assyrians meet an other in the field or in the latter's home territory, and further encourages us to separate any analysis of the impact of such encounters by registering the cultural responses of both envoys/locals and Assyrians.[17]

There is, of course, a huge scholarly literature on "the gift" from Durkheim and Mauss to the present, which provides a basis for

---

[15] Curtis and Tallis (eds.), *The Balawat Gates,* 2008, pl. 56. I am grateful to Yan Jia for conversations regarding these gates, which are the subject of her dissertation, currently in progress.

[16] Winter, 'Le Banquet royal assyrien', 2013; Grayson, *Royal Inscriptions of Mesopotamia: Assyria* 2, 1991, pp. 175–176, §682.

[17] Note, for example, that in the Ninurta Temple inscription (Grayson, *Royal Inscriptions* 2, 1991, p. 143, § 585) we are told that Assurnasirpal also staged a banquet in a conquered palace in the western state of Patina, for which only battle scenes are preserved in relief.

investigations in our field.[18] The delegations depicted on the Apadana reliefs of Persepolis in the Achaemenid Period have served as the iconic instance of gifting associated with royal celebration (Fig. 6a & b). I mention the Persians here because so much has been said about continuity of Assyrian representational tropes that were subsequently adopted into the arts of the Achaemenids. And yet, the multiplicity of delegations and the extent of the tribute depicted at Persepolis go well beyond what was shown on Assyrian reliefs – even in the expanded registers of Assurnasirpal II's gate bands from Balawat and the reliefs of Sargon II at Khorsabad.

The delegates are distinguished by dress, often hairstyle and headgear, as well as frequently by the gifts they bear. The best of the "other" is thus displayed as contributing to, even being absorbed by, the center in the course of an asymmetrical encounter.[19]

Figure 6a. Tribute bearers, Apadana, Persepolis.

[18] Liverani, 'Dono, tribute, commercio', 1979; Zaccagnini, 'La circolazione dei bene', 1984; and the articles in Briant (ed.), *La tribute dans l'empire perse,* 1989, along with those in Klinkott et al. (eds.), *Geschenke und Steuern, Zölle und Tribut*, 2007, especially Klinkott, 'Steuern, Zölle, Tribute', pp. 263–290.

[19] See also the discussion of booty as the countersign of tribute in Feldman, 'Assyrian Representations', 2011, pp. 140ff. What is interesting here is Feldman's observation, citing Cifarelli, 'Gesture and Alterity', 1998, pp. 24–28, that even tributaries seem to slouch in posture, thereby rendering them subsidiary in style no less than in narrative action.

Figure 6b. Detail, tribute bearer carrying bracelets, Apadana, Persepolis.

What would be interesting at this point in scholarship, especially now that the frequently-labeled bronze bands of Assurnasirpal II from Balawat have been published, would be to take the entire corpus of textual and visual representation of tribute-bearing/gift-bearing delegations through both the Assyrian and the Persian Periods, and plot on a map, reign by reign, where delegates come from with respect to the capital and the territorial boundaries of the represented polities. It would be useful as well, to pursue Michelle Marcus' rejection of the overly-binary

"Center::Periphery" model for the more nuanced and tripartite differentiation between "Center::*Province*::Periphery" (italics mine), or whatever other division of units may be deemed appropriate.[20] With such a study, one might be able to see whether various Assyrian rulers' delegation imagery of guests brought into the center or tributaries following battle represent a map-able circuit of dependent or autonomous territories. Perhaps one might then be better able to distinguish between enemy "not us" beyond a certain distance from the center and the assimilated/absorbed/acceptable/acculturated "not us but with us" – a class of recognizable outsiders joined to the center by mutual, if hierarchical, relationships of political alliance, treaty, cultural affinity or trade.[21]

---

[20] Marcus, 'Centre, Province, and Periphery', 1990. For the ancient Near Eastern field, see also the recent work of Bagg, *Assyrien und das Westland*, 2011; Cannavò, 'The Role of Cyprus', 2010, pp. 184–187; Lanfranchi, 'Consensus to Empire', 1997; MacGinnis and Matney, 'Archaeology at the Frontiers', 2009; Parker, *The Mechanics of Empire,* 2001; Pedde, 'The Assyrian Heartland', 2012; Tadmor, 'World Dominion', 1999; Winter, 'The "Local Style"', 1977; Yamada, *The Construction of the Assyrian Empire*, 2000 – a number of which focus upon specific regions in contact with Assyria or under Assyrian control. For yet another category of settlement within the widely-defined Assyrian 'center', see also Van Soldt et al., 'Satu Qala', 2013. Like Balawat, Satu Qala was within the immediate hinterland controlled by Assyria, but differentiated from the capital, and has produced a very Neo-Assyrian material culture, with objects and textual fragments very much in evidence (Van Soldt et al., cited above, Figs. 4, 5, 6, 7, 14, 15, 21, 22, 24, 25, 26, for which pre-print I am grateful to Cinzia Pappi). Note also that MacGinnis and Matney, cited above, p. 6, also attempt a typology, suggesting 'sites exclusively Assyrian', 'sites predominantly Assyrian', 'sites belonging to indigenous populations with some evidence of Assyrian contact', and 'sites belonging to indigenous populations with no evidence of Assyrian contact.' For a more theoretical framework, see Campbell, 'Toward a Networks and Boundaries Approach', 2009, which deals with Bronze Age China, where the author schematizes his polity by a diagram, distinguishing three concentric circles, including the area of the political capital and center, then extended to dependent subordinates and allies, and finally an outer perimeter of polities designated enemy, rebels and 'barbarians', p. 837, fig. 7. The diagram references 'contact' distances, rather than rigid and regular geographical distances.

[21] On this with respect to the Roman Empire, see Woolf, 'Romancing the Celts', 1998; with respect to the Hebrew Bible, see Kennedy, *Ethnic Identity in the Ancestral Narratives of Genesis*, 2011. One of the questions one must ask is to what extent the incorporated 'other' undergoes acculturation in the process of political absorption, and then to what extent this has an impact on the intensity of positive response on both sides to 'encounter.' Furthermore, in a domain not considered in the present article, it is interesting to see how religion factors into such incorporations: whether the center's gods are introduced into/imposed upon incorporated territories, or whether indigenous religion continues without intervention (on which, see the early study by Cogan, *Imperialism and Religion*, 1974, and the more recent Aster, 'Transmission', 2007, and Berlejung, 'Shared Fates', 2012, specifically with respect to Judah).

I mention this issue here because it raises an important point, both with respect to identifiable foreigners fighting with the Assyrian army and identifiable tributaries, about the nature of the polity depicting itself and its designated others beyond the class of 'enemy.' If there may always be assumed to be an 'other' lurking behind any definition of group identity,[22] then it may just be possible to see a developmental sequence of types of representation of the other depending not only upon historical events (i.e., diachronic changes in status and hence degrees of closeness/ incorporation), but also upon the respective structural organizations involved and the nature of the relationship between the socio-political units involved.

4. Territorial Incorporation

An issue in recognizing the values attached to cultural and geographical absorption is that an incorporated province, for example, can be considered neither as an enemy/former enemy, nor an independent ally, but as a territory. That is, it can be defined as *identifiably other, but now within the geographical boundaries of the 'us'* or *now counted as one of us*. Therefore, each case of territorial absorption needs to be examined separately to see what values are attached, and how this matches up with known history. One of the telling differences between the Assyrian and Persian images representing the "incorporated other" is to be seen in the figures symbolically supporting the ruler as part of his throne iconography. In the campaign of Sennacherib (704–681 BCE) against Lachish, on the reliefs of Room 36 in the Southwest Palace at Nineveh (Fig. 7), we see the king seated on a high-backed chair the sides of which are decorated with semi-divine figures with raised arms in atlantid/supporting posture, as he receives booty and captives from the successful campaign.[23]

---

[22] On which, see Pongratz-Leisten, 'The Other and the Enemy', 2001 and 'Comments on the Translatability', 2011; also Hughes, *The Invention of Jewish Identity*, 2010.

[23] Barnett, *Sculptures from the Southwest Palace*, 1998, Slab 11 (BM WAA 124911), Room 36. John Curtis has recently published a study of these figures, referring to them as "Protective figures" – see Curtis, '*Stützfiguren* in Mesopotamia', 1995, pls. 13–17. They recur on a number of Neo-Assyrian works, including a sculptured relief of a carried throne from Façade L of Sargon II's palace at Khorsabad and in a wall painting of an enthroned Assyrian ruler, probably Tiglath Pileser III, from Til-Barsib (our fig. 18, discussed below), and so must be considered characteristic of Assyrian rulers' thrones at least in the 8th century BCE.

Figure 7. Relief of Sennacherib: siege of Lachish. Southwest Palace, Room 36, Slabs 11/12. Nineveh. British Museum, London, ME 124911. (Photograph courtesy of the Trustees, The British Museum.)

The similarly-shaped throne of Darius II on door-jambs at Persepolis and the supporting platforms depicted on royal tomb facades at nearby Naqsh-i-Rustam make use of a related trope of support for the ruler; however there we see a wide range of apparently non-divine figures in varying dress comparable to those depicted in the Apadana processional reliefs – figures thought to be persons or personifications of the various satrapies of the Persian Empire, bearing tribute (Fig. 8).[24] This may well be the most radical element of the present article, although one might ask why this difference is deemed radical (or, why I am radical for dwelling on this difference). Because I think there are important implications when one attempts to account for the difference. And the question must then be posed, if not answered systematically here, whether cultural encounters

[24] Schmidt, *Persepolis III*, 1970, Tombs of Darius I and Artaxerxes I, frontispiece and pls. 19-22, 48–51; Klinkott, 'Steuern, Zöllen, Tribut', 2007.

taking place under conditions of empire differ from those associated with other sorts of polities.

Figure 8. Tomb of Darius, Naqsh-i-Rustam: detail of platform/support structure for the ruler.

The Assyrian polity, like the Ur III and the Akkadian before it, has often been referred to as an empire, because of the extent of territory incorporated into the state as the result of conquest or treaty and the ensuing bureaucratic structures developed to ensure the administration of the state.[25] I have remained un-persuaded of the appropriateness of using the term empire, even for the early Neo-Assyrian Period, especially if one sees a developmental sequence along a scale from city-state to nation-

[25] Liverani, *Akkad, the First World Empire*, 1993; Barjamovic, 'The Mesopotamian Empires', 2012; Bedford, 'The Neo-Assyrian Empire', 2009; Joannès, *The Age of Empires*, 2004; Parker, *The Mechanics of Empire*, 2001; Tadmor, 'Assyria and the West', 1975. But see also Postgate, 'The Debris of Government', 2010, p. 35, who is careful not to refer to Ur III as an 'empire', but rather as simply a 'state.'

state or kingdom, and from there through the phase of an expanding "territorial state" to true "empire."[26]

Work over the last three decades has examined instances of the governance and representational imagery of empire in the Near East, particularly with respect to the Roman and Ottoman Periods.[27] In virtually all cases under scrutiny, including the Persian, one of the primary criteria for identifying an empire is the creation of a multi-ethnic state characterized by diversity and hybridity. This diversity is even marked in the Hebrew Bible account known as the Scroll of Esther, set in the Achaemenid Period (whenever it may have been redacted). When the Persian king required that his word be recorded and disseminated throughout the realm, he ordered that each component unit was to be written to in its own script, and sent to every people in their own language (Esther 1:22; 3:12; 8:9). It is precisely that recognition of diversity that I believe is demonstrated in the Persepolis and Naqsh-i Rustam reliefs, with each of the administrative sub-polities/satrapies embodied by a representative of its indigenous people, each in their own dress, constituting as a collective the extent of the polity that has absorbed such a diversity of peoples.

By contrast, in the Neo-Assyrian records, one sees consistent attempts to incorporate subject peoples into the center, through actual population movements in practice and by phrases like: I conquered [such-and-such a people] "*and counted them Assyrians*" (italics mine).[28]

---

[26] Lest this sound overly linear in evolutionary sequence, I would note the discussion in Barjamovic, 'The Mesopotamian Empires', 2012, esp. fig. 1 and pp. 4–8, which allows for oscillations between centralization and fragmentation throughout the historical sequence. He also makes clear (p. 7) that by using the term 'empire' for a number of centralized polities from the 3rd through the 1st millennium, the term has been "left intentionally vague to denote any type of larger territorial state that held political hegemony…through military power…", and he is cognizant of the fact that "some would reject such broad classification in favor of a more fine-grained terminology." I find myself in the latter category at present, putting together the issue of naturalizing modern terms/concepts and then retrojecting them into the past, as discussed by Leve, 'Identity', 2011, cited in fn. 2, above, along with the later comments by Morehart, 'What if the Aztec Empire never Existed?' 2012. That said, I, too, am not unaware that the category 'territorial state' requires a definition that would distinguish it from 'empire' – an exercise that has not yet been rigorously undertaken.

[27] On this topic, see the papers included in Laurence & Berry (eds.), *Cultural Identity*, 1998, plus the work of Bru, *Le pouvoir impérial,* 2011. And, more generally, Alcock et al., *Empires*, 2001 and C. Sinopoli, 'The Archaeology of Empires', 1994.

[28] See, for example, the deportees depicted by Sennacherib from Lachish and elsewhere (Barnett et al., *Sculptures from the Southwest Palace*, 1998, pl. 322, slabs 9-12; also pl. VI from his Babylonian campaign). For the text, Tadmor, *Inscriptions of Tiglath-Pileser* III, 1994, Ann. 9, 10, 13, pp. 42–43, 44–45, 66–67 resp., and see also, CAD M1, *manû*, "to count."

The representational repertoire may distinguish such new citizens or incorporated populations by exposing their origins through details of dress and hairstyle; but the polity as a whole does not subscribe to the same degree of acceptable heterogeneity as subsequent, more fully-developed "empires." I could elaborate on this at length, but suffice to say in the present context that I am not persuaded either the Akkadian or the Ur III polities represented true empire, but rather expanding kingdoms accruing territory. Similarly, I wonder whether the Middle- and Neo-Assyrian phenomena, at least through the early expansions of the 9th century BCE, are not better described as "territorial states," in which expansion incorporates formerly autonomous regions into the center. While such expansion may also be characteristic of and a necessary condition for empire, one could argue that this is not a sufficient criterion in and of itself. If instead, one requires diversity and rhetorically-recognized difference, plus a complex administrative organization distributed throughout the territory, as necessary to empire, then at best we see the beginning of the shift toward imperial structures in the Assyrian period only in the 8th century with the reigns of Adad-nērari III, Tiglath Pileser III and Sargon II. At that time, former allies and tributary states become incorporated as provinces, with the administrative officers governing those provinces appointed by the center and holding quite high status within the center.[29]

It is this distinction that I believe accounts for the difference in the atlantid supports of the royal throne or podium in the two periods – particularly where, in the Neo-Assyrian Period, the ruler's title does not change from "king" to a new Akkadian equivalent of augmented status equivalent to "emperor," one that would mark consciousness of a new organizational and political structure of governance. To pursue other changes in the royal titulary is beyond the purview of the present study, however much it might warrant investigation. The point here is that there does not seem to be a cluster of observable differences in the visual record to mark the organizational and structural shifts I would identify with empire.

Wherever one lands in this debate, its relevance in the present paper is to put in question whether the distinction between empire and kingdom, or territorial state, would make a difference in describing relationships

---

[29] On this process, see Masetti-Rouault, 'Globalisation', 2014; Gerlach, 'Tradition-Adaptation—Innovation', 2000, Gilan, 'Überlegungen', 2004, Lanfranchi, 'Consensus to Empire', 1997, pp. 81–87 and Tadmor, 'Assyria and the West', 1975. I would like to thank Maria-Grazia Masetti-Rouault for making her manuscript available to me prior to publication, as well as Gojko Barjamovic and Eckart Frahm for stimulating conversations on this topic.

with incorporated peoples, or with peoples/territory beyond the boundaries of incorporation: that is, how heterogeneity is conceived, how and under what conditions a former enemy may become an ally, how the 'us/not us' dichotomy may have to be redefined, how the flow of benefits may be diagrammed given new boundaries. In short, what are the spatio-temporal coordinates and consequences of a given encounter, based upon the type of engagement plus the kind(s) of polities involved?

If we are, indeed, dealing with representations of an expanding territorial state in the early Neo-Assyrian Period but not quite 'empire', then the accumulation of wealth, gifts, trade access and reciprocal hospitality in both text and image can be understood through that lens just as easily. Power relations are no less in play, yet difference matters. For example, on Assurnasirpal II's Court D reliefs, and on that ruler's bronze door bands from Balawat (see fig. 5a & b), only gifts brought to the king are depicted,[30] and yet, one might anticipate that if the ruler was as lavish in his hospitality as is recounted in the text of the "Banquet Stela," some gifts were likely to have been distributed *to* the king's guests at the inauguration of the Northwest Palace, as is well-documented in other accounts of elite ceremonial reception and subsequent gifting (for example, in the Homeric account of a silver mixing bowl given to Telemachus, son of Odysseus, by the ruler of Sparta on the occasion of the former's visit – *Odyssey* 4.614–619). In the verbal rhetoric of the center, and in political practice, the host must be shown to adhere to rules of hospitality; in the visual rhetoric of the palace, by contrast, on the very wall separating the courtyard from the Throne Room, it is only the king who receives – the display of asymmetry essential to the rhetoric of representation in the royal palace.

Indeed, even when seeming equality between polities is represented, as on the front of throne base of the Assyrian ruler Shalmaneser III from Nimrud (Fig. 9), where the king and the ruler of Babylon seem to be clasping hands and one might construct a 'positive' category of interaction between equals, I would argue that Assyrian rhetoric is still likely to have governed the imagery, since traditional battle/tribute scenes are depicted on the sides, clearly to the benefit of and suggesting the political and economic dominion by Assyria.[31]

---

[30] Meuszynski, *Rekonstruktion*, 1981.

[31] Mallowan, *Nimrud and its Remains*, Vol. II, 1966, pp. 444–450 and fig. 447d, found in the throne room, TR T1, in Fort Shalmaneser. The Assyrian king is represented at the right, the Babylonian ruler, Marduk-zakir-šumi, at the left. The tribute processions include a delegation from southern Babylonia being received by Shalmaneser. The special yet complex relationship between Assyria and Babylonia can be traced throughout the Assyrian Period, and is implied most clearly here on the Shalmaneser Throne Base.

Figure 9. Detail, Throne base of Shalmaneser III, Fort Shalmaneser, Room T1, Nimrud. Iraq Museum, Baghdad.

Figure 10. Drawing of relief of Sennacherib: booty from conquered citadel, Southwest Palace, Nineveh, Room 38, slabs 17–18. British Museum, London, Or. Dr. IV, 60 (original lost).

I would like, therefore, to look next at how we may understand the directional arrows of agency through visual expressions of cultural exchanges, arguing that such analyses may be useful in marking sub-sets of cultural encounters "of the Assyrian kind."

5. GIFTING/LOOTING/TRADE IN; EMULATION OUT

Directional arrows point *into* the center when booty and tribute are collected, gifts received, artisans imported, and/or treaties redacted in order to regulate certain goods to the benefit of the center. I would underscore the fact that, once again, the perspective with respect to assessing encounter is that *of* the center (positive), while donor populations may not perceive anything but burden (negative). For example, we see the armies of Sennacherib making off with high-end luxury goods following a campaign depicted in the Southwest Palace of Nineveh (Fig. 10), to the clear benefit of Assyria, but not to the donor site.[32] These same goods or their congeners are still in use two reigns later,

Figure 11. Relief of Assurbanipal: garden scene. North Palace, Room Nineveh, Room S'. British Museum, London, ME 124920. (Photograph courtesy of the Trustees, The British Museum.)

[32] Barnett et al., *Sculptures from the Southwest Palace*, 1998, pl. 365, = Room 38, slabs 17–18, Cat. No. 453. The campaign was clearly undertaken in a mountainous region. Note that a similar procession with almost identical furniture emerges from quite a different location, a Babylonian campaign, in Room 48, slabs, pl. 411 and 413, Cat. Nos. 524–5. For more on this issue, see below, fn. 61.

as in the "Garden Scene" of Assurbanipal (668–627 BCE) from the North Palace, where the furniture of couch and table replicate the shape if not the exact iconographic detail of the booty taken (Fig. 11), and the small objects such as the pyxis on the table before the ruler, match very closely actual pyxides known to have been coming from Syria – both in ivory and in stone.

Figure 12. Relief of Assurnasirpal II: chariot battle. Throneroom B, Northwest Palace, Nimrud. British Museum, London, ME 124553. (Photograph courtesy of the Trustees, The British Museum.)

Whatever is selected for representation in the royal palace notwithstanding, not all activity moves things into the major political center. Once contact has been made, the provinces and the periphery are exposed to material culture and practices *of* the given center as well. That is what has been observed archaeologically when Assyrian objects and Assyrian motifs are found or depicted outside. On their own terms, such loci function as centers themselves. One such case is well-attested at the 9th-century site of Hasanlu in Northwestern Iran. Objects found at the site include Assyrian works, along with works executed in what has been called a "Local Style" heavily dependent upon Assyria (Figs. 12 & 13). In this situation, I have argued elsewhere for an avoidance of the monolithic term "influence" to account for the Assyrian impress on Hasanlu, congruent with the campaigns of Assurnasirpal II and

Shalmaneser III onto the Iranian plateau.[33] Rather, I suggested that we must understand the phenomenon as reflecting local agency in the selection process, such that the residents/craftsmen of Hasanlu were active participants in choosing just *which* elements were to be incorporated and which rejected. And for this reason, I substituted terms like "emulation," and "absorption," to reflect that local agency, as it may be distinguished from the passivity implied in "influence."

Figure 13. Detail, Silver Beaker, Hasanlu, Burned Building II, 9th c BCE. Iran Archaeological Museum, Teheran, HAS 58–427. (Photograph courtesy of the Hasanlu Project, University of Pennsylvania.)

At that point, any locus can be discussed as a 'center' in its own right; its relationship to other 'centers' being dependent upon issues of power, wealth, access to raw materials, and cultural affinity or dissonance. For example, in another instance, during the later years of the Neo-Assyrian period, one may observe active absorption of Assyrian imagery in the sealing practices of the Levant – as with an 8th/7th-century stamp seal found recently in an Iron II building excavated in Jerusalem (see modern

[33] Winter, 'The "Local Style" of Hasanlu IVB', 1977. Note that one could describe the phenomenon of absorption at Hasanlu as 'assyrianizing', to the extent that the site both incorporates finished objects of Assyrian manufacture and also translates Assyrian elements into a distanctly local vocabulary and style. This process may be contrasted with what Feldman ('Assyrian Representations', 2011, p. 143) discusses as 'Assyrianization', in which the dominant center itself absorbs elements from outside the center and makes of them their own – a subject to which we turn in the next section.

impression, fig. 14).[34] Here, a recognizably assyrianizing figure of a bowman seems to have been absorbed into Judah, itself formerly an autonomous polity, albeit on a considerably smaller scale than the Assyrian, ultimately absorbed into the larger state. However, once again, with the region's own agency in operation, the image does not appear in the original narrative context of extended battle scenes known from Assyrian relief carvings (compare Figs. 3 & 4).[35] Instead – perhaps stimulated by intermediaries in other media, as suggested by Ornan et al. – the single visual element was extracted and adapted to meet local needs of sealing practices in Judah that also included an inscription in Hebrew, "(belonging) to Hagab."

Figure 14. Seal of Hagab (modern impression), from Jerusalem, Iron II building, Room 1. Israel Antiquities Authority no. 2011–1334. (Photograph courtesy of Benny Sass.)

[34] Ornan et al., 'Four Hebrew Seals', 2008, fig. 7 and discussion, pp. 117–127. My thanks to Tali Ornan for having brought this seal and publication to my attention, and to Benny Sass for permission to publish his photograph of the seal impression.

[35] Cf. also Barnett et al., *Sculptures from the Southwest Palace of Sennacherib*, 1998, Room V and pl. 55, Room XXXVI and pl. 71, cited in Ornan et al., 'Four Hebrew Seals', 2008, p. 123. I include fig. 4, to emphasize the interesting parallel of the 'foreigner' fighting with Tiglath Pileser's army, who by his haircurls can be identified with the West, while his garment rather resembles that depicted on the Hagab seal. For other instances of the interaction between an Assyrian presence and the indigenous tradition, see Masetti-Rouault, 'Globalisation', 2014, and 'Rural Economy', 2010, for the Middle Euphrates; Gerlach, 'Tradition-Adaptation-Innovation', 2000, for North Syria/Southeast Anatolia; Tanyeri-Erdemir, 'Tradition vs. Innovation', 2005, especially Ch. 4, for Urartu.

6. Moving the Center into the Provinces and the Periphery

On a list of cultural encounters worth pursuing in the visual record, I would also point to major Neo-Assyrian works erected in relatively newly-incorporated territories – such as royal stelae and rock reliefs positioned at notable points in the landscape or at settlement gateways. One such case is the royal stelae found in areas east, west, north and south of the center – as, for example, those of Esarhaddon from Til Barsib on the Euphrates, renamed Kar Shalmaneser in the second half of the 9th century, and from Zincirli, ancient Sam'al, further to the west (Fig. 15). The former was the seat of prominent Assyrian provincial governors from the 8th century, the latter also a province and, before that, an ally.[36] Assyrian officials governing in the provinces frequently utilized imagery on their personal seals that replicated palace iconography of the center, and sometimes set up their own stelae.[37] In the case of the Esarhaddon stelae in particular, placement at important public gates open to general view, rather than in restricted contexts, must have been important for the assertion of Assyrian presence. And it is to be noted that the imagery on the stelae was on the obverse, projecting outward from place of installation, with the inscriptions, when added, on the reverse, so hidden from immediate view, suggesting that the visual would have been more 'readable' to the local audience.

At the same time, local rulers in early contact with Assyria tended to adopt Assyrian dress and modes of representation post-incorporation, as on the Incirli stela found near the North Syrian site of Sakcegözü that must be dated to the 8th century reign of Tiglath Pileser III, after the area had become an Assyrian province.[38]

---

[36] For Til Barsib: Robaert, 'A Neo-Assyrian Statue from Til Barsib', 1996; Bunnens, 'Til Barsip under Assyrian Domination', 1997; Porter, 'The Importance of Place', 2001; for Zincirli, Porter, loc. cit., plus Eph'al, 'Esarhaddon, Egypt and Shubria', 2005, pp. 106–109, and 'Stages and Aims in the Royal Historiography of Esarhaddon', 2014. In general, see Masetti-Rouault, 'Globalisation', 2014; Harmanşah, 'Beyond Aššur', 2012; Shafer, 'Assyrian Royal Monuments', 2007. Now that we have the textual evidence from Tell Masaikh that the good crossing site on the Middle Euphrates site had its name changed to Kar Assurnasirpal in the 9th century (Masetti-Rouault, loc. cit., n. 28 and passim), it makes sense with respect to the taking of the site and river crossing of Til Barsib that it should be re-named Kar Shalmaneser in the later 9th century. Kar-Assurnasirpal, too, became the seat of an important and often relatively independent Assyrian governor.

[37] Winter, '*Le palais imaginaire*', 2000, for the seals; Dalley, 'Shamshi-ilu', 2000, and Masetti-Rouault, 'Globalisation', 2014, for relatively independent governors' stelae.

[38] Dodd, 'Squeezing Blood', 2012.

Figure 15. Stela of Esarhaddon of Assyria, found Zincirli, ca. 671 BCE. Basalt. Vorderasiatisches Museen, Berlin, VA 2708.

What is important to stress in these cases is the role of the vantage point when assessing evidence for the 'type' of encounter and its valuation: that is, what is positive to the center in asserting its presence outside of the center may be either positive or negative to those outside of the center. On the one hand, visible signs of Assyrian presence or influence may be positive to the locals, suggesting affiliation and deterrence in the face of possible third-party threats. On the other hand, they may reflect political expediency but unwelcome dominance grudgingly acknowledged and sometimes simultaneously subverted. Each case must therefore be assessed on its own terms before generalizations can be attempted.

In this vein, one could also consider relationships manifest in bilingual texts erected in display contexts, such as at the sites of Karatepe and Tell Fakhariyeh (Fig. 16), along with the trilingual inscription of the Incirli stela mentioned above, to assess what they signify in terms of history, multiplicity of audience and hegemony. For the present, I would only observe that the 'bilingual' Luwian and Phoenician versions of the Karatepe inscription are mirrored by two styles of relief carvings found at the site: one more Neo-Hittite, the other more Levantine. Here, chronology is crucial. For, if these relief styles represent a chronological difference, from the 9th to the 8th century BCE, subsequently brought together in a late rebuilding, then one may perhaps read a sequential history of developing encounters, replicated for purposes of stress in a new rendering parallel to the old.[39] However, if in fact they were contemporary, as argued recently by Halet Çambel and Asli Özyar,[40] one could suggest that the two styles, along with the bilingual versions of the text, were directed at different linguistic and cultural groups in the contemporary audience, and may well signal relations between the local and the non-local. Whether or not the disparity in style of the reliefs reflects a significant difference of date, not just of style, brings into play quite different issues of social reception, and thereby 'encounter.'

For the bilingual text of the Fakhariyah statue, inscribed on the standing ruler-figure's skirt and written in Assyrian dialect Akkadian and Aramaic, it is interesting to note that the Akkadian text is the more visible when viewed from the front. In the Akkadian version, the local ruler is referred to with the title of "governor," probably in deference to the putative political domination of Assyria at the time; however in the

---

[39] Winter, 'On the Problems of Karatepe', 1979; see also the 2nd millennium case discussed in Winter, 'Theran Painting', 2000.

[40] Çambel & Özyar, *Karatepe-Arslantaş: Azatiwataya*, 2003.

Figure 16. Statue of Hadad-it'i, ruler of Guzana, with bilingual inscription, found Tell Fakhariyeh, 8th c BCE. Damascus Museum, Damascus.

Aramaic version, he is given the title of "king."[41] Whether this in fact constitutes an act of sedition remains to be examined, but the difference in titles assumed is striking.[42] The local center may even exercise both

[41] Abou-Assaf et al., *La Statue de Tell Fekheriye,* 1982.

[42] Scott, *The Art of Not Being Governed,* 2011, which raises throughout the dialectic between states and indigenous populations (or provinces) who perceive themselves to be more self-governed/autonomous than the territorial power [I thank M. T. Larsen for suggesting this reference]. As our archaeological (hence, both textual and visual) evidence is by definition partial, however, the caution must remain firmly in mind that new materials may shift significantly the perspective discernible at present. Nevertheless, issues of

deference and sedition at the same time. In any case, the encounter must be probed for its significance to both the dominant political power at a distance and the absorbed, formerly autonomous or semi-autonomous local polity.

7. Absorption into the dominant Center

The Hasanlu and Karatepe cases bring forward the reminder that cultural encounters occur in historical chains that need to be understood diachronically as well as synchronically, and for this, the chronology – both relative and absolute – based upon archaeological, historical or scientific analysis is again crucial. Thus, the 10th/early 9th century BCE stone orthostats depicting chariot hunts and battles encountered by later 9th century Assyrian rulers when passing through North Syrian sites such as Carchemish (Fig. 17) had first to be incorporated into the Assyrian center (Fig. 12) before the encountered motifs could be processed, then passed on to/absorbed further east by sites such as Hasanlu (Fig. 13).[43]

In both of these cases, it is important to stress once again how dependent upon chronology is any argument regarding impact resulting from cultural encounters. As the dating of some sites and rulers has shifted over time with new evidence, the directional arrows of impact have sometimes had to be revised. This has been the case, for example, with the far greater control we now have over the sequence of Neo-Hittite monuments and rulers in the states of Northern Syria and Southeastern Anatolia with respect to the sequence in Assyria proper.[44] This was alluded to just above with respect to the chariot battle motif moving from west to east, which is just one of multiple instances. Such phenomena demonstrate that the degree to which the center itself absorbs is a significant sub-set of cultural encounters. As such, they might well provide distinctions with respect to the sort of borrowings evident in the formative years of a given polity and those observable at moments of subsequent structural or ideological change. In this analysis, I would include not merely the goods brought into the center as booty, tribute or trade, but also the absorption of cultural/religious practices and technologies encountered outside and then reflected internally in visual

resistance and/or power shifts manifest in the record can sometimes attested. For our period, see the case of Tell Masaikh in the Middle Euphrates, for example [Masetti-Rouault, 'Globalisation', 2014; 'Rural Economy', 2010]. See also the several papers in Liew (ed.), *Post-Colonial Interventions*, 2009, particularly those of Moore, Gossai and Boer with respect to ancient Israel.

43 Winter, 'Art as Evidence', 1982.

44 See especially, Hawkins, *Corpus of Hieroglyphic Luwian Inscriptions*, 2000; and for the reliefs, Gilibert, *Syro-Hittite Monumental Art*, 2011.

(and textual) imagery. In short, appropriation or absorption *by* the center is an important consequence of "cultural encounter."

Figure 17. Relief, Long Wall, Carchemish: chariot scene, 10th–9th c BCE. Archaeological Museum, Ankara, Inv. 10068.

The incorporation of foreign soldiers into the Assyrian army under Tiglath Pileser III has already been noted, and complements the texts of local Syrian rulers, acknowledging their military engagement in the service of the Assyrian ruler (e.g., fig. 4).[45] On a different plane, however, it is also the case that the same Tiglath Pileser is represented enthroned holding a lotus flower in one hand (Fig. 18) – a detail not attested earlier in Assyria, yet familiar from the Late Bronze Age into the Iron Age in the West.

[45] Discussed in Winter, 'Art as Evidence', 1982, p. 366, particularly from Sam'al/Zincirli. And, see more recent discussions above, fn. 13.

Figure 18. Relief of Tiglath Pileser III: seated king with lotus. Central Palace, Nimrud. Rijksmuseum van Oudheden, Leiden, A 1934/6 1.

Illustrated here is an image showing Bar Rakib of Sam'al (Fig. 19), a vassal of Tiglath Pileser III in the 8th century, but the motif is also evident on a stela of his 9th century predecessor, Kilamuwa, and on the earlier sarcophagus of Ahiram of Byblos.[46] If depiction of this signifier is indeed

[46] See Barnett & Falkner, *The Sculptures of Assurnasirpal II,* 1962, pl. XIX, and the discussion in Winter, 'Art as Evidence', 1982, p. 366. More recently, see Rehm, *Der Ahiram-Sarkophag*, 2005, and Brown, 'The Kilamuwa Relief', 2008, for 10th–9th century examples of local rulers holding a blossom in the Levant/North Syria, and Pommerening, 'The Early Dynastic origin of the water-lily motif', 2010, for its origins in Egypt. Once introduced into Assyria, it continues to be represented, as when Sargon II at Khorsabad is

new to Assyria (and one must leave room for accidents of archaeological preservation), then a sign of the representational schema of rule has been brought into the center from the provinces at exactly the same time as new practices in territorial governance and the consolidation of holdings in the West is being established.[47]

Figure 19. Stela of Bar Rakib of Sam'al: king with lotus, found Zincirli, ca. 730 BCE. Basalt. Vorderasiatisches Museen, Berlin, VA 2817.

---

shown in his chariot in Room 7, slab 11, of the royal palace (Albenda, *Palace of Sargon,* 1986, pl. 89) and is held by Assurbanipal in his 'garden scene', our fig. 11. It also continues in use as an attribute in the west, as is clear from the Incirli stela (Dodd, 'Squeezing Blood', 2012). The motif seems to have originated quite early in Egypt during the Old Kingdom. It therefore makes sense for it to have appeared first in the Levant, in regular contact with Egypt, before being adopted by Assyria in the mid-8th century, as a consequence of its territorial encounters with the west. That it was initially associated with funerary iconography (see on this, Markoe, 1987, for Cyprus, and Rehm, 2005, for the Ahiram sarcophagus), does not necessaitate that this meaning had to be relevant for Assyria, however.

[47] Tadmor, 'Assyria and the West', 1975.

Had such an emblem been attested only in Assyrian representations executed in and for the provinces, as on the 8th century wall painting known from the Assyrian governor's palace at Til Barsib palace (Fig. 20), one could surmise that the Assyrian state apparatus was consciously using an *indigenous* visual vocabulary to convey Assyrian rule by deploying previously known emblems for a local and newly incorporated audience.[48]

Figure 20. Wall painting, Til Barsib, Governor's Palace, Room 47: seated king with lotus, 8th c BCE.

Depicted on reliefs in the Central Palace at Nimrud, however, one must consider that the motif has been absorbed into the symbolic vocabulary of the center itself, becoming part of Tiglath Pileser's 'self-representation', as it were. And furthermore, that the center has responded to at least this selected sign from the "other" as its own identity changes

[48] Thureau-Dangin & Dunand, *Til Barsip*, 1936, Room 47; Bunnens, 'Til Barsip', 1997.

– specifically by addressing a broader community of membership in the polity at large precisely at a time of structural change within the Assyrian state, if I am correct in arguing for a shift in 'kind' of polity from the mid-8th century. A portion of the newly-conceptualized and organized constituency would then recognize its own vocabulary as part of the dominant center's system of communication and identity. The desirability of such recognition would have resulted in an expansion of the vocabulary of the center, and at the same time, conceivably have served to make the Western provinces feel closer to the center.[49]

Another instance of the absorption of features into the center is seen in the statement of several 8th and 7th century Assyrian rulers that they have included architectural elements in their building schemes clearly identified with the West – in particular, the well-known *bīt-hilāni* from the land of Hatti, thought to be comprised of a portico marked by columns and perhaps also a windowed upper storey.[50] Thus, material practices and symbols reflecting cultural encounter can be observed as having been absorbed into the built environment, no less than through imported elite objects.

If one reads some sense of "value" vested in what has been absorbed into a given polity, then it is important to point out that such incorporations into the Assyrian center tend to come more often from the West than the North or East, as if elements absorbed into self-

[49] Barnett and Falkner, *The Sculptures*, 1962, pl. XIX and p. 11. Note that the relief here illustrated (our fig. 18), although the most frequently reproduced, was not alone in showing a lotus held by the ruler among the reliefs of Tiglath Pileser III from the Central Palace at Nimrud (see also Barnett & Falkner, *The Sculptures,* 1962, pls. VIII and LXIII), which would suggest that the motif was actually well-integrated into the center at this time, strengthening its signifying role. Another example of such incorporation of western practices of representation into Assyria is discussed by Melville, *The Role of Naqia/Zakutu*, 1999, pp. 13–16, where the West Semitic/Anatolian practice of showing a woman holding a mirror appears for the first time in Sargonid representations. In this domain of incorporating into the center, one might also consider the role of active 'collecting' of works for purposes of display – on which, see Thomason, *Luxury and Legitimation*, 2005. I am indebted to Izabela Eph'al for conversations on this issue, particularly the likely mutuality of agenda and response, and yet the complexity of evaluating the same. For, while use of the lotus motif is empirically attested, and the iconography can be recognized as significant, whether the signal sent by the king is "I am close to you," or "I use your emblem of royalty to indicated you are now subservient to me," or both simultaneously, is more difficult to ascertain.

[50] E.g., Tadmor, *Inscriptions of Tiglath-Pileser* III, 1994, Ann. 28, ll. 1'-2' and Summary Inscription I, l. 18', pp. 86–87 and 172–173: "…a *bīt-hilāni* modeled after a palace of the land of Hatti," on which there is a large literature, including most recently, Sinopoli, *Il re e il palazzo,* 2005, plus Harrison & Osborne, 'Building XVI', 2012. See also Thomason, *Luxury and Legitimation*, 2005, with respect to plants and trees similarly brought in to the royal gardens of the center from all parts of the domain.

representation had been selected according to discriminating principles of the desirable and differential notions of relationship with respect to differing geo-political areas.

I would also stress that there is a long tradition in the Ancient Near East of people – i.e., skilled craftsmen, musicians, and court women – being incorporated into the center along with objects and concepts, both through peaceful means and through conquest/displacement. In the Neo-Assyrian period, there seems to be evidence that women who ultimately became royal wives not-infrequently had personal names that reflected non-Assyrian origins, ethnic and/or linguistic. An example of this is seen not only in the name of the mother of 7th century Assyrian ruler Esarhaddon, Naqia/Zakutu, but also apparently in the names of the 8th century queens buried in Tomb 2 of the Northwest Palace at Nimrud.[51] These royal women seem to have been accompanied by objects and ornaments that can be identified as produced and in use *in* the West, once one compares the finds to Phoenician or Syrian products. Such marriages of course reflect yet another political dimension of "encounters," as can be demonstrated in the 2nd millennium BCE as well. The recent work of Amy Gansell has explored notions of ideal feminine beauty through images in ivory.[52] The adherence of court women to demonstrable ideals of beauty, particularly foreign women, makes of them no less "ornaments" than the luxury goods in the royal surround.

The social dynamic surrounding such women and their ornaments raises questions of whether the accompanying objects were, in the Neo-Assyrian Period at least, also recognized for their places of origin, as well as for the quality of their artisanship and precious material, such that the prior "encounter" is constantly reinforced in the works' (and the women's) display.[53] This would represent a different social context from

[51] Melville, *The Role of Naqia/Zakutu*, 1999 – especially pp. 13–16 and the bronze relief depicting Naqia and her son in the Louvre (cited and illustrated, p. 26, fig. 1). Melville notes that the motif of a woman holding a mirror is Syrian/Anatolian in origin, and seems to appear in Assyrian art here for the first time, just as the king holding a lotus seems to appear with Tiglath Pileser III. On Naqia and Assyrian royal women, see also Dalley, 'The Identity of the Princesses', 2008; Macgregor, *Beyond Hearth and Home*, 2012; Wicke, 'Die Goldschale', 2010; Collon, 'Getting it Wrong in Assyria', 2010.

[52] Gansell, 'The Iconography of Ideal Feminine Beauty', 2014.

[53] For an interesting opening of this question, see Hales & Hodos (eds.), *Material Culture and Social Identities*, 2010, where the construction of identity is explored in terms of the ownership and display of material objects, particularly in the articles of Antonaccio, Hingley, Riva and Sommer. [See also the electronic review by A. Ibarra, *Bryn Mawr Classical Review*, 2010.08.29.] In addition, the study of Glatz, 'Empire as network', 2009, documents for Late Bronze Age Anatolia the ways in which material objects function in cultural interaction.

that demonstrated by Marian Feldman for the Late Bronze Age in the Levant,[54] where the place of origin of high-end luxury goods was purposefully obscured in favor of signaling a broad *koine* of intercultural relations, thereby erasing cultural difference. The degree to which the first millennium's notions of political community were marked stylistically and iconographically would need to be accounted for in the light of how the expanded socio-political community of the Iron Age designated, and intended to signal, both similarity and difference.

For the Neo-Assyrian moment, it is useful to stress that the center is absorbing goods, motifs, building practices and people, along with wealth in natural resources; and that ideas/knowledge are often the product of such incorporations.[55] The patterns of consumption then become part of the historical profile and identity of the center.

8. Encounters in Image :: Encounters in Text

In citing this case close to the end of my paper, I pose the question of the relationship of the textual record to visual display, including instances where imagery may be viewed as complementarity to text, not mere duplication. What I have not done is to explore in depth for the 1st millennium BCE instances, such as is evident on the Stela of Eannatum of Lagash from 3rd millennium Sumer, when imagery offers information or stress different from what has been provided by text. Equally unexplored is the issue of representation of landscape/topography in the reliefs and how the same lands are described in text. The text of Sargon II's 8th campaign and some of Sennacherib's campaign accounts notwithstanding, landscape as depicted in Assyrian reliefs by the Sargonid rulers may be a good case for visual representation on occasion surpassing in detail the textual representation of place. Two issues also open for further consideration are the large-scale deportations/movements of populations that can generate intense cultural encounters, rather than those resulting from occasional interactions such as diplomatic banquets/visits or military presence (as seen in the reliefs of Tiglath Pileser III and Sennacherib), as well as evidence for the impact upon religious practices and deities following cultural encounters. These

[54] Feldman, *Diplomacy by Design*, 2006, and see also her forthcoming *Communities of Style: Portable Luxury Arts, Identity and Collective Memory in the Iron Age Levant* for the difference between 2nd millennium and 1st millennium conditions and artistic patterns.
[55] Bonatz, 'Objekte der Kleinkunst', 2004.

questions, while important, are less documentable from visual sources, and so have not been addressed here; however, they should be noted.[56]

On the basis of what *has* been addressed, I have insisted that "ideology" and "identity" are no less evident in the visual record than in the textual. I would further stress that the historian (whether using image, text, or text-and-image) needs to explore multiple directions and multiple dimensions of interaction and agency in assessing the impact of given cultural encounters.[57] Also, if it may be said that politics to some extent underlies *all* encounters, however much 'culture' may determine the content and style of the message, then before one seeks to determine whether or not, or to what extent, the political is coded into representation, one must examine the total field of available evidence for cultural interactions, not work with isolated sets of data.

A lexicon of well-defined key words and concepts – both in "their" languages and in our own – is necessary to assessing cultural encounters. Terms like "influence" and "ideology" have been used for some time in modern scholarship; but more recently, more nuanced discriminations between "emulation," "appropriation", and "absorption" have been introduced, while complex notions of "hybridity," memory, and "identity" have more recently been brought into intellectual discourse. All of these intellectual constructs are now expected to be part of the analytical frame. The degree to which "encounters" produce knowledge as well as materials and experience remains up to us as historians to assess. The *mimma šumšu* – something special, something exotic – requested by an Old Assyrian Period wife in Assur of her husband in Kültepe/Kanesh, or the better technology of an 8-spoked chariot wheel of North Syria eventually adopted in Assyria reminds us that both experience and knowledge come as by-products of encounter. It seems important, therefore, to work toward a more systematic typology of interactions characteristic of "encounters," using relatively well-documented test cases like the Neo-Assyrian and others examined in the present volume, to produce not just an historically and/or culturally-

---

56 For visual depictions of deportations, see Barnett & Falkner, *The Sculptures*, 1962, and Barnett et al., *Sculptures from the Southwest Palace*, 1998. The one place where the impact of encounter upon religion can be visually documented is in representations of iconoclasm. See on this, most recently, May, 'Iconoclasm and Text Destruction', 2013, esp. p. 16. For a discussion of the translatability of deities across cultural borders with the emergence of empire, see now Pongratz-Leisten, 'Comments on the Translatability', 2011.

57 As case studies of such movements of goods and ideas, see Hoffmann, *Imports and Immigrants*, 1997; Matthäus, 'Das griechische Symposion', 1999-2000; Braun-Holzinger & Rehm (eds.), *Orientalischer Import*, 2005; Kyrieleis, 'Intercultural Commerce', 2009; Cannavò, 'The Role of Cyprus', 2010; and the papers in Darbandi & Zournatzi (eds.), *Ancient Greece and Ancient Iran*, 2008.

specific lexicon or inventory, but also begin to accumulate those categories and markers that may permit broader generalization.

9. ENCOUNTERS AS SUCH

In the end, I am persuaded that "encounters" have to be understood in terms of a variety of interactions and relationships. Meetings of definable political, cultural, linguistic and ethnic entities take place in describable historical contexts and geographical loci. What is more, these contexts and loci come with cultural memories and prior histories understood by all parties. These parties are then not unaware when changes in status are being marked, especially with respect to peoples/territories newly incorporated into the political center that are then distinguished from those beyond the boundaries of incorporation.

On such occasions, some impact of one upon the other, or both upon each other, may be discerned. Furthermore, encounters can and do occur under a variety of conditions. They can be instantiated between peoples, places, and things; and can result in the transmission of knowledge as well as material entities. At the same time, representations cannot be said to be ideological alone. Visual depictions in the "center" of foreign landscapes, exotic objects, and local dress may also feed insiders' curiosity, as well as shaping attitudes by declaring the value and status of outsiders, their homelands and their products. Or, and perhaps simultaneously, they may function to establish a sense of internal collective identity through the expression of difference.

An initial inquiry into some consequences resulting from encounter(s) has been attempted here; much more is outlined with an eye to future studies in the field. For example, what makes an encounter "cultural" as distinct from "historical" has not yet been systematically examined, since the semantic range of the two terms and how they may overlap remain under-defined. But I would submit that any encounter, once identified, must be assessed across a broad field of interactions: whether between equals, dependents of high status, subordinates or enemy; whether resulting from movements of people or materials from a distance; whether in emulation or as part of a re-definition of identity. Therefore, both reception and impact need to be investigated, not assumed. In addition, although I have not done so here, archaeological evidence needs to be incorporated beyond elite works and sites: e.g., evidence for architectural features of known origin outside the area of origin; the range of burial practices (and distinctive food preferences) apparent through excavation;[58] and the distribution and standardization of ceramic types that can mark "encounters" and/or identify sub-groups in populations.[59]

Only then can we hope to establish an adequate typology for "encounters" of however many kinds – a typology that takes into consideration recent "network theory," which would permit the historian – both visual and textual – to go beyond mere recognition of the signs of encounter, toward setting a social scale for evaluating the specific domain(s), valuation and impact of such encounters and the range of possible, polyvalent responses. Greater precision in evaluating signs of encounter, it is argued, will then enable us to find correlations between individual cases, moving from case studies to systematic comparison and finally, to generalizable social theory.[60]

As a start, I have suggested that the identity of the representing "us" be parsed not assumed, and that one way to achieve this is through representations of that "us" in opposition to a designated "not us." I have further suggested that it is important to avoid assuming an essentialized and over-simplified "other" to cover all such cases. The category "other," the "not us," needs to be broken down into a variety of sub-categories, since the manner and subject matter of representation differed depending upon how that other was viewed by the "us" (here, Assyria) at any given moment.

In the identified sub-sets of encounter(s), differing degrees of alterity are likely to be in inverse relation to socio-cultural/political proximity and the desire to convey or build a community of discourse. For example, although I have drawn most of my examples from Assyrian interactions with the West and East, it is clear that relations with Babylonia in the South throughout the Neo-Assyrian Period, and with Urartu in the North in at least the 8th–7th centuries, would provide as interesting (and rather different) pictures of "encounter" from those I have cited: the former acknowledged as a foundational cultural tradition for Assyria, but with perpetual difficulties in political and economic relationships; the latter

---

58 As pursued in Carroll & Rempel (eds.), *Living through the Dead,* 2011.

59 Duistermaat, *The Pots and Potters*, 2008; Anastasio, *Atlas of the Assyrian Pottery,* 2010; Postgate, 'The Debris of Government', 2010.

60 Campbell, 'Toward a Network and Borders Approach', 2009; Scheidel (ed.), *Rome and China*, 2009; and the papers in Bang & Bayley (eds.), *The Medieval History Journal* 6 (2003), including 'Introduction', pp. 169-187; also Barjamovic, 'Propaganda and Practice in Assyrian and Persian imperial culture', 2012. See also Darbandi & Zournatzi (eds.), *Ancient Greece and Ancient Iran*, 2009, and *The Stanford Ancient Chinese and Mediterranean Empires Comparative History Project (ACME)*, <http://www.stanford.edu/~scheidel/acme.htm>.

frequently oppositional militarily, and seeming to draw more from Assyria than contributing to it.[61]

All of the indicators of encounter, pictorial and material no less than textual, may at a given moment be geared toward changing rather than reifying already-existing tropes of community- and identity-formation. And what is more, it has been stressed that arrows of impact can move in both directions along with artifacts, motifs and people.[62] In some instances the Assyrians as they expanded politically and territorially viewed (and represented) certain others with curiosity and appreciation, incorporating elite material culture identified with that 'other' and absorbing aspects of that other into the semantic system of the center. In contrasting instances, the Assyrians used representation as a means of de-humanizing or dominating specific others in keeping with their larger political agenda.

Finally, I have suggested that the visual record should not be understood merely as illustrative of a given textual record. Rather, it can serve as an independent source of evidence, yielding to analysis and providing perspective on the domains and strengths of impact in cultural

---

[61] See, for example, the dissertation of Tanyeri-Erdemir, 2005, in which she examines Urartean absorption of Assyrian imagery and material culture in the 8th century. For elite objects, things may be quite complicated. Jeffers, 'Fifth-campaign reliefs', 2011, argues that the military campaign of Room 38, slabs 17–18 (our fig. 10) in the Southwest Palace at Nineveh actually is to be identified as taking place in the north, against Urartu, during Sennacherib's 5th Campaign, rather than in the west during the king's 3rd Campaign. In that case, imagery of booty, including furniture, would require us to re-assess the proposition that this high-end furniture being carried off by Assyrian soldiers from an enemy citadel was produced in and received from the West alone. Indeed, it is conceivable that elites in a variety of locations may well have shared a high-end material culture, in some media at least, with similar objects then coming to Nineveh from several directions, wherever they may have been manufactured (see fn. 27), or having been manufactured in multiple places initially. Manufacture in a single place and subsequent distribution would not be precluded, particularly as the number of instances where places of use or booty are known seem to privilege the West (for example, a couch of a similar shape on which the ruler of Patina/Palastina in the West reclines as depicted on the Balawat Gates of Shalmaneser III (Left side, band 3), but this would have to be subject to close analysis. In any case, if representations of booty taken are not tied to materials from a single place of origin, the works could as well have been copied in the absorbing center after their own fashion. [The 'Woman/Women at the Window' decorative panels on the legs of Assurbanipal's couch, that correspond in theme to, but in detail differ from, actual ivory fragments found in various Assyrian capitals, have been the subject of such speculation, as discussed in Feldman, 'Assyrian Representations', 2011, p. 145.]

[62] On this, see also, and most recently, Stockhammer, 'From Hybridity to Practice', 2013, especially p. 17, where the author distinguishes between *regional* and *material entanglements* (emphasis mine), for which one might substitute the term *encounters*. It is proposed that such a distinction would contribute to a more rigorous analysis of trans-cultural (or cross-cultural) engagements and how they ramify, particularly in the realm of resulting hybridity.

encounters. Only as a second step should the two records, visual and verbal, along with other categories of data, be put together in order to assess the intensity of and attitude toward encounter(s) at any given moment, as well as the changing parameters of encounter(s) over time.[63]

In brief, with a more sophisticated analytical framework it becomes possible to (1) develop an analytical dimension that allows for degrees of "otherness," along with (2) a scale to measure intensity of "impact," which in turn can then be tested by a number of case studies. These case studies would permit the scholar to (3) explore how the "self" and the "other" are represented (and conceptualized) in specific instances of encounter, and (4) establish the degree to which the universe of visual representation contributes to a discernible agenda across a wide spectrum of time and space.

At present we are just at the beginning stages of accumulating case studies in order to identify a range of patterns typical of particular encounters. The challenge before us presently, it seems to me, is to develop greater rigor in description, classification and terminology when assessing degrees of impact and importance in the scholarly evaluation of cultural encounters. Only then will it be possible to undertake any systematic comparative exercise, toward uncovering the range of "cultural encounters" represented in the art of the Neo-Assyrian Period, as well as throughout the Mesopotamian sequence and beyond.

BIBLIOGRAPHY

Abou-Assaf, A., et al. *La Statue de Tell Fekheriye et son inscription bilingue assyro-arraméene.* (Études Assyriologiques, Cahiers 7.) Paris, 1982.

[63] As noted at the beginning, one reason for having an art historian examine this topic, has been to test whether for any given cultural/historical moment the visual and verbal records are identical, overlap partially (and if so, where), or differ. Such a case of difference is most apparent in the SW Palace at Nineveh, Room 36, where the battle against Lachish is depicted from approach to conclusion, while Lachish does not appear in the text that refers to Sennacheribs's 5th campaign in Judah. Conversely, Jerusalem, mentioned in text but not conquered in that campaign, does not appear in imagery. A second case would be the representation of Assurbanipal's Elamite campaign at the Ulai River, where the complex imagery that folds in on itself from beginning to end is anchored by a series of 37 epigraphic texts added to the reliefs, thereby providing a far more complete narrative sequence that is preserved in any textual account. On this latter sequence, see Kaelin, *Ein assyrisches Bildexperiment,* 1999; also Bahrani, 'The King's Head', 2005; Bonatz, 'Ashurbanipal's Headhunt', 2005; and Watanabe, 'The "Continuous Style"', 2005 – all of which appear in Collon and George (eds.), *Nineveh,* 2005.

Albenda, P. *The Palace of Sargon, King of Assyria*. Paris, 1986.
Alcock, S. E., et al. (eds). *Empires: Perspective from Archaeology and History*. Cambridge, 2001.
Allen, L. 'Reading Identity from the Robe: Achaemenid Garment Inscriptions at Pasargadae, Susa and Persepolis.' Paper delivered at the Annual Meetings of the American Oriental Society, March 2012.
Anastasio, S. *Atlas of the Assyrian Pottery of the Iron Age*. (Subartu 24.) Turnhout, 2010.
Assman, J. *Cultural Memory and Early Civilization: Writing, Remembrance, and Political Imagination*. Cambridge, 2011. [Originally published in German, 1994].
Aster, S. Z. 'Transmission of Neo-Assyrian Claims of Empire to Judah in the late Eighth Century B.C.E.' *Hebrew Union College Annual* 78 (2007), pp. 1–44.
Ataç, M-A. *The Mythology of Kingship in Neo-Assyrian Art*. Cambridge, 2010.
Bagg, A. M. *Die Assyrer und das Westland: Studien zur historischen Geographie und Herrschaftspraxis in der Levante in 1 Jh. v. u. Z.* Leuven, 2011.
Bahrani, Z. 'The King's Head.' D. Collon & A. George (eds.), *Nineveh. Papers of the XLIXe Rencontre Assyriologique Internationale, London, 7–11 July 2003*. London, 2005, pp. 115–119.
Bang, P. F., and C. A. Bayley. 'Introduction: Comparing pre-modern empires.' *The Medieval History Journal* 6 (2003), pp. 169–187.
Bär, J. *Der assyrische Tribut und seine Darstellung. Eine Untersuchung zur imperialen Ideologie im neuassyrischen Reich*. (Alter Orient und Altes Testament 243.) Neukirchen-Vluyn, 1996.
Barjamovic, G. 'The Mesopotamian Empires.' P. F. Bang & W. Scheidel (eds.), *The Oxford Handbook of the Ancient State: The Near East and the Mediterranean*. Oxford, 2012, pp. 2–40.
– 'Propaganda and Practice in Assyrian and Persian Imperial Culture.' P. F. Bang & D. Kolodziejczyk (eds.), *Universal Empire: A comparative approach to imperial culture and representation in Eurasian history*. Cambridge, 2012.
Barnett, R. D., et al. *Sculptures from the Southwest Palace of Sennacherib at Nineveh*. London, 1998.
Barnett, R. D. & M. Falkner. *The Sculptures of Assurnasirpal II, Tiglath Pileser III and Esarhaddon from the Central and Southwest Palaces at Nimrud*. London, 1962.
Bedford, P. R. 'The Neo-Assyrian Empire.' I. Morris & W. Scheidel (eds.), *The Dynamics of Ancient Empires: State power from Assyria to Byzantium*. New York, 2009, pp. 30–65.

Berlejung, A. 'Shared Fates: Gaza and Ekron as Examples for the Assyrian Religious Policy in the West.' N. May (ed.), *Iconoclasm and Text Destruction.* (Oriental Institute Seminars 8.) Chicago, 2012, pp. 125–149.

Bonatz, D. 'Ashurbanipal's Headhunt: An Anthropological Perspective.' D. Collon & A. George (eds.), *Nineveh. Papers of the XLIXe Rencontre Assyriologique Internationale, London, 7–11 July 2003.* London, 2005, pp. 93–101.

– 'Objecte der Kleinkunst als Ideenträger zwischen dem syro-anatolischen und dem assyrischen Raum: Das Problem der Elfenbeine.' M. Novák et al. (eds.), *Die Aussenwirkung des späthethitischen Kulturraumes.* Münster, 2004, pp. 387–404.

Braun-Holzinger, E. & E. Rehm (eds.). *Orientalischer Import in Griechenland im frühen 1. Jahrtausend v. Chr.* (Alter Orient und Altes Testament 328.) Münster, 2005.

Briant, P. (ed.). *Le tribute dans l'empire perse. Actes de la Table Ronde de Paris, 12–13 Décembre 1986.* Paris, 1989

Brown, B. 'The Kilamuwa Relief: Ethnicity, Class and Power in Iron Age North Syria.' J. M. Córdoba et al. (eds.), *Proceedings of the 5th ICAANE.* Madrid, 2008, pp. 339–356.

Bru, H. *Le pouvoir impérial dans les provinces syriennes. Représentations et célébrations d'Auguste à Constantin (31 av. J.-C. – 337 ap. J.-C.).* Leiden – Boston, 2012.

Brusasco, P. *The Archaeology of Verbal and Nonverbal Meaning: Mesopotamian Domestic Architecture and its Textual Dimension.* (BAR International Series 1631.) London, 2007.

Bunnens, G. 'Til Barsip under Assyrian Domination: A brief account of the Melbourne University excavations at Tell Ahmar.' S. Parpola & R. Whiting (eds.), *Assyria 1995. Proceedings of the 10th Anniversary Symposium of the Neo-Assyrian Text Corpus Project, Helsinki, 7–11 September.* Helsinki, 1997, pp. 17–28.

Çambel, H. & A. Özyar. *Karatepe-Arslantaş: Azatiwataya. Die Bildwerke.* Mainz, 2003.

Campbell, R. B. 'Toward a Networks and Boundaries Approach to Early Complex Polities: The Late Shang Case.' *Current Anthropology 50:6* (2009), pp. 821–848.

Cannavò, A. 'The Role of Cyprus in the Neo-Assyrian Economic System: Analysis of the Textual Evidence.' *Rivista di Studi Fenici* 35 (2010), pp. 179–190.

Carroll, M. & J. Rempel (eds.). *Living through the Dead: Burial and Commemoration in the Classical World.* (Studies in Funerary Archaeology 5.) Oxford, 2011

Cifarelli, M. 'Gesture and Alterity in the Art of Assurnasirpal II of Assyria.' *Art Bulletin 80* (1998), pp. 210–228.

Cogan, M. *Imperialism and Religion: Assyria, Judah and Israel in the Eighth and Seventh Centuries B.C.E.* Missoula, 1974.

Collon, D. 'Getting it Wrong in Assyria: Some Bracelets from Nimrud.' *Iraq* 72 (2010), pp. 149–162.

Collon, D. & A. George (eds.), *Nineveh. Papers of the XLIXe Rencontre Assyriologique Internationale, London, 7–11 July 2003*. London, 2005.

Curtis, J. '*Stützfiguren* in Mesopotamia.' U. Finkbeiner et al. (eds.), *Beiträge zur Kulturgeschichte Vorderasiens. Festschrift Rainer Michael Boehmer*. Mainz, 1995, pp. 77–86.

Curtis, J. & N. Tallis (eds.). *The Balawat Gates of Ashurnasirpal II.* London, 2008.

Dalley, S. 'The Identity of the Princesses in Tomb II and a new analysis of events in 701 B.C.' J. Curtis et al. (eds.), *New Light on Nimrud – Proceedings of the Nimrud Conference, 11–13 March, 2002.* London, 2008, pp. 171–175.

– 'Shamshi-ilu, Language and Power in the Western Assyrian Empire.' G. Bunnens (ed.), *Essays on Syria in the Iron Age.* (Ancient Near Eastern Studies Supplement 7.) Leuven, 2000, pp. 79–88.

van Damme, W. 'Cultural Encounters: Western Scholarship and Fang Statuary from Equatorial Africa.' Inaugural Lecture, Tilburg University. The Netherlands, 2011.

Darbandi, S. M. R. & A. Zournatzi (eds.). *Ancient Greece and Ancient Iran: Cross-Cultural Encounters*. Athens, 2008.

Dodd, L. S. 'Squeezing Blood from a Stone: The Archaeological Context of the Incirli Inscription.' M. J. Lundberg et al. (eds.), *Puzzling Out the Past: Studies in Northwest Semitic Languages and Literatures in Honor of Bruce Zuckerman.* Leiden – Boston, 2012, pp. 214–232. Cf. <http://www.humnet.ucla.edu/humnet/nelc/stelasite/stelainfo.html> and <http://balshanut.wordpress.com/2009/01/26> for description and reconstruction(s) of the inscription.

Donner, H. and W. Röllig. *Kanaanäische und Aramäische Inschriften I.* Wiesbaden, 1962.

Eph'al, I. 'Stages and Aims in the Royal Historiography of Essarhaddon.' *Orient* 49 (2014), pp. 51–68.

– 'Esarhaddon, Egypt, and Shubria: Politics and Propaganda.' *Journal of Cuneiform Studies* 57 (2005), pp. 99–111.

Fales. F. M. 'The Enemy in Assyrian Royal Inscriptions: The "Moral Judgment".' H.-J. Nissen & J. Renger (eds.), *Mesopotamien und seine Nachbarn: Politische und kulturelle Wechselbeziehungen im Alten*

Vorderasien vom 4. bis 1. Jahrtausend v. Chr. Berlin, 1982, pp. 425–435.

Feldman, M. H. *Diplomacy by Design: Luxury Arts and an 'International Style' in the Ancient Near East, 1400 – 1200 BCE.* Chicago, 2006.

– 'Assyrian Representations of Booty and Tribute as a Self-Portrayal of Empire.' B. E. Kelle et al. (eds.), *Interpreting Exile: Displacement and Deportation in Biblical and Modern Contexts*. Atlanta, 2011, pp. 135–150.

Gansell, A. 'The Iconography of Ideal Feminine Beauty Represented in the Hebrew Bible and Iron Age Levantine Ivory Sculpture.' J. M. LeMon et al. (eds.), *Image – Text – Exegesis*. New York, 2014.

Gerlach, I. 'Tradition-Adaptation-Innovation: Zur Reliefkunst nordsyrien/südanatoliens in Neuassyrische Zeit.' G. Bunnens (ed.), *Essays on Syria in the Iron Age.* (Ancient Near Eastern Studies Supplement 7.) Louvain – Paris – Sterling VA, 2000, pp. 235–257.

Gilan, A. 'Überlegungen zu "Kultur" und "Aussenwirkung".' M. Novák et al. (eds.), *Die Aussenwirkung des späthethitischen Kulturraumes.* Münster, 2004, pp. 9-20.

Gilibert, A. *Syro-Hittite Monumental Art and the Archaeology of Performance: The Stone Reliefs at Carchemish and Zincirli in the Earlier First Millennium BCE.* (Topoi Berlin Studies of the Ancient World 2.) Berlin, 2011.

Glatz, C. 'Empire as network: Spheres of material interaction in LBA Anatolia.' *Journal of Anthropological Archaeology 28* (2009), pp. 127–141.

Grayson, A. K. *Royal Inscriptions of Mesopotamia: Assyria*, vol. 2. Toronto, 1991.

Gruen, E. (ed.). *Cultural Identity in the Ancient Mediterranean, Issues and Debates*. Los Angeles, 2010.

Halbwachs, M. *On Cultural Memory*. Chicago, 1992. [Originally published in French, 1952.]

Hales, S. and T. Hodos (eds.). *Material Culture and Social Identities in the Ancient World.* Cambridge – New York, 2009.

Harmanşah, Ö. 'Beyond Aššur: New Cities and the Assyrian Politics of Landscape.' *Bulletin of the American Schools of Oriental Research* 365 (2012), pp. 54–77.

Harrison, T. P. & J. F. Osborne. 'Building XVI and the Neo-Assyrian Sacred Precinct at Tell Tayinat.' *Journal of Cuneiform Studies* 64 (2012), pp. 113–131.

Hawkins, J. D. *Corpus of Hieroglyphic Luwian Inscriptions*. Berlin, 2000.

Hoffmann, G. L. *Imports and Immigrants: Near Eastern Contacts with Iron Age Crete*. Ann Arbor, 1997.

Hughes, A. W. *The Invention of Jewish Identity: Bible, Philosophy, and the Art of Translation*. Bloomington, IN, 2010.

Jeffers, J. 'Fifth-campaign reliefs in Sennacherib's "Palace Without Rival" at Nineveh.' *Iraq* 73 (2011), pp. 87–116.

Joannès, F. *The Age of Empires: Mesopotamia in the first millennium BC*. Edinburgh, 2004.

Kaelin, O. *Ein assyrisches Bildexperiment nach ägyptischem Vorbild. Zur Planung und Ausführung der 'Schlact am Ulai'*. (Alter Orient und Altes Testament 266.) Munich, 1999.

Kennedy, E. R. *Ethnic Identity in the Ancestral Narratives of Genesis*. Leiden, 2011.

Kertai, D. 'Kalhu's palaces of war and peace: Palace architecture at Nimrud in the ninth century BC.' *Iraq* 73 (2011), pp. 71–86.

Kinnier Wilson, J. V. 'Lines 40–52 of the Banquet Stele of Assurnasirpal II.' *Iraq 50* (1988), pp. 79–82.

Klinkott, H. 'Steuern, Zöllen, Tribut in Achaemenidenreichs.' H. Klinkott et al. (eds.), *Geschenke und Steuern, Zölle und Tribut: Antike Abgabenformen in Auspruch und Wirklichkeit*. Leiden & Boston, 2007, pp. 263–290.

Kyrieleis, H. 'Intercultural Commerce and Diplomacy: Near Eastern, Egyptian and Cypriote Artefacts from the Heraion of Samos.' V. Karageorghis & O. Kouka (eds.), *Cyprus and the East Aegean: Intercultural Contacts from 3000 to 500 BC, An International Archaeological Symposium held at Pythagoreion, Samos, 17–18 October 2008*. Nicosia, 2009, pp. 139–143.

Lanfranchi, G. B. 'Consensus to Empire: Some Aspects of Sargon II's Foreign Policy.' H. Waetzoldt & H. Hauptmann (eds.), *Assyrien im Wandel der Zeiten. XXXIX Rencontre Assyriologique International (Heidelberg 6–10 Juli 1992)*. Heidelberg, 1997, pp. 81–87.

Laurence, R. & J. Berry (eds.). *Cultural Identity in the Roman Empire*. London – New York, 1998.

Leve, L. 'Identity.' *Current Anthropology* 52 (2011), pp. 513–535.

Lieu, T. B. *Postcolonial Interventions: Essays in Honor of R. S. Sugirtharajah*. (The Bible in the Modern World 23.) Sheffield, 2009.

Liverani, M. (ed.). *Akkad, the first world empire: structure, ideology traditions*. Padua, 1993.

– 'Dono, tributo, commercio: ideologia dello scambio nella tarda eta del bronzo.' *Annali dell'Istituto Italiano di Numismatica* 26 (1979), pp. 9–28.

MacGinnis, J. D. A. and T. Matney. 'Archaeology at the Frontiers: Excavating a Provincial Capital of the Assyrian Empire.' *Journal of Assyrian Academic Studies* 23 (2009), pp. 3–21.

Macgregor, S. L. *Beyond Hearth and Home: Women in the Public Sphere in Neo-Assyrian Society.* (State Archives of Assyria 21.) Helsinki, 2012.

Machinist, P. 'Assyrians on Assyria in the First Millennium B.C.' K. Raaflaub & E. Müller-Luckner (eds.), *Anfänge politischen Denkens in der Antike*. Munich, 1993, pp. 77–104.

Mallowan, M. E. L. *Nimrud and its Remains*, Vol. II. New York, 1966.

Marcus, M. I. 'Centre, *Province*, and Periphery: A New Paradigm from Iron-Age Iran.' *Art History* 13 (1990), pp. 129–150.

Markoe, G. 'The Funerary Iconography of the Lotus in Iron Age Cyprus and the Levant.' Paper given at the annual meetings of the Society for Biblical Literature, Denver CO, 1987.

Masetti-Rouault, M. G. 'Globalization and Imperialism: Political and Ideological Reactions to the Assyrian Presence in Syria (IXth–VIIIth century BCE). M. Geller (ed.), *The Ancient World in an Age of Globalization.* (Melammu Symposium 6.) Berlin, 2014, pp. 49–68.

– 'Rural Economy and Steppe Management in an Assyrian Colony in the West: A View from Tell Masaikh, Lower Middle Euphrates, Syria.' H. Kühne (ed.) *Dur-Katlimmu 2008 and Beyond.* (Studia Chaburensia 1.) Wiesbaden, 2010, pp. 129–149.

Matthäus, H. 'Das griechische Symposion und der Orient.' *Nürnberger Blätter zur Archäologie* 16 (1999–2000), pp. 41–64.

May, N. 'Iconoclasm and Text Destruction in the Ancient Near East.' N. May (ed.), *Iconoclasm and Text Destruction.* (Oriental Institute Seminars 8.) Chicago, 2012, pp. 11–36.

Meuszynski, J. *Rekonstruktion der Reliefdarstellungen und ihre Anordnung im Nordwestpapast von Kalhu (Nimrud).* (Baghdader Forschungen 2.) Mainz am Rhein, 1981.

Morehart, C. T. 'What if the Aztec Empire Never Existed? The Prerequisites of Empire and the Politics of Plausible Alternative Histories.' *American Anthropologist* 114 (2012), pp. 267–281.

Ornan, T. et al. 'Four Hebrew Seals, one depicting an Assyrian-like Archer, from the Western Wall Plaza Excavations, Jerusalem.' *Atiqot* 60 (2008), pp. 115–130.

Parker, B. J. *The Mechanics of Empire: The northern frontier of Assyria as a case study in imperial dynamics*. Helsinki, 2001.

Pedde, F. 'The Assyrian Heartland.' D. T. Potts (ed.), *A Companion to the Archaeology of the Ancient Near East, vol. II.* Oxford – Malden MA, 2012, pp. 851–866.

Pommerening, T. et al. 'The Early Dynastic origin of the *water-lily* motif.' *Chronique d'Égypte* 85 (2010), pp. 14–40.

Pongratz-Leisten, B. 'The Other and the Enemy in the Mesopotamian Conception of the World.' R. M. Whiting (ed.), *Mythology and Mythologies.* (Melammu Symposia 2.) Helsinki, 2001, pp. 195–231.

– 'Comments on the Translatability of Divinity: Cultic and Theological Responses to the Presence of the Other in the Ancient Near East.' C. Bonnet et al. (eds.), *Les représentations des dieux des autres.* Palermo, 2011, pp. 83–110.

Porter, B. N. 'The Importance of Place: Esarhaddon's Stelae at Til Barsip and Sam'al.' T. Abusch et al. (eds.), *Historiography in the Cuneiform World.* Bethesda, MD, 2001, pp. 374–390.

Postgate, J. N. 'The Debris of Government: Reconstructing the Middle Assyrian State Apparatus from Tablets and Potsherds.' *Iraq* 72 (2010), pp. 19–37.

Raja, R. *Urban Development and Regional Identity in the Eastern Roman Provinces, 50 BC – AD 250.* Copenhagen, 2012.

Rehm, E. *Der Ahiram-Sarkophag. Dynastensarkophage mit szenischen Reliefs aus Byblos und Zypern.* Mainz am Rhein, 2005.

Robaert, A. 'A Neo-Assyrian Statue from Til Barsib.' *Iraq* 58 (1996), pp. 79–87.

Scheidel, W. (ed.). *Rome and China: Comparative perspectives on ancient world empires*. Oxford, 2009.

– 'The monetary systems of the Han and Roman empires.' W. Scheidel (ed.). *Rome and China: Comparative perspectives on ancient world empires*. Oxford, 2009, pp. 137–207.

Scott, J. C. *The Art of Not Being Governed: An Anarchist History of Upland Southeast Asia.* (Yale Agrarian Studies Series.) New Haven, 2011.

Schmidt, E. *Persepolis III.* Chicago, 1970.

Shafer, A. 'Assyrian Royal Monuments on the Periphery: Ritual and the Making of Imperial Space.' J. Cheng & M. H. Feldman (eds.), *Ancient Near Eastern Art in Context: Studies in Honor of Irene J. Winter by her Students.* Leiden – Boston, 2007, pp. 133–160.

Sinopoli, C. M. 'The Archaeology of Empires.' *Annual Review of Anthropology* 23 (1994), pp. 159–180.

Sinopoli, G. *Il re e il palazzo. Studi sull'architettura del Vicino Oriente: il* bīt hilāni. San Giuliano Terme, 2005.

Van Soldt, W. H. et al. 'Satu Qala: A Preliminary Report on the Seasons 2010–2011.' *Anatolica* 39 (2013), pp. 1–43.

Stockhammer, P. W. 'From Hybridity to Enganglement, From Essentialism to Practice.' *Archaeological Review from Cambridge* 28 (2013), pp. 11–28.

Tadmor, H. 'World Dominion: The Expanding Horizon of the Assyrian Empire.' L. Milano (ed.), *Landscapes, Territories, Frontiers and Horizons in the Ancient Near East. Papers presented to the XLIV Rencontre Assyriologique Internationale (Venezia, 7–11 July 1997)*. Padova, 1999, pp. 55–62.

– *The Inscriptions of Tiglath-Pileser III King of Assyria: Critical Edition, with Introductions, Translations and Commentary*. Jerusalem, 1994.

– 'Assyria and the West: The Ninth Century and its Aftermath.' H. Goedicke & J. M. Roberts (eds.), *Unity and Diversity*. Baltimore, 1975, pp. 36–43.

Tanyeri-Erdemir, T. *Tradition vs. Innovation: A stylistic analysis of Imperial and Material Change under Rusa II of Urartu*. Unpublished PhD thesis, Boston University, 2005.

Thomason, A. K. *Luxury and Legitimation: Royal Collecting in Ancient Mesopotamia*. Burlington VT, 2005.

Thureau-Dangin, F. & M. Dunand. *Til Barsib*. Paris, 1936.

Wäffler, M. *Nicht-Assyrer neuassyrischer Darstellungen*. (Alter Orient und Altes Testament 26.) Neukirchen – Vluyn, 1975.

Watanabe, C. 'The "Continuous Style" in the Narrative Scheme of Assurbanipal's Reliefs.' D. Collon & A. George (eds.), *Nineveh. Papers of the XLIXe Rencontre Assyriologique Internationale, London, 7–11 July 2003*. London, 2005, pp. 103–114.

Wicke, D. 'Die Goldschale der Iabâ – eine levantinische Antiquität.' *Zeitschrift für Assyriologie und Vorderasiatische Archäologie* 100 (2010), pp. 109–141.

Winter, I. J. 'Le banquet royal assyrien: mise en oeuvre de la rhétorique de l'abondance.' C. Grandjean et al. (eds.), *Le banquet du monarque dans le monde ancien*. Rennes – Tours, 2013, pp. 287–311.

– 'Theran Painting in the Light of the Ancient Near East: Questions of Methodology and Interpretation.' S. Sherratt (ed.), *The Wall Paintings of Thera: Proceedings of the First International Colloquium*, Vol. 2. Athens, 2000, pp. 745–762.

– '*Le palais imaginaire:* scale and meaning in the iconography of Neo-Assyrian cylinder seals.' C. Uehlinger (ed.), *Images as media: Sources for the cultural history of the Near East and the Eastern Mediterranean (1st millennium BCE)*. Fribourg, 2000, pp. 51–87.

– 'The Body of the Able Ruler: Toward an Understanding of the Statues of Gudea.' H. Behrens, D. Loding and M. T. Roth (eds.), *DUMU-E2-DUB-BA-A: Studies in Honor of Åke W. Sjöberg*. Philadelphia, 1989, pp. 573–583.

– 'Art as Evidence for Interaction: Relations between the Assyrian Empire and North Syria.' H. J. Nissen & J. Renger (eds.), *Mesopotamien und seine Nachbarn: Politische und kulturelle Wechselbeziehungen im Alten Vorderasien vom 4. bis 1. Jahrtausend v. Chr.* Berlin, 1982, pp. 355–382.

– 'On the Problems of Karatepe: The Reliefs and their Context.' *Anatolian Studies* 29 (1979), pp. 115–151.

– 'The "Local Style" of Hasanlu IVB: A study in receptivity.' L. D. Levine & T. C. Young, Jr. (eds.), *Mountains and Lowlands: Essays in the Archaeology of Greater Mesopotamia.* Malibu CA, 1977, pp. 371–386.

Wiseman, D. J. 'A New Stela of Assurnasirpal II.' *Iraq* 14 (1952), pp. 22–44.

Woolf, A. 'Romancing the Celts: A segmentary approach to acculturation.' R. Laurence & J. Berry (eds.), *Cultural Identity.* London, 1998, pp. 111–124.

Yamada, S. *The Construction of the Assyrian Empire: A Historical Study of the Inscriptions of Shalmaneser III (859–824 BC) Relating to his Campaigns to the West.* (Culture and History of the Ancient Near East 3.) Leiden – Boston, 2000.

Zaccagnini, C. 'The Enemy in the Neo-Assyrian Royal Inscriptions: The "ethnographic" description.' H.-J. Nissen & J. Renger (eds.), *Mesopotamien und seine Nachbarn: politische und kulturelle Wechselbeziehungen im alten Vorderasien vom 4. bis 1. Jahrtausend v. Chr.* Berlin, 1982, pp. 409–424.

– 'La circolazione dei beni di lusso nelle fonti neo-assire (IX–VII sec. a. C.).' *Opus 3* (1984), pp. 235–252.